THE ART OF PITY

MEDIEVAL & RENAISSANCE LITERARY STUDIES
Rebecca Totaro and Reginald A. Wilburn, Series Editors

The Art of Pity: Aesthetics, Ethics, and Compassion
in Sidney, Spenser, and Shakespeare
DANIELLE A. ST. HILAIRE

The Art of Pity

*Aesthetics, Ethics, and Compassion in Sidney,
Spenser, and Shakespeare*

DANIELLE A. ST. HILAIRE

The Kent State University Press

KENT, OHIO

For Hélène,
who always picks up the phone when I need her

© 2025 by The Kent State University Press, Kent, Ohio 44242
All rights reserved
ISBN 978-1-60635-491-9
Published in the United States of America

No part of this book may be used or reproduced, in any manner whatsoever, without written permission from the Publisher, except in the case of short quotations in critical reviews or articles.

Cataloging information for this title is available at the Library of Congress.

29 28 27 26 25   5 4 3 2 1

⊹⟦ CONTENTS ⟧⊹

Acknowledgments   vii

Introduction   1

1 Sidney Between Two Worlds: Pity, Delight, and the
Failure of Instrumental Aesthetics   29

2 Virtuous Pity and Spenser's Aesthetic Doubt:
The Rise of Literary Autonomy   53

3 Alternate Realities: Shakespearean Aesthetics,
Pity, and *King Lear*   89

Conclusion   131

Notes   137

Bibliography   155

Index   163

ACKNOWLEDGMENTS

This book has been the labor of seven years, and in that time I have been helped along and supported by more people than I can possibly name, all of whom have my gratitude. I am grateful to Duquesne University for offering financial support for this project in the form of a Paluse grant in 2018 and a Presidential Scholarship Award in 2021, both of which enabled me to dedicate my time to writing over the summers. I also received a 2019 NEH Summer Stipend to support my writing, which provided both the resources and the encouragement I needed to see this project through.

My colleagues at Duquesne have been a tremendous source of support, material and emotional, over the years. I am grateful to my research assistants who helped me research for this project: Shawn Watkins, Courtney Mullis, and Courtney Druzak. Without their help finding books and articles, this book would have taken much longer to write. Many thanks also to the many colleagues, at Duquesne and elsewhere, who have read chapters and provided feedback, including John Mitcham, Matt Ussia, and Laura Engel, three people who provided me encouragement when I needed it most, as well as Anna Gibson-Knowles, Ben Parris, and Bradley Irish. It is never a small thing to agree to read another person's drafts; thank you for the gift of your time and your insight. I am also very grateful to Rebecca Totaro and an anonymous reader for Kent State University Press; both saw merit in this book and provided feedback to help it reach its present form. Tremendous thanks also to Susan Wadsworth-Booth, who has always provided good advice and has supported my work for many years now.

I am grateful to the conference and panel organizers who have given me space to work through the ideas in this book, including the Renaissance Society of America and American Comparative Literature Association, as well as to conference attendees who provided questions and feedback. I am also indebted to Richard Strier and *Modern Philology,* who published my essay "Pity and the Failures of Justice in Shakespeare's *King Lear,*" upon which the third chapter of this book draws heavily and which was in many ways the starting point of this entire project.

Last but certainly not least, I give my eternal gratitude to my family, near and far, who have supported me over the years. To my father and my sister, I am thankful that you have always believed in me. To my mother, I can never repay the patience and kindness you've shown: you've been my rock in bad times and my cheerleader in good times. I could not have written this without your care and love. I would also be remiss not to acknowledge my furry "research assistants," Erasmus, Leonidas, Echo (may she rest in peace), and Phoenix, who made sure I never spent too much time at the computer and who rewarded me with snuggles, antics, and walks throughout this process. Most of all, thanks to my spouse, Robin Sowards, who has read every word of this book many times over, who has supported me every step of the way, and whose love and care give more meaning to everything I do.

╬ INTRODUCTION ╬

What does it mean that literature makes us feel? How do the feelings provoked by literature affect our lives? These two questions are at the heart of this book because they are at the heart of late sixteenth- and early seventeenth-century theories of literature. Whereas modern aesthetics begins from the proposition of the autonomy of the artwork, early modern discussions of poetry focused instead on questions of its social value: is literature good for us (and by extension for society) or not? Because of a tradition extending from Aristotle into the seventeenth century that emphasized emotion's role in virtue, that value was at least in part dependent on literature's ability to provoke feelings in the audience. As a result, early modern aesthetics focused on an element of aesthetic experience that has gone underdiscussed in literary study's current return to aesthetics: our emotional engagement with art. The works discussed in this book all ask the question: how do the emotions provoked by literature—whether delight or other strong emotions like pity and fear—affect literature's ethical force?

Early moderns inherited this question from the history of aesthetic inquiry that preceded the early modern period. In appraisals of literature from Plato to Aristotle to Augustine, the question of the ethical value of literature—which was the central matter of debate—was deeply bound up with the emotions literature can provoke. Writers like Sir Philip Sidney, Edmund Spenser, and William Shakespeare drew disparately upon these earlier discussions as they attempted to define and defend literature.

What they discovered as they did, however, were the seeds of the autonomy thesis that wouldn't see its full articulation until the work of Immanuel Kant late in the eighteenth century. These seeds enable Sidney, in his *Defence of Poesy,* to proclaim that the poet "nothing affirms, and therefore never lieth."[1] At the same time, however, elaborating upon the view of aesthetic experience as something separate from real-life experience posed serious problems for early moderns who defended literature's value by relying on the Horatian platitude that literature teaches and delights. Aesthetic delight, which sat in an uneasy relationship with other feelings provoked by literary experience, was treated as the vehicle of moral instruction while also causing writers like Sidney and Spenser, in particular, to stumble over the argument that literature can teach us to feel emotions that promote virtue.

This book makes two main arguments. First, a careful examination shows that what troubled early modern attempts to locate the value of poetry in its ethical effects was a difficulty in reconciling those ethical effects with an increasing sense of the artwork's autonomy. Specifically, the tendency to link ethical effects with literature's ability to engage our emotions ran headlong into a question about the relationship between aesthetic and ethical emotions arising from the recognition that artworks have a reality different than our own. This conflict in large part coalesces around the experience of pity. As an emotional response to various kinds of human experience, pity—understood broadly in terms of sympathy or compassion—plays an important role both in discussions of aesthetics and of ethics that preceded the early modern period. Examining how early modern writers discussed and represented pity, especially when considering Sidney and Spenser, reveals a fault line between aesthetic and ethical experience that points to a burgeoning recognition of literature's autonomy from lived experience.

Second, I show that early modern discussions of literary value can open a way to think about the significance of the emotions that art makes us feel and the importance of those emotions in our ethical lives, without sacrificing the autonomy of the artwork. Modern aesthetics, at least as practiced by literary scholars, tends to focus on how the artwork as an autonomous entity is nevertheless situated in relation to the world as it is. At the same time, perhaps as a result of the

Kantian claim that our experience of art is disinterested, that relationship tends to be framed cognitively and moves away from questions about how reading literature affects us emotionally.[2] But the struggles of early modern writers with this divide between aesthetic autonomy and emotional experience, and particularly the dramatic explorations of these questions in Shakespeare, suggest that the autonomy of the art nevertheless provokes emotional responses that can travel beyond the experience of the playhouse. Reintegrating our emotional engagement with literary works into aesthetics in order to ask how literature can affect our behaviors in the world provides aesthetics with powerful arguments for why literature is valuable and why it should be studied.

My purpose in this introductory chapter is to trace the conceptual distinctions that my readings of Sidney, Spenser, and Shakespeare will rely upon, as well as to make the case for why we should pay attention to emotion in discussing early modern aesthetics. To do so, I will first outline what we miss when we read early modern theories of literature too much in the light of modern aesthetics: specifically, the insistence on literature's ability to *move* the audience that emphasized our emotional responses to literature as part of its value. To understand how these responses were understood, we must consider some of the theories early moderns inherited from previous periods. The question of literature's value was often entangled with discussions of how these works provoke pity in the audience, and so the various valuations Plato, Aristotle, and Augustine developed of literature and of literary emotion provide a framework for understanding the conflicts early modern writers were negotiating. For the writers explored here, these conflicts were both the source material they were working with and part of larger cultural debates about the role of emotion in ethics and the role of literature in society. At the same time, their engagement with these ancient and medieval conflicts was distinctly their own, even as it looked forward to the rise of aesthetics as such in the eighteenth century.

I. MODERN VERSUS EARLY MODERN AESTHETICS

Critical discussions of early modern aesthetics tend to pull in two directions. One examines how early modern literature prefigures the rise of aesthetic autonomy in the eighteenth century; the other seeks to recover a pre-eighteenth-century aesthetics from the sixteenth and seventeenth centuries. The two currents registered by these opposed critical positions—one pulling toward the Enlightenment and critical theory, the other looking back to older theories of mimesis—form the central dynamic troubling late sixteenth and early seventeenth-century English theories of literature. While early modern literature was beginning to develop the notion of literature's autonomy as an entity distinct from the world as it is, it was at the same time deeply engaged with earlier debates about the value of literature.

On the one hand, modern critical discussions focused on those earlier debates have sometimes overemphasized Kantian disinterestedness and thereby missed the way that early modern texts speak to modern theories. On the other hand, discussions recognizing a continuity between early modern and modern aesthetics have generally overlooked the significance of emotion in those earlier debates. What gets lost in the conversation is how older philosophical engagements with literature might be integrated with modern aesthetics to be more responsive to the emotional dimension of aesthetic experience and its ethical significance.

Talking about "early modern aesthetics" always opens the door to charges of anachronism. As a discrete field of philosophical inquiry, "aesthetics" arises more than a hundred years after the death of the last author this book considers. Moreover, as Andrew Bowie argues, this philosophical field arises partly in response to the shift away from understanding art as mimetic and toward understanding it as autonomous.[3] To the extent that early modern discussions of literature often frame it as a representational art form (as we will see in more detail shortly), there are thus good reasons to resist the idea of applying the term "aesthetics" to early modern discussions of literature, at least without significantly qualifying the term.

That resistance largely focuses on the difficulty of applying a theory of autonomy—understood in part through the Kantian claim that our experience of the beautiful is disinterested—to texts that very clearly wanted readers to see them as directly relevant to their lived ethical experience. Genevieve Guenther, for instance, argues that we need to take a pre-Kantian approach to thinking about what she calls early modern "instrumental aesthetics": "The literature that espoused or performed an instrumental aesthetic in early modern England composed neither an autonomous sphere constructed to be disinterested nor merely one site among others for cultural contestation. It was, rather, the producer of effects not to be found in other cultural sites and a discourse explicitly interested in the instrumental ends such effects might have in social and political life."[4]

Accounts like Guenther's or Charles Whitney's, which looks for "ante-aesthetics" in Shakespeare's work, rightly emphasize the incongruity of reading early modern texts as disinterested.[5] Defenders of poetry like Sidney and Thomas Lodge explicitly claim that literature can have a positive effect on the social order, while detractors like Stephen Gosson argue that literature has negative social effects. Guenther's argument that early modern English writers saw their fictional work as instrumental in various ways is simply incontrovertible. The linking of aesthetic autonomy to Kantian disinterestedness, however, misses twentieth- and twenty-first- century development of eighteenth-century aesthetics that asks how artworks interact with the social world. Modern aesthetics, while descended from Kant, nevertheless tends to recognize the incongruities of the third *Critique* and looks "for a concept of autonomy that isn't about being divorced from the world as it is, but that ... 'discovers the world in new ways ... rather than copying or representing what is known to be already there.'"[6]

Pushing back against "a formulation of the aesthetic that is derivative of an 'over-simplified Kantianism'"[7]—something like Gauthier's "*l'art pour l'art*" thesis—critics engaged with modern philosophical aesthetics look to twentieth-century theorists, Theodor Adorno in particular, to identify ways in which artworks are relevant to and in dialogue with real world experience, even as they resist that real world. While Adorno claimed that "Artworks detach themselves from the empirical world and bring forth another world, one opposed to the empirical world,"[8] the very fact of opposing the empirical world opens the possibility for critique of and resistance to the world that is. If Adorno refused the position that art has a "social function,"[9] he nevertheless articulated the relation between the artwork and the social world in such a way that "art's very 'alienation' and 'isolation' ... provides the grounds for its political and philosophical potential in modernity."[10]

In this account, art is autonomous to the extent that it makes its own rules for itself; but those rules speak through their difference to our own, allowing us to imagine "the possibility that the world and its objects might be otherwise than they are."[11] For many early modernists, there is something familiar about this proposition. When Sidney imagines, in his *Defence,* the poet "freely ranging within the zodiac of his own wit" in order to "deliver a golden" instead of a "brazen" world (216), we might see, as Mark Robson argues, that Sidney's idea of poetry "is co-extensive with the world but opens a space for critical engagement with that world."[12] In discussing Spenser, Rachel Eisendrath sees a similar dynamic, in which the poem pushes "its readers to try to imagine . . . a meaning that lies somehow beyond the poem itself. The poem becomes, to use Adorno's language, 'nonidentical' with itself."[13] And Hugh Grady, in looking at *A Midsummer Night's Dream,* argues the play offers "one of the fundamental possibilities of aesthetic representation: to distantiate us from the familiar human world, to lead us into imagining other modes of living and loving, to look critically into received ideologies of love and marriage."[14]

None of these readings via modern aesthetics argues that the moral worlds of early modern literature are divorced from the lives of the audience. An instrumental aesthetics, in which writers see their literary works as interventions in the audience members' ethical lives, is therefore not necessarily at odds with a modern understanding of aesthetic autonomy. In defining the relationship between early modern and modern aesthetics, the important question is not *whether* early modern writers sought ethical effects in their work: it is *how* those works achieve ethical effects. This was the question that the early modern writers under consideration here sought to answer. In doing so, they highlighted an increasing belief in aesthetic autonomy that was at odds with theories of representation deriving largely from Plato.

What modern aesthetics largely overlooks, however, is the crucial role emotions play for early modern writers in answering these questions. One of these emotions was delight: the feeling of pleasure an audience experienced when reading literature or watching a play. The Horatian platitude, that literature teaches and delights, was a commonplace in the period. More specifically, as Guenther has argued, for the English early moderns literature "teaches *by delighting.*"[15] Thus, for instance, in his reply to Stephen Gosson's antipoetical polemic *The School of Abuse,* Thomas Lodge argues that "What so [poets] wrot, it was to this purpose, in the way of pleasure to draw men to wisedom," while Sidney claims that the poet "cometh to you with words set in delightful proportion, either accompanied with, or prepared for, the well enchanting skill of music. . . . And, pretending no more, doth intend the winning of the mind from wickedness to virtue."[16] As we will see in more detail in the next chapter, questions of what produces this delight and how delight transforms into teaching were not easily answered. Early modern writers nevertheless remained committed to the role of delight in making literature ethically valuable.

But other emotions—not just the general enjoyment we feel in experiencing art but the emotions evoked by the specific artwork with which we are engaging—were important, too. In the *Defence,* Sidney runs through a range of emotive responses that literature "teaches," from pity to sorrow to scorn. The notion that it might be important to *teach* emotions is not one with much currency today, when deontic and utilitarian frameworks dominate ethics. But Thomist-Aristotelian virtue ethics formed part of the backdrop against which Sidney, Spenser, and Shakespeare were writing. This way of thinking about ethics held that learning to feel emotions in the right way was vital for virtue; moreover, virtue ethics emphasized that emotion was often needed to move a person not just to virtuous internal response but to virtuous action in the world.[17] While, as Christopher Tilmouth has argued, sixteenth-century England was heavily influenced by rationalist, anti-emotion ethical traditions deriving from Stoicism, critics like Richard Strier have demonstrated that there remained in the period significant resistance to the idea that reason's job was to repress or restrain emotion.[18] For writers eager to defend the value of literature, its ability to evoke and thereby teach ethical emotions was what set literature above even philosophy for its value to society.

Additionally here, literature does not just teach virtuous emotions, but those emotions are believed to be crucial for moving the audience to take ethical *action.* Sidney argues that "no learning is so good as that which teacheth and moveth to virtue; and . . . none can both teach and move thereto so much as poetry" (234). As many scholars have noted, theories of literature in the period relied heavily on rhetoric,[19] "which aimed not only to teach people but also, as Cicero put it, to move them."[20] Thus, for example, in his 1560 *Arte of Rhetoric,* Thomas Wilson identified the ends of rhetoric as "To teach. To delight. To perswade," repeating the Horatian platitude beloved of defenders of poetry with the addition of persuasion.[21] Rhetorical discourses from Aristotle onward recognized that one of the best ways to persuade is to provoke emotion in the audience.[22] This conviction crosses over from the domain of rhetoric into ethics. As Tilmouth demonstrates, even a relatively rationalist treatise like Thomas Rogers's 1576 *Anatomie of the Minde* nevertheless makes the Aristotelian argument that emotions "are the components of desire which reason must necessarily appropriate to achieve its ends" because "they alone move man to act."[23] Indeed, the emphasis on our emotions' ability to move us was so prevalent in the period that Richard Meek and Erin Sullivan hypothesize this emphasis drove the transition from the word "passion" to the word "emotion," evoking the idea of movement, in the period.[24]

One of the emotions most associated with Christian ethics was pity. In describing the value of the passions for virtue, Augustine in *City of God* turns to *misericordia*—pity or compassion—to defend emotion from the Stoics. Quoting Cicero's comment to Caesar that "Of all your virtues, none was more admirable, none more attractive, than your compassion," he calls this sentiment "Far more creditable, more humane, and more in harmony with the feelings of true religion" than the usual Stoic "condemnation" of pity.[25] In the sixteenth and early seventeenth centuries, this emphasis on compassion continued in thinkers as different as John Calvin and Thomas Wright. In his commentary on Seneca, Calvin explicitly rejects the Stoic's comments on *misericordia* on the basis that "he who feels no pity cannot be a good man," while Wright argues early in *Passions of the Minde* that "Passions, are not onely, not wholy to be extinguished (as the Stoicks seemed to affirme) but sometimes to be moved, and stirred up for the service of virtue . . . : for mercie and compassion will move us often to pitty, as it did Job."[26] It was specifically pity that these early modern writers sought to rescue from the ebbing tide of sixteenth-century Stoicism, and it was specifically pity's ability to move us—the same power Sidney attributes to poetry to justify its ethical value—that made it worth rescuing.

It is worth pausing to note here a certain terminological difficulty that arises out of this tension between Christian pity and Stoic virtue. The passage from Wright just quoted aligns mercy, compassion, and pity, and for many writers thinking of the Christian tradition, these three words can all serve as translations of *misericordia*.[27] The Stoic tradition, however, opposed *misericordia*, understood as an emotion, to the virtue of *clementia*, understood as a rational decision to remit a punishment in order to attain some benefit. In *De Clementia,* Seneca argues that, contrary to *misericordia,* "Mercy [*clementia*] joins in with reason," and so it is superior to *misericordia* because the "Sadness [caused by pity] is ill adapted for seeing how things are, for thinking out what might be useful."[28] Stoic mercy, in other words, eschews fellow-feeling in favor of remitting a punishment when it will be of value to a ruler. Unhelpfully, Stoic *clementia* was also often translated in the period as "mercy." Thus, whereas for writers espousing an Augustinian concept of *misericordia,* "mercy" and "pity" are synonyms, for writers operating in a Stoic framework, pity is often *opposed* to mercy. *Clementia* is further discussed in chapters two and three, but, unless otherwise noted, the pity and mercy that suffuse the texts under consideration here align with *misericordia,* often specifically resisting Stoic *clementia.*

Emotion thus was at the center of early modern English aesthetic thought because these writers believed in the value of emotion for teaching, persuading, and moving to ethical action. The theory of emotion that underwrites this belief differs significantly from the humoralism that so much early twenty-first-century criticism in the field has emphasized, which examines the role of the body in the transmission of feeling from person to person.[29] But a growing body of scholarship recognizes that Galenism was not the only and perhaps not even the dominant framework for thinking about emotion in the period. As Richard Meek has recently argued, emotions like "pity and compassion from this period are far more concerned with imagination, projection, and self-recognition" than they are with bodily experience.[30] Moreover, as others have noted, Thomist ideas about the soul, which in turn draw heavily on Aristotle, likewise maintained currency through the sixteenth and into the seventeenth centuries. These Thomist-Aristotelian ideas saw emotions not as motions of the body but as a form of thought or judgment. As Benedict Robinson notes, "In virtually every premodern theory of the passions, the passions are forms of intentionality, ways of seeing, and therefore also perceptions and modes of cognition."[31] These theories, as Robinson, Meek, Julie Solomon, and others have argued, continued to have influence when Sidney, Spenser, and Shakespeare were writing.[32]

These theories illuminate how emotion could function not just as a force for persuading but for teaching. The cognitive tradition of thinking about emotion provided a framework that saw emotion not as a force divorced from rationality but one that participates in it. Despite arriving at disparate conclusions about the role of emotion in ethics, Stoicism and Aristotelian virtue ethics held in common the premise that emotional responses are a form of judgment. In modern philosophy of emotion, this has become a dominant theory in the last fifty years, though it is not one with much cultural currency. Philosophers like Robert C. Solomon and Martha C. Nussbaum trace this position, often called the "cognitive theory of emotions," back to the Stoics in particular, though, as Stephen Halliwell notes, Aristotle's theories clearly also demonstrate a cognitive view.[33] To be sure, for the Stoics emotions most often constitute *incorrect* judgments, but Nussbaum develops their theories while rejecting their conclusions, in part by engaging heavily with Aristotle. She argues that "Emotions...involve judgments about important things, judgments in which, in appraising an external object as salient for our own well-being, we acknowledge our own neediness and incompleteness before parts of the world that we do not fully control."[34] For example, in defining pity in *Rhetoric*, Aristotle states that it is "a feeling of pain at an apparent evil, destructive or painful, which befalls one who does not deserve it, and which we might expect to befall ourselves or some friend of ours." Aristotle's pity, Nussbaum explains, thus comprises a judgment "that the suffering is serious rather than trivial," that "the person does not deserve the suffering," and that "the possibilities of the person who experiences the emotion are similar to those of the sufferer."[35]

The cognitive theory of emotion as a form of judgment—specifically a judgment of *value,* as Nussbaum argues—is useful for understanding early modern aesthetic theories both because it is based in the same history of ideas that early modern English writers were drawing on and because it provides a framework for understanding how emotional experience relates to ethical action and our rational faculties. To feel a particular way about a character or an event constitutes an ethical judgment for the writers discussed here. For Shakespeare, the recognition of this judgment opens the door to questions about the ethical value of individual judgments—*should* we feel the way that we feel?—questions that offer a way to reconcile the autonomy of the artwork with claims for literature's ethical merits. While Sidney and Spenser do not get so far in questioning the value of our emotional response to aesthetic experience, the ethical potentials of emotional experience raise literature above all other forms of learning for all three of these writers.

This is what most distinguishes early modern aesthetics from modern. When modern aesthetics discusses the social or ethical value of aesthetic experience, it tends to do so in rationalist terms: "the role of aesthetic experience in education is to extend the possibility of *thinking* otherwise."[36] The early moderns, however, believed that we access *thinking* otherwise by *feeling* otherwise; early modern theories of literature were particularly attuned to this dynamic.

II. LITERATURE, PITY, AND THE EARLY MODERN INHERITANCE

If modern aesthetics focuses relatively little on our emotional experience of art, the ancient debates about literature that formed the intellectual inheritance of the early modern period focused on nearly nothing but. The question of the value of literature was deeply entangled with the question of the value of emotions. Poetry is dangerous for Plato in part because the emotions it provokes are dangerous. For Aristotle, who saw a positive role for emotions in ethical life, poetry was instructive *because* of the emotions it provoked. In either case, our emotional experience of literature is fundamental to the question of how art affects its audience and therefore of the social effects of literature.

These discussions about the value of aesthetic emotions, however, raise a second question: are the emotions provoked by aesthetic experience of the same kind as the emotions we experience in the real world? Plato and Aristotle both take a position on this question by simply assuming it as the ground of their evaluations. Not until Augustine does a clear division between aesthetic emotion and ethical emotion—emotion in response to real-world experience that affects our real-world behavior—arise. While Augustine's reflections on theater recapitulate the dispute between Plato and Aristotle, it is his expansion on what I will call Aristotelian "aesthetic distance" that plants the first recognizable seeds of the autonomy thesis.

At stake in these questions was the nature of *representation* as an aesthetic term. These ancient debates that examined the nature of aesthetic "reality" via the ability of emotion to travel across the boundary between reality and fiction established both the terms and fault lines that early modern writers had to contend with as they developed their own theories. We must examine these terms and fault lines in order to establish the framework through which the following chapters will read the works of Sidney, Spenser, and Shakespeare.

The key emotion that cuts across these discussions is pity, largely due to the central role tragedy plays in the history of philosophical aesthetics. As Halliwell notes, a "series of classical sources, from Herodotus to Isocrates, and including Aristotle's *Poetics,* attests that the experience of tragedy was consistently associated with the strong, open display of emotion—especially pity—by mass audiences."[37] The conflict between Plato and Aristotle in particular on this subject provides an important model for distinguishing different ways of understanding the relation between our emotional engagement with literature and our actions in the world.

In critiquing the role of poets in his Republic, Plato repeatedly returns to tragic stories to provide evidence for poetry's potentially damaging effects. Just before he banishes the poets, for instance, Plato argues that pity destroys the good citizen's constitution: "The very best of us, when we hear Homer or some other of the makers of tragedy imitate one of the heroes who is in grief, and is delivering a long tirade in his lamentations or chanting and beating his breast, feel pleasure, and abandon ourselves and accompany the representation with sympathy and eagerness, and we praise as an excellent poet the one who most strongly affects us in this way."[38] Part of the pleasure of poetry, according to Plato, is that we all want to lament every now and then, and poetry gives us that opportunity. "Part of the soul," Socrates claims, "has hungered for tears and a good cry and satisfaction, but it is its nature to desire these things." Such desires are, however, "forcibly restrained" in a good person by a rational faculty that knows such responses are dangerous, and so poetry is a destructive indulgence because it teaches us the bad habit of giving freer rein to our emotional desires: "For after feeding fat the emotion of pity there, it is not easy to restrain it in our own sufferings."[39] Because for Plato pity is dangerous, so then is poetry. In allowing ourselves to lament alongside characters in poems, we inadvertently become more likely to allow ourselves the same experience of emotion in our own lives.

Aristotle similarly puts pity at the center of his discussion of literature, though of course he values it differently from Plato. "Tragedy," Aristotle explains, "is the imitation of an action that is serious and also, as having magnitude, complete in the parts of the work; in a dramatic, not in a narrative form; with incidents arousing pity and fear, wherewith to accomplish its *catharsis* of such emotions."[40] Here, as in Plato, pity is one of the defining characteristics of tragedy, alongside fear, both of which together are means to catharsis. *Poetics* does not clearly pronounce one way or the other on the moral value of these emotions in themselves:[41] as Halliwell notes, however, insofar as Aristotle sees poetry as a means of learning, he clearly does not think that the arousal of pity and fear by tragedy is dangerous in the way that Plato does, but instead he sees these emotions as rational judgments consistent with virtue.[42] Aristotle states that pity "is occasioned by undeserved misfortune," while its counterpart, fear, is what we feel for "one like ourselves."[43] Pity in this sense is an ethical judgment regarding what a person does or does not deserve. To the extent that justice is an ethical end, encouraging a pitiful response to the sight of someone "suffering undeservedly" can be a form of ethical instruction, insofar as it teaches us to respond negatively to injustice. As Nussbaum argues in her discussion of *Poetics*, "these emotions can be genuine sources of understanding, showing the spectator possibilities that are there for good people" faced with terrible situations.[44]

Beyond their different valuations of emotion, Plato and Aristotle also provide significantly different accounts of artistic mimesis or representation in the way each describes the emotional effect of poetry on the audience—a difference that will prove crucial to subsequent attempts to defend (or denounce) literature. Plato's theory of mimesis involves two main arguments. The first relates to what it means to *write* a poem: the art of the poet, Plato argues, is mere imitation of the visible world, which itself is merely an imitation of divine Forms, so that poetry moves away from the Form of the Good, rather than toward it.[45] The second relates to what it means to *read* a poem. Because the poet "know[s] nothing but to imitate," he "lays on with words and phrases the colors of the several arts in such fashion that others equally ignorant ... will deem his words most excellent, whether he speaks in rhythm, meter, and harmony.... So mighty is the spell that these adornments naturally exercise."[46] For Plato, aesthetic language—language full of "adornments"—circumvents the rational judgment of the content of that language so that the works of the poets seem excellent regardless of whether they actually are.[47] Poetry casts a magic "spell" on the audience such that we fail to notice that we are experiencing a copy of a copy of the real world, far removed from the Form of the Good.[48]

Thus he argues, in the passage previously examined, that tragic scenes in poetry are bad for us because, "after feeding fat the emotion of pity [by reading poetry], it is not easy to restrain it in our own sufferings." Plato's assumption, then, is that "there is continuity, even equivalence, between our relations to people and things in the real world and to people and things presented in mimetic art."[49] Halliwell notes this dynamic in Plato's *Philebus,* in which "tragic theater, where the spectators 'derive pleasure from weeping,' is held up as an instance" of "mixed emotional experiences of pleasure and pain. . . . Socrates declares: 'So our argument shows that pains and pleasures are mixed together in outpourings of grief . . . and in tragedies—not only in stage-plays, but in the entire tragedy and comedy of life.'"[50] In other words, just as art mimics real life, so too do our *responses* to art mimic our responses to real life. To the extent that the "outpourings of grief" associated with compassionate responses to suffering are destructive to the good life and to the well-ordered republic, tragic narratives are thus unethical because they cast spells that bypass our reason in order to teach us the bad habit of giving free rein to strong and (in Plato's account) irrational emotions rather than teaching us to be guided at all times by the dictates of reason.

Aristotle, on the other hand, frames mimesis somewhat differently. Whereas Plato claims the poet tries to pass off an imitation of the world for the real thing, Aristotle seems to describe the activity of the poem as something more in line with the word's root, *poeien,* meaning "to make." He clearly states that "the poet's function is to describe, not the thing that has happened, but a kind of thing that might happen," so that the poet is a "maker of plots."[51] Moreover, Aristotle claims that we *do not* experience aesthetic representations the same way we experience the real thing: "though the objects themselves may be painful to see, we delight to view the most realistic representations of them in art, the forms for example of the lowest animals and of dead bodies."[52] Despite the fact that the attraction of art is in part its "realism," Aristotle nevertheless also marks out aesthetic experience as something distinct from other kinds of real-world experiences. Halliwell (in language seemingly influenced by Sidney) summarizes the difference. For Plato, "Mimesis is taken to be crudely parasitic on reality: the artist's aim . . . is to produce the effect of a mirror held up to the world of the senses." Aristotle, in contrast, "reacts against this view of mimesis by releasing the artist from the obligation of transcribing or reproducing reality in any straightforward way, by charging mimesis with the power of embodying universals rather than particulars, and by treating the poet not as an affirmer . . . but as a skillful maker of dramatic fictions."[53]

This distinction between reality and fiction is crucial to the role of strong emotion, particularly pity, insofar as our pity reflects our distance from—rather than continuity with—the representation. Fear and pity exist for Aristotle in a delicate balance. In his *Rhetoric*, he writes, "Pity may be defined as a feeling of pain at an apparent evil, destructive or painful, which befalls one who does not deserve it, and which we might expect to befall ourselves or some friend of ours." He goes on, however, to qualify the notion that we identify with the object of pity, saying that we pity "those whom we know, if only they are not very closely related to us—in that case we feel about them as if we were in danger ourselves." When we feel in danger ourselves, Aristotle claims, the experience is simply "terrible" and will "produce the opposite of pity." From this Aristotle derives the principle that "what we fear for ourselves excites our pity when it happens to others."[54] In other words, too close an identification between the subject and the object of pity creates only fear, which chases away pity.

Halliwell, who likewise reads Aristotle's theory of pity in *Poetics* with reference to *Rhetoric*, summarizes this dynamic in Aristotle: "Pity, in sum, seems to involve a degree of sympathy or fellow feeling . . . , but a sympathy that does not erase the sense of difference between oneself and the object of pity."[55] In other words, pity requires distance—and in the case of tragedy, this is a specifically *aesthetic distance.* We know the figures on the stage are imitations—otherwise we would not experience pleasure in them. We can hold fear and pity in balance because those imitations never present us with an immediate sense of danger to ourselves or to our most beloved friends and family.

While for Plato pity means sharing the emotional reactions of the characters before us, for Aristotle our aesthetic distance means that our sufferings are not those of the characters at all, but meaningfully different from the emotions being imitated on stage. While, as Halliwell demonstrates, Aristotle never goes so far as to suggest that aesthetic emotions are qualitatively different from real-life emotions, the fact that our responses are elicited by a dramatic structure that presents itself as fiction means that we do not experience these emotions, as Plato would argue, "as overwhelming waves of feeling, but as part of an integrated response to the structured material of poetic drama: the framework for the experience of these emotions is nothing other than the cognitive understanding of the mimetic representation of human action and character."[56] Oedipus does not pity himself; he experiences the terror of discovering he is an incestuous patricide. But we, as the audience, pity him because, while we might recognize that we, too, could have undeserved misfortune befall us, we're not actually experiencing the fear we would have if we discovered the same about ourselves.

This difference opens up a gap for reflection that enables reason to enter the experience in a way it doesn't for Plato.[57] Thus Aristotle ties poetic imitation to learning, arguing that readers "enjoy seeing images, therefore, ... because as they look at them they have the experience of learning and reasoning out what each thing represents, concluding, for example, that 'this is so and so.'"[58] In making space for a poetic audience to "reason out" what they are experiencing in a poetic imitation, Aristotle disputes the Platonic argument that poetry is simply "the vehicle of a worldview."[59] Instead, an artwork is an object for reflection, something whose meanings and lessons involve the active, thinking participation of the audience, rather than, as for Plato, our merely passive reception. Thus when we leave the theater, as both Halliwell and Nussbaum argue, what we take with us is not undirected emotion, but a better understanding of human character and vulnerability—what Aristotle terms *catharsis*.[60]

The distinction between these two understandings of *mimesis*—the one that sees aesthetic experience as continuous with other forms of experience, the other that sees it as a different form of experience—is crucial for early modern discussions of literature. On the one hand, writers like Sidney did not often mark the distinction and so would slide back and forth between the two models of artistic representation without entirely noticing the conceptual havoc it wreaks to overlay one model on the other. On the other, Aristotelian mimesis offered early moderns a model for recognizing the uniqueness of literary experience, a recognition that is necessary for arriving at the theory of art's autonomy.

It is not Aristotle, however, but Augustine who more fully articulates the division of aesthetic from real-world experience and spells out the difficulty that aesthetic distance posed for locating art's value in its ability to evoke ethical emotions. In his *Confessions,* Augustine famously repudiates classical literature and tragic theater, pointing explicitly to the kind of pity (*misericordia*) they evoke as the source of the problem. Given the deep influence Platonism exerted on Augustine, the resemblance between some of his remarks and Plato's is unsurprising. Excoriating tragic theater, he writes, "the more anyone is moved by these scenes, the less free he is from similar passions," echoing Plato's fear that responding to literature with pity creates bad habits of mind.[61]

Contrary to Plato's position, however, Augustine's complaint doesn't grow from the assumption that the feelings we experience while viewing aesthetic objects are the same as those we experience in real life. Instead, he takes the position that aesthetic pity is qualitatively different from the kind of pity we do—and, importantly, *should*—feel when we regard a real person's misfortune: "But what quality of mercy [*qualis misericordia*] is it in fictitious and theatrical inventions? A member of the audience is not excited to offer help, but invited only to grieve."[62] The problem, according to Augustine, is that the kind of feeling tragic literature teaches us is the wrong kind of pity. Augustine defines the right kind of pity in *City of God:* it is "a heartfelt sympathy [*compassio*] for another's distress, impelling us to succor him if we can."[63] Augustine disapproves of tragic theater because it teaches us to feel a *misericordia* wherein we are "not excited to offer help," not impelled to provide "succor." Emotion can provide a powerful call to action, as noted above, but for Augustine not *every* emotion will do that. Specifically aesthetic emotion, he argues, is inert. For him, virtuous Christian pity is thus at odds with the kind of pity inspired by literature.

Thomas Aquinas elaborates on Augustine's concept of Christian pity in a manner that paradoxically clarifies the distance between Aristotle and Augustine on the value of tragedy by attempting to align them. Starting with Augustine's definition of *misericordia* in *City of God,* Aquinas combines this with Aristotle's claim that pity arises in people viewing others' misfortunes "because it makes them realize that the same may happen to themselves," a connection Aquinas calls "real union."[64] But Aquinas modifies Aristotle to fit Augustine's definition of Christian pity by ignoring the distance Aristotle places between the subject and object of pity in *Rhetoric* and instead turning to *Nicomachean Ethics*. Aquinas asserts that, in *misericordia,* there is an even closer identification between subject and object, called "union of the affections, which is the effect of love. For, since he who loves another *looks upon his friend as another self,* he counts his friend's hurt as his own, so that he grieves for his friend's hurt as though he were hurt himself."[65] The emphasized language is taken directly from book 9 of *Nicomachean Ethics,* where Aristotle is discussing the virtue of friendship.[66] Anthony Keaty notes that, for Aquinas, the "union of affections" is the important factor in making pity a virtue rather than simply a passion—that is, in making it "an operative habit inclining a person to a certain act."[67] For Aquinas, Augustine's understanding of Christian pity embraces an Aristotelian virtue ethics, wherein a passion combines with action—aid on behalf of the other that is spurred on by emotion—to produce virtue.

Aquinas's expansion of Augustine's definition of *misericordia* clearly accords with Augustine's rejection of tragic pity and illuminates Augustine's expansion of Aristotle's distinction between real-world and aesthetic emotion. Augustine takes issue with the fact that watching a tragic play does not create a "union of affections" but instead places an aesthetic distance between the subject and object of pity: "Hence came my love for sufferings, but not of a kind that pierced me very deeply; for my longing was not to experience myself miseries such as I saw on stage. I wanted only to hear stories and imaginary legends of sufferings which, as it were, scratched me on the surface."[68] If we feel the sufferings of others as our own pain, we will want to remove the source of that pain; but if we see a distance between ourselves and the one who suffers—because the suffering is only "stories and imaginary legends"—we can take pleasure in the suffering and perhaps wish it to continue rather than to abate.

In *Confessions* Augustine identifies two different kinds of pity that correspond with two different kinds of experience: ethical, Christian pity, which causes us to move to help a real person through a close identification with their real-world suffering, and tragic or aesthetic pity, which relies on the kind of distance Aristotle recognizes as a key component of his own notion of pity. In Augustine, then, the terms of

INTRODUCTION 19

the classical debate over the ethical value of the aesthetic are rewritten. Like Plato, Augustine believes literature can provoke responses that carry out into the world. Unlike Plato, he finds a fundamental difference between our responses to things in the world and our responses to aesthetic objects. Like Aristotle, Augustine believes tragic pity creates a distance between the subject and object who pities. Unlike Aristotle, Augustine frames this as a specifically *aesthetic* response, set against a different *qualis misericordia*—Christian pity—which is an *ethical* response to the world around us. Where Plato critiques poetry for causing us to identify too strongly with its characters and Aristotle praises it for doing the opposite, Augustine critiques it for not causing us to identify strongly enough.

Long before Kant, and in much stronger terms than Aristotle, Augustine provides an account of aesthetic response that is qualitatively different from our experience of the world and that is fundamentally disinterested—that carries no force into the world—because it can only "scratch [us] on the surface." Through the virtue of Christian pity, Augustine identifies a division between aesthetic and ethical emotional responses that calls into question how—or whether—literature could be a vehicle for ethical instruction by positing that our emotional experience of art is qualitatively different from our experience of other things in the world. Our delight in watching a tragedy is a marker of that distinction, and it creates a boundary between the aesthetic world and reality that our emotional experience does not cross.

III. EARLY MODERN ENGAGEMENTS WITH THE PAST

Early modern writers thus inherited a tradition of linking the value of literature—whether positive or negative—to the emotions it can produce and their ethical effects. But that tradition offered a variety of conflicting models of aesthetic representation that raised questions about how aesthetic experience relates to real-world experience and therefore how the emotions we feel when we experience literature relate to the ethical emotions that were recognized by Christian virtue ethics. The seeds of the autonomy thesis—and with them the move away from understanding literature as a copy of the world to understanding it as governed by its own fictional structures—were planted long before the sixteenth century. In grappling with the value of literature, early modern writers cultivated those seeds, largely by recapitulating and then transforming these earlier debates.

The antipoetic sentiment that gave rise to several defenses of literature in the late sixteenth century demonstrates how deeply indebted these early modern debates were to their ancient antecedents. In his famous attack on the theater, *The School of Abuse*, Stephen Gosson explicitly cites Plato, who he claims "saw the doctrines of these teachers [poets], neither for profit, necessary, nor to be wished for pleasure," before arguing that "the allurement" of poetry "draws the mind from virtue, and confoundeth the wit."[69] Like Plato, Gosson argues that, through its "allurement," poetry bypasses reason. The result is to encourage us to feel more than to think: "There set they abroach strange consorts of melody, to tickle the ear; costly apparel, to flatter the sight; effeminate gestures, to ravish the sense; and wanton speech, to whet desire to inordinate lust. . . . These by the privy entries of the ear slip down into the heart, and with gunshot affection gall the mind, where reason and virtue should rule the roost."[70] The Platonic rejection of pleasure, the belief that poetry usurps reason for feeling, and the notion that audiences will uncritically imbibe whatever pleasures the theater provides all appear here.

In his reply to Gosson, Thomas Lodge rebuts Gosson's claims by taking a positive view of aesthetic emotion, defending both the value of pleasure and of the arts' ability to move the audience. He accuses Gosson of creating "a new sect of serius stoikes," implicitly criticizing him for his absolute rejection of all pleasure and emotion, and instead argues that poets seek "in the way of pleasure to draw men to wisedom: for seeing the world in those days was unperfect, yt was necessary that they like good Phisions: should so frame their potions, that they might be appliable to the quesie stomaks of their werish patients."[71] Moreover, in responding to Gosson's particular critique of the effects of music in the theater, Lodge makes the case that "The Seas shall not swallowe *Arion* whilst he singeth, nether shall hee perish while he harpeth, a doleful tuner of a diing musitian can moue a Monster of the sea," noting the power of this kind of art to transform a "monster" via appeal to the affections.[72]

What is striking about Lodge's reply to Gosson is the extent to which it accepts the broadly Platonic framework within which Gosson operates. While he defends the value of the pleasure and emotion that literature or theater can evoke, Lodge does not challenge Gosson's more or less Platonic understanding of literature as something whose pleasures can transmit a worldview to the audience. Lodge's use of the physician metaphor above responds to a similar accusation made at the very beginning of Gosson's attack. "I must confess," Gosson begins, "that poets are the whetstones of wit, notwithstanding that wit is dearly bought: where honey and gall are mixed, it will be hard to sever the one from the other. The deceitful physician gives sweet syrups to make his poison go down the smoother."[73] Both see the pleasures of literature as a vehicle for introducing some kind of content into the audience. The only question is whether that content is a medicine delivered by a "good physician" or a "poison" delivered by a "deceitful physician."

The physician metaphor had a long history through the Italian and into the English Renaissance and cleaves closely to Platonic concerns about the coercive power of poetry's pleasurable effects. While Plato does not himself use this metaphor, his positioning of the pleasures of poetry as a "spell" identifies how poetry works as a "vehicle of a worldview." Verse provides pleasures via verbal, formal effects, and those pleasures lead us to take in the content of those words as truth, regardless of whether or not they are. As Bernard Weinberg notes in his discussion of Platonic influences (including the physician metaphor) in similar Italian Renaissance theories of literature, "Whether the critics take the position favorable to poetry or its opposite, they remain within the same framework of discussion."[74]

As a defense of poetry, Lodge's version of the physician metaphor is unlikely to convince anyone who isn't already convinced. If poetry's delights cast a spell that coerces our consent to the conceptual content of the work, regardless of whether that content is actually ethical, then Plato may be right that it's safer to banish the poets altogether and concentrate on philosophy. Early modern writers looking to defend poetry thus needed to develop alternate models to frame their arguments. Sidney's claim that the poet is a "maker" "freely ranging only within the zodiac of his own wit" is one of those alternatives (215, 216). A similar idea appears at the very beginning of George Puttenham's 1589 *The Art of English Poesie,* where he opens with the proclamation, "A poet is as much to say as a maker" and goes on to suggest of poets that "if they be able to devise and make all these things of themselves, without any subject of verity, that they be . . . as creating gods."[75]

To understand the poet as a "maker," following Aristotle, is to distance the poet from Platonic imitators who badly represent what they do not know well and therefore deceive people about the nature of reality. Instead, Puttenham's and Sidney's approach in these moments moves closer to a conception of aesthetic autonomy. Instead of imagining that artworks try to and either succeed or fail at representing "truth"—the difference between Lodge's good physician and Gosson's deceitful one—the poet-as-maker metaphor opens the possibility that the poet imagines a world distinct from ours that perhaps plays by its own rules and whose truth-value lies elsewhere than in its correspondence to nature. This concept allows defenders of poetry to redirect the conversation about the value of poetry away from poetry's "charming" effects and the Platonic concern that poetry bypasses reason to force us to imbibe a falsehood.

In doing so, however, defenders of literature run the risk of divorcing aesthetic from ethical experience. If poetry is a world of its own, how then does it relate to our real-world experience? And how do our emotional responses to literature affect us outside of the world of the poem? In the next chapter, I'll explore how Sidney, in particular, struggled with these issues. For now, it's important to note that the difficulty of reconciling autonomous art with ethical experience—a problem developed by Augustine—led early modern defenses of literature to combine Platonic with Aristotelian modes of mimesis. Thus Puttenham, despite comparing some kinds of poets to gods, nevertheless also claims that "a poet may in some sort be said a follower or imitator, because he can express the true and lively of every thing is set before him, . . . and so in that respect is both a maker and a counterfeiter, and poesy an art not only of making, but also of imitation."[76]

A Platonic model of mimesis, which sees representations of the world being communicated wholesale by the artwork, very clearly offered literature the ability to "teach" in the way early modern defenders of poetry claimed made it valuable. Because of the *way* it teaches, however, by passing off a representation as the real thing, this model was open to the kind of critique Plato and writers like Gosson leveled against it. The Aristotelian, proto-autonomy model offered a way to protect against that attack. But this position, while granting the poet exceptional powers of world-building and granting the poem the status of a reality of its own, did not clearly lay a path to the ethical claims that were central to early modern defenses of literature. Because those ethical claims were deeply intertwined with the emotional experience of literature, building a bridge between the separate world of the text and the feelings it generates in the audience became, I argue, a significant part of the project of defending literature in the period.

IV. THE ART OF PITY

This book reconstructs that bridge. In the next chapter, we see that Sidney's work lays bare the contradictions posed by disparate understandings of mimesis that will eventually lead to mimesis being replaced by the idea of aesthetic autonomy. His *Defence* is widely read as unstable and contradictory, as it tries to reconcile the disparate aesthetic discourses that formed the early modern inheritance. What primarily drives this instability is his struggle to combine a sense of the artwork's autonomy with what he believes are its ethical effects. Sidney hints that our emotional responses to literature were not simply the vehicle of ethical instruction, as he argues explicitly, but also part of the *content* of that ethical instruction, insofar as literature might be able to train us to have the "right"—that is, Christian—emotional responses to the world around us. At the same time, however, he struggles to reconcile the ethical emotional response provoked by literary experience with his recognition that these responses are mediated by another, explicitly aesthetic emotion: the "delight" of artistic experience that marks literature as something different from other kinds of objects we encounter in the world. This problem becomes particularly clear in *Astrophil and Stella,* where Sidney's own theory of art in the *Defence* is refuted by his poems, which meditate on their failure to produce ethical pity in Stella. These sonnets, then, demonstrate a concept of aesthetic distance in their representation of pity that resists the argument that poetry can move its audience to action in the world.

Sidney's struggle and ultimate failure to reconcile our emotional engagement with literature with a model of aesthetic autonomy lays the groundwork that enables Spenser to engage in a much fuller exploration of this problem. *The Faerie Queene* cynically exploits the tensions

Sidney explored in order to signal the collapse of the *Faerie Queene*'s ethical project in the 1596 version of the poem. The philosophical engagements of Spenser's "Letter of the Authors," the explanatory text appended to the three-book, 1590 publication of the poem, also conflate Platonic and Aristotelian elements much as in Sidney's *Defence*. Spenser, however, demonstrates considerably more skepticism about the value of the specifically aesthetic, ornamental aspects of literature than does Sidney, a skepticism informed by a Platonism that unsettles the didactic claims Spenser makes for art. Turning then to the 1596 *Faerie Queene*, chapter 2 examines the poem's insistence on an Aristotelian ethical framework; in particular, book 4 relies on a Thomist modification to Aristotle's ideas about friendship that emphasizes pity's virtuous potential. In contrast to depictions of pity elsewhere in the poem, book 4 relies on pity as the virtue that enables friendship.

Through Spenser's insistence on the didactic power of "ensamples," he suggests that book 4 has the power to teach us how to be better friends by evoking readerly pity for his characters, hinting through the narrator's expressions of sympathy that our emotional response to the book can, as Sidney also imagines, transmit virtue to us by training our responses to suffering in a properly Christian direction. But this hint takes a bitter turn for Spenser. He uses an ultimately ironic performance of narrative pity to note the qualitative difference between the sad compassion the poem's friends feel for each other and the pity mediated by aesthetic delight that we experience as readers. Poking fun at our sadness that isn't *really* sad, Spenser's narrator signals his abandonment of the original, didactic purpose of his poem. His earlier Platonist suspicion of aesthetic pleasure gives way to the more Augustinian position that our pleasure marks aesthetic emotions as too distant from our ethical experience to produce positive change. Instead of providing "ensamples," the poem shows us that its world is not ours. For Spenser, this autonomy ultimately stands between the reader and an ethical experience.

While Spenser's response to the perceived incompatibility of ethical-emotional response and autonomous art is to side with autonomy against an instrumental aesthetics, Shakespeare offers a way to reconcile autonomy with the ethical value of the emotions literature provokes. Shakespeare, particularly in *King Lear*, demonstrates one model of how aesthetic pity *can* potentially generate ethical pity, as he creates a model of audience response that more fully integrates emotional and rational responses than his predecessors' accounts. Put simply, for Shakespeare, an audience's affective response to tragedy has the power to change how we think.

Examining metatheatrical moments in *A Midsummer Night's Dream, The Tempest,* and *Hamlet,* chapter 3 first outlines a Shakespearean aesthetic theory in which the experience of art is immersive in the moment, imposing on the viewer a worldview that includes both affective and cognitive responses. This worldview dominates our thinking for the duration of the play but afterward invites our consent while recognizing its inability to coerce it. Much as it does for Aristotle, aesthetic enjoyment rests largely in that moment of reflection, in the movement from our acceptance of the world of the play to our decision at the play's end about what to *do* with that world.

The chapter then turns to consider how Shakespeare rewrites tragic pity in *King Lear* away from a form of Aristotelian judgment—this person does or does not deserve to suffer—into an alternate mode of relation to the people around us; specifically, Cordelia's pity in the play asks us to make judgments on the basis of *need* rather than *merit*. This form of pity is not simply about feeling sadness for another's suffering but about a way of viewing the world through the ties of community, through a Thomist notion of the union of will and affections rather than according to the divisions of justice. To experience the play and to sympathize with Cordelia's pity is thus likewise to engage in this reoriented way of viewing others, to take in with our experience not just the emotional reaction but the altered worldview that enables us to pity an old man Aristotle would likely condemn.

The lessons of pity in this Shakespearean framework become available to cognition at the play's conclusion, with the reflection that enables us to understand the rational content of the pity Cordelia experiences. We do not have to feel exactly as Cordelia feels to learn how our pity offers us a different way of relating to other people in the world. The vehicle of aesthetic instruction thus becomes not, as Sidney and Spenser describe, a precept carried on an emotion, but a cognitive awareness of the way that emotions are structured by worldviews and the possibility that literature can lead us toward alternatives not available merely through rational thought. Shakespeare thus offers, implicitly if not explicitly, a model for aesthetic experience to intersect with our emotional lives that embraces the aesthetic autonomy that troubled Sidney and Spenser. Literature, Shakespeare's work shows, can use our emotional responses to the text to teach us new ways of seeing the world *outside* the text. What to *do* with these new ways of learning—how to mobilize them to ethical ends—the plays must leave to us.

The art of pity is at the heart of all these discussions. It is both art that represents pity and art that tries to evoke our own pity, and thereby asks us to consider the relationship—including the distance—between those two forms of emotion. To the extent that, as Aristotle argues and the authors considered here contend, an emotion like pity provides motive to act, understanding the role of that emotion in our experience of literature is crucial for understanding what ethical import it might have. The aesthetic realm may be autonomous, but insofar as it forms an important part of human experience, we can carry some part of that experience into the rest of our lives. As Sidney and Spenser demonstrate, emotions cannot communicate across the boundary between artwork and audience because the feelings evoked by aesthetic experience are mediated by our awareness of (and pleasure at) the distinction between the world of the text and our own. What Shakespeare shows, however, is that those emotions nevertheless form powerful motivations to engage in the kinds of reflection that can refine or alter our own worldviews. The boundary between the aesthetic world and our own means that the artwork can never determine the outcome of that reflection: the artwork can make us feel, but it is up to us to decide what those feelings mean—and how to act on them.

While this book focuses on a particular point in time and space— late sixteenth- and early seventeenth-century England—the debates and questions I discuss here have in many ways never left us. In 2024, the American Library Association documented that 2023 saw a 65 percent rise in the numbers of book ban attempts over the previous year, which represented an all-time high for the 21st century.[77] The attempt to remove books from public availability signals an awareness that literature has ethical effects and is driven by the fear that literature, as Plato argued, inspires mindless imitation. Oscar Wilde defended books in the nineteenth century by claiming that "the sphere of art and the sphere of ethics are absolutely distinct,"[78] but we can embrace literature's ethical potential without falling into the Scylla of naïve moralism or the Charybdis of aestheticism. As we will see, literary texts engage our emotions in a way that invests us in the worlds they offer. When we recognize, as Shakespeare did, that those emotions are mediated by aesthetic structures that prompt reflection on those emotions and the meanings they carry, we can recognize that literature poses important ethical questions without insisting that it offers all the answers.

✦ CHAPTER 1 ✦

Sidney Between Two Worlds

Pity, Delight, and the Failure of Instrumental Aesthetics

When Sir Philip Sidney sat down to compose his *Defence of Poesy*—probably around 1580 and likely in response to Gosson's *School of Abuse*—the ethical and aesthetic traditions outlined in the introduction were simultaneously the intellectual foundations upon which sixteenth-century European culture was built; a transmuted hodgepodge of ideas broken down, mixed, and reconstituted in the belly of the medieval and Italian Renaissance commentary tradition; and a relic overthrown by the Protestant Reformation. The *Defence* itself infamously bears out this mixed inheritance. Critical discussions of the text have long noted the work's indebtedness to Plato, to Aristotle, to the Italian commentary tradition, and to Protestant ideology,[1] as well as the conceptual muddiness of the essay's argument. A generous understanding of Sidney's approach is that the *Defence*'s "rhetorical oscillations," which "create an impression of confusion and even inconsistency," should be read with an understanding that "persuasion, not logical clarity, is its aim."[2] A more typical reading is Gavin Alexander's note that "when critics apply too much logic to the *Defence* it tends to fall apart or at least to feel the strain."[3]

But this strain grows out of the dynamic I traced toward the end of the introduction. Sidney, like many of his contemporaries, moves between an understanding of artistic mimesis in the Platonic sense—in which literature provokes what Jenefer Robinson calls "life emotions"

30 THE ART OF PITY

and thereby becomes, in Halliwell's words, a "vehicle for a worldview"—
and a growing sense of the artwork's autonomy.[4] These two incompatible views of aesthetic experience answer different imperatives in the
Defence. The first enables Sidney to develop powerful arguments for the
good that literature can do, largely through the way poetry engages us
emotionally. The second allows Sidney to defend against claims about
the evil literature can do—at the expense, I will show here, of his arguments about poetry's ethical potential. Sidney tries to have it both
ways in the *Defence,* creating the often-noted conceptual confusion of
the argument. When he tries to put these ideas into practice in his sonnet sequence *Astrophil and Stella,* he discovers the incompatibility of
these two approaches.

As we shall find, Sidney's early formulations of the autonomy thesis
interrupt the ethical claims he makes in literature's defense. In addition, the emphasis he gives to emotion's role in aesthetic experience
exposes what modern criticism loses when we focus too much on Sidney's forward-looking theories at the expense of his claims for literature's ethical potential. Critical discussions of Sidney's claims about
the ethical value of poetry have largely focused on Sidney's argument
that literature communicates moral precepts, an idea central to the
Defence's argument that the poet combines the techniques of the historian and of the moral philosopher, providing the precepts of the one
clothed in the particular story of the other. Thus in older discussions
of Sidney's engagement with his philosophical tradition, the "fore-
conceit" and the "speaking picture" take center stage: Sidney thinks,
the argument runs, that poetry enables us to see moral truths and
thereby to learn those truths.[5] As David Glimp and Margaret Ferguson have noted, however, the ability of poetry specifically to *move* its
audience—to produce emotional responses that can in turn generate
ethical action—is also central to Sidney's argument about the ethical
potentials of literature.[6] For Sidney, the ethics of poetry are not just
about communicating ethical *ideas* but also ethical *feelings.*

The autonomy thesis disrupts this argument to the extent that it
calls into question whether those feelings can carry forward into the
world or whether they are mediated by aesthetic experience in such a
way that our feelings never travel beyond the text. Ironically, this mediation is itself emotional: our experience of delight is what ultimately
interferes with aesthetic emotion becoming ethical in Sidney's work.

If we examine how Sidney discusses our emotional engagement with literature, first our delight and then our capacity to be moved, we see how these theories of emotional aesthetic experience both complement each other and resist each other. Insofar as they resist each other, it is because Sidney's understanding of aesthetic delight merges with an Augustinian sense that aesthetic emotions are precisely *not* life emotions—or at least that they do not carry out of the artwork into our lives. A closer look at moments of failed lessons in the virtuous emotion of pity in the *Defence* and *Astrophil and Stella* demonstrates that Sidney's aesthetics seeks to reconcile a growing sense of the autonomy of literature with the ethical effects he argues literature can have; this ultimately fails, however, because he is unable to imagine how emotion can traverse the boundaries of the artwork.

I. AESTHETICS, ETHICS, AND EMOTION IN THE *DEFENCE*

Sidney's *Defence* has a dual emphasis. On the one hand, Sidney argues that literature can communicate ethical ideas better than any other method. On the other, he argues that literature exceeds other forms of moral instruction because only poetry has the power not only to teach us but to move us to action. In both cases, our emotional engagement with literature plays a starring role. It is the element of delight, he argues again and again, that enables us to imbibe hard truths that we might otherwise resist. And it is the ability to move the audience—to evoke strong emotion—that pushes the ethical instruction poetry provides out of the realm of mere theory and into practice. Without the element of emotional engagement, poetry would have no particular claim to superiority among the intellectual arts, and so understanding Sidney's instrumental aesthetics requires an understanding of how the ethical teaching provided by poetry interacts with the emotional responses poetry provokes.

At some moments in Sidney's argument, delight—a response to aesthetic form—is a vehicle for ethical content. Our emotions are engaged in a way that enables ethical ideas to travel directly into our intellects (even against our wills). At other moments in Sidney's argument, however, our emotions play a role in ethical ideas themselves so that part of the "teaching" offered by literature is not just ethical precepts but a training in virtuous emotional responses. Both approaches suggest a model of mimesis whereby we take what we experience in literary works directly into our lives—something close to the Platonic model discussed earlier. Yet this approach to defending literature is undermined by moments in the *Defence* that move toward an autonomy model of aesthetics. Sidney makes various arguments about the relationship between our intellectual engagement with art and our emotional one, and this lays the groundwork—never fully realized in his own work—for a model of aesthetics that incorporates emotional engagement and its ethical import.

The simplest version of the relationship between ethical ideas and our emotional experience of literature found in the *Defence* is the Horatian platitude: poetry, Sidney claims, "is an art of imitation, for so Aristotle termeth it in the word *mimesis* . . . with this end, to teach and delight" (217). As Weinberg notes, this is well-worn territory by the time Sidney was writing; Horace's *Ars Poetica* was, at the dawn of the Renaissance in Italy, the most widely known work of literary criticism and the only such work "which had some currency during the Middle Ages and which came to the humanistic period and the Renaissance as a part of their more immediate intellectual heritage."[7] In particular, the tradition of commentary on the *Ars* throughout the Quattrocento and Cinquecento emphasized Horace's claim that the poetry that "combines pleasure with usefulness [*utile dulci*] wins every suffrage, delighting the reader and also giving him advice,"[8] refiguring Horace's advice for selling books into the argument that poetry should be socially useful.[9]

The means by which it becomes useful is specifically *delight*. This emotion, Sidney argues, makes us receptive to ethical ideas that we might otherwise resist. Drawing on the physician metaphor that Lodge also uses to defend literature, Sidney argues that

> even those hard-hearted evil men who think virtue a school name, and know no other good but *indulgere genio,* and therefore despise the austere admonitions of the philosopher, and feel not the inward reason they stand upon, yet will be content to be delighted—which is all the good fellow poet seemeth to promise—and so steal to see the form of goodness, which seen they cannot but love ere themselves be aware, as if they took a medicine of cherries. (227)

This metaphor, as we have seen, makes the delight afforded by poetry into a vehicle by which ethical instruction is communicated into the mind of the reader. Such is the power of delight, Sidney argues, that even those who resist virtue will nevertheless learn it from literature because they "will be content to be delighted."

The source of delight for Sidney, at least in this metaphor, lies in the formal characteristics of poetry rather than in its content. Just before this passage, he argues that the poet "comes to you with words set in delightful proportion, either accompanied with, or prepared for, the well-enchanting skill of music," so that it is the "proportion" of the words, enabling them to be "either accompanied with, or prepared for" music, that produces the cherry-flavor in the medicine. Narrative also provides its charms, insofar as the poet offers "a tale with holdeth children from play." The poet in this way, "pretending no more, doth intend the winning of the mind from wickedness to virtue—even as the child is often brought to take most wholesome things by hiding them in such other as have a pleasant taste" (227). Insofar as the poet is "pretending no more" than to offer "words set in delightful proportion" and a tale that can make a five-year-old sit still (a mighty power indeed!), the delight Sidney refers to derives not from ethical content but from structure: musical poetic rhythms, engrossing narrative forms. In other words, in this metaphor aesthetic texts can present ethical ideas within forms that make them appealing—an appeal those ideas do not have on their own.[10] According to this argument, narrative structures and rhythm produce pleasurable feelings in us. While we are enjoying ourselves listening, we take in "wholesome things" and so are instructed without realizing that is what is happening to us.

Alongside these arguments for literature's ability to communicate ethical *ideas,* however, the *Defence* also emphasizes its ability to produce ethical *feelings.* "Truly," Sidney notes, "I have known men that even with reading *Amadis de Gaule* . . . have found their hearts moved to the exercise of courtesy, liberality, and especially courage" (227). *Amadis* affects not the mind but the heart, and it does so through the act of moving the heart to virtuous emotions. Similarly, he argues that the elegist "surely is to be praised, either for compassionate accompanying just causes of lamentations, or for rightly painting out how weak be the passions of woefulness" (229). And in making the case for tragedy, Sidney writes: "But how much it can move, Plutarch yieldeth a notable testimony of the abominable tyrant Alexander Pheraeus, from whose eyes a tragedy, well made and represented, drew abundance of tears, who, without all pity, had murdered infinite numbers, and some of his own blood, so as he, that was not ashamed to make matters for tragedies, yet could not resist the sweet violence of a tragedy" (230). In all of these examples, Sidney pins poetry's ethical potential on the feelings it provokes—specifically feelings that are traditionally linked to virtue. In the case of the final example, it is able to do so even in someone who has lacked that virtuous feeling in his own life. Just as delight can make "hard-hearted evil men" imbibe lessons of virtue, so too can poetry teach even merciless tyrants to feel the pangs of pity.

These virtuous feelings are important, moreover, because they are able to move us to ethical action. It is this aspect of poetry that leads Sidney to set the work of the poet above the work of the philosopher:

> Yet do I think that no man is so much *philophilosophos* as to compare the philosopher in moving with the poet. And that moving is of a higher degree than teaching, it may by this appear, that it is well nigh both the cause and effect of teaching. For who will be taught, if he be not moved with desire to be taught? And what so much good doth that teaching bring forth (I speak still of moral doctrine) as that it moveth one to do that which it doth teach? For, as Aristotle saith, it is not *gnosis* but *praxis* must be the fruit. And how praxis can be, without being moved to practise, it is no hard matter to consider. (226)

Both poetry and philosophy offer instruction in ethics, Sidney claims— but poetry surpasses philosophy not because of the superiority of its teachings but because of its ability to produce movement, both internally and externally, to make a person both *want to learn* and then to *want to act* on that learning. Sidney continues, "Learned men have learnedly thought that where once reason hath so much overmastered passion as that the mind hath a free desire to do well, the inward light each mind hath in itself is as good as a philosopher's book.... But to be moved to do that which we know, or to be moved with desire to know: *hoc opus, hic labor est*" (226).

Here Sidney perhaps makes his most important claim for the value of emotion, though he makes it implicitly. If we can "overmaster" passion, our minds will be as philosopher's books, clearly laying out the truth in rational terms. But even then, Sidney suggests, something would be missing: "to be moved to do that which we know." Only literature—specifically the aesthetic delight that, by stirring the passions, "moves" us—can compel this last step. More than two hundred years after Sidney, Hegel would write that, once in the course of human progress our rationality had become sufficiently developed, art would eventually be rendered useless and philosophy would take its place.[11] Sidney here offers us an argument against Hegel that is based in the implicit assumption that reason alone can never be enough to move human beings to action in the world because emotions are fundamental to ethical life. The philosopher can tell us what to do, Sidney argues, but she can never make us want to do it. The poet, on the other hand, "doth not only show the way, but giveth so sweet a prospect into the way, as will entice any man to enter into it" (226).

Sidney follows other sixteenth-century writers who understood emotion as *necessary* for action, and therefore an important component of any attempt to persuade or otherwise induce ethical behavior.[12] This idea is evident in the history of the rhetorical tradition beginning with Aristotle and carrying through to the early modern period, in which appeal to emotion was considered fundamental. Aristotle devotes a great deal of time to discussing different emotions an orator might seek to evoke in their audience precisely as a way to persuade, to "move" the audience to choose or act a specific way. Similarly, when Thomas Wilson notes that the three ends of rhetoric are to teach, to delight, and to persuade, he then explains that, in order to persuade, the orator "must move the affections of his hearers in such wise, that they shall be forced to yield unto his saying."[13]

This emphasis on the role of the emotions in persuasion for both Wilson and Sidney speaks to a larger belief that the entire project of human civilization relies on people's affective engagements. Wilson argues that, without the persuasive force of rhetoric, no one would be content to labor while others ruled.[14] Sidney paints a similar picture in one of his earliest and most literal claims about literature's ability to "move" others, where he describes Amphion who "was said to move stones with his poetry to build Thebes" (213). In the story Sidney refers to here, Amphion builds a city by quite literally singing it into existence: his song causes the stones to follow him to the site of his new city and to form a wall of their own volition. Just as Wilson claims that "mov[ing] the affections" is necessary to create civilization, Sidney chooses a tale wherein the poet's ability to physically move its audience builds a great city, creating order from chaos.

Modern ethics is dominated by deontic and utilitarian/consequentialist theories, which rely on some form of rational calculation to motivate ethical behavior. These theories tend to argue that people *should* make decisions according to reason alone.[15] Sidney and his contemporaries, however, were much more interested in how people *do* make decisions and thus understood emotion to play a key role in the kind of ethical teaching that would produce stable societies. This understanding leads Sidney to an aesthetics wherein poetry's value rests in no small part in its ability to stir strong emotions in us. Those emotions then follow us out of the confines of the text and into the world, where they can prompt us to act on the virtuous emotions taught to us by the work of poetry.

This argument is significantly different from Sidney's claim that poetry makes us receptive to ethical ideas via delight—indeed, they are ultimately incompatible claims. It is worth noting, however, that both rely on a sense of continuity between aesthetic and "real life" experience. In discussing delight, Sidney frames the power of poetry much like Plato in the *Republic*, wherein Plato claims that the "adornments" of poetry, its "rhythm, meter, and harmony," cast a "spell" over the audience that compels our consent to the world of the text. He also argues that it teaches us to feel for ourselves and others whatever the poem compels us to feel for the characters so that, "after feeding fat the emotion of pity" in poetry, "it is not easy to restrain it in our own sufferings."[16] Like Plato, Sidney relies on a model of aesthetic mimesis in which the text bleeds into life. Whether our emotional responses make us susceptible to poetry's ideas or whether the emotional responses are themselves what we carry forward into the world, poetry's ethical value for Sidney derives from arguments that poetry is a "vehicle for a worldview."

Indeed, Sidney's arguments about the effects of poetry on the audience are closer to Plato's than they are either to Horace or to Lucretius, whose *De Rerum Natura* is the origin of the physician metaphor.[17] That Sidney uses Horatian and Lucretian framing to make these arguments signals an awareness of a problem he is skirting: that these claims for how literature works are just as easily used to attack literature as to defend it. In a concession to the poet-haters, he acknowledges later in the text that "poesy may not only be abused, but . . . being abused, by the reason of his sweet charming force, it can do more hurt than any other army of words" (236), before comparing the power of poetry to that of a sword which can be used equally to kill one's father as to defend one's country (237). Poems don't kill people, he argues: people kill people. But even Sidney doesn't seem convinced. As Guenther notes, the *Defence* demonstrates an anxiety over the way that poetry affects us despite ourselves in his allusions to magical practice. Sidney, she argues, "seems to imagine that poetry has a magical power that works automatically, like a spell"—a belief also advanced by Plato in critiquing poetry.[18] However much Sidney might couch the Platonism of this part of his argument in other terms, he is working within a mimetic framework that cannot rescue poetry from the charge of being at least potentially dangerous.

Because this model of artistic representation was replaced by the autonomy thesis in the eighteenth century, it is unsurprising that most recent discussions of Sidney's *Defence* do not focus much attention on this part of his argument—particularly not when he offers much more forward-looking aesthetic theories elsewhere in the text. What most modern discussions therefore miss, however, is an aesthetic model that not only accounts for our emotional experience of literature but that puts that experience at the center of poetry's ethical potential. While the model Sidney presents falters by relying on a Platonic framework, it nevertheless reminds us that our investment in literature derives from emotional experience—both delight and more unpleasant emotions like fear and pity—and raises the possibility that that experience affects us when we leave the text behind. To the extent that emotions are powerful motivators of action, and literature is characterized by its ability to arouse strong emotions, what could be better suited to create change in the world than literature? To the extent that we have not arrived at Hegel's age of rationality, Sidney reminds us that poetry is uniquely positioned to speak to both our reasoning and emotional faculties, offering a more holistic understanding of literature's ethical potential.

II. AUTONOMY, REFLECTION, AND DELIGHT

If Sidney offers a provocative reminder *that* our emotional engagement with literature forms the greatest part of its power as a social force, he nevertheless struggles to articulate exactly *how*. At times, the *Defence* accords with Leigh A. DeNeef's reading in which "Sidney's psychology of moving the reader" means that a "reader must imitate the poet's imitating."[19] At other moments, however, Sidney's examples suggest that we might do just the opposite, that through literature we learn to *avoid* imitating what we see. The *Defence* does not provide an account of how a reader might decide whether to imitate or to avoid, but this second claim signals a different understanding of aesthetic experience than the first, one closer to Aristotle's version of mimesis and related to those moments in the *Defence* that presage the autonomy thesis.

These forward-looking passages, which have received the bulk of recent critical attention, offer a vision of the artwork as a world of its own, not bound by the rules of this one. While these passages have less to say about how the audience relates to this more autonomous model of poetry, it is this way of thinking about literature, I would argue, that underwrites moments in Sidney's argument where his model of aesthetic experience involves distance for reflection. These moments trouble the argument that poetry can teach us via the transmission of ideas and emotion from text to audience. Put simply, the nascent autonomy thesis conflicts with Sidney's account of literature's ethical potential by suggesting that our emotional experiences are mediated by an aesthetic distance that transforms that emotional experience.

The most often-noted passages in the *Defence* that look forward to modern theories are the "golden world" section from early in the text and then the claim that the poet "nothing affirms, and therefore never lieth" from several sections later. Both present a starkly different account of artistic representation than the Platonic model Sidney accepts elsewhere in the argument. In the first passage, Sidney describes the poet "disdaining to be tied to any such subjection [to nature], lifted up with the vigour of his own invention," so that he "doth grow in effect another nature." This poet, according to Sidney, "goeth hand in hand with nature, not enclosed within the narrow warrant of her gifts, but freely ranging only within the zodiac of his own wit." Whereas nature's "world is brazen, the poets only deliver a golden" (216). As many critics have observed of this passage, Sidney here grants poets the ability to produce worlds in literature that operate at least to some extent autonomously from the world as it is.[20]

If this is a forward-looking moment in Sidney, however, it also has roots in Aristotle. The image of the poet creating his own nature evokes Aristotle's argument that the work of the poet is superior to the historian's because the historian "describes the thing that has been," while the poet describes "a kind of thing that might be." This argument is one of the ways that Aristotle's account of poetry distinguishes itself from Plato's: it is a refutation of the idea that the poet sets out to imitate the world as it is. For Sidney, who cites precisely this passage in Aristotle a few pages later (223), the Aristotelian poet who describes "a kind of thing that might be" offers a way to refute the Platonic claims of the *misomousoi* like Gosson. Poetry can show us a way to a better world, Sidney suggests, because it is *not* bound to represent the world as it currently is.

The seeds of the autonomy thesis are scattered throughout Aristotle's *Poetics,* and Sidney's *Defence* germinates those seeds. Somewhat later in the *Defence,* he overgoes Aristotle's claims for poetry's independence from the world by claiming that the poet "nothing affirms, and therefore never lieth" (235). Taking aim at the Platonic argument that poetry is "the mother of lies" (234), Sidney not only rejects the idea that poetry falsely represents the world but in this statement divorces poetry from propositional content entirely. This is a significantly more daring idea than anything else in the *Defence.* Beyond arguing that poets can overgo the work of historians by offering us a "golden world," Sidney suggests the possibility that poetry might not say anything about our world at all—it might, on the strongest reading of this claim, speak only about itself.[21]

As Sidney elaborates on this idea, it becomes clear that the reasoning behind this assertion has to do with our experience of poetry—specifically, the fact that we are always *aware* we are having an aesthetic experience. "What child is there," he continues, "that, coming to a play, and seeing *Thebes* written in great letters upon an old door, doth believe that it is Thebes?" (235). This emphasis on the audience's awareness that their experience is fictional evinces both a more Aristotelian model of mimesis and one more consonant with modern theories than the model of poetic transmission described in the previous section. Part of what distinguishes Aristotle's mimetic theory from Plato's is that, for Aristotle, the audience is always aware of the fiction; we do not experience representations in poetry as we do "real life" events because we are never confused about the fact that what we see on the stage is a reality of its own. Sidney builds on that idea here but takes it a step further with the audacious argument that poetry "nothing affirms." To recognize aesthetic experience as something distinct from real-world experience is to entertain the possibility that such experience refers only to itself, that its meaning is confined to the sphere of the aesthetic.

As Daniel Jacobson notes, the strong reading of Sidney's argument here is not compatible with many other claims in the *Defence,* including some made only a few lines after Sidney's famous proclamation.[22] Rather than suggesting that we should look for other meaning in Sidney's words, however, he argues that this incompatibly evinces a fundamental tension for Sidney between his humanist commitments and his need to rescue poetry from charges of hedonism. This divided commitment, I contend, leads Sidney to work with two different models of mimesis that are incompatible—at least as far as he is able to imagine them. When he wants to demonstrate the ethical potential of poetry, he relies on a model wherein poetry produces virtuous emotions in us that we carry out into our daily lives. When he wants to defend poetry from the charge that it is dangerous, however, he turns to the argument that poetry exists in a sphere of its own.

These conflicts aren't confined to separate arguments in the *Defence;* they complicate and undermine moments where Sidney is making the case for literature's ethical potential, in part because Sidney seems more convinced by his forward-looking arguments than his Platonic ones. The fissures in the argument appear in some of the examples already examined. The example of *Amadis de Gaule,* in which readers "have found their hearts moved to the exercise of courtesy, liberality, and especially courage," demonstrates literature moving us to imitate the virtuous emotions of the text's heroes. But the case of elegy muddies the waters. If the elegist "is to be praised, either for compassionate accompanying just causes of lamentations, or for rightly painting out how weak be the passions of woefulness," then are we learning to pity suffering or to avoid such pity? Sidney's argument is that, if the elegist gives us "just causes of lamentations," we are supposed to respond with compassion, joining our sense of sorrow to the lamentations of the speaker. But if the elegist is "painting out how weak be the passions of woefulness," we learn to scorn and therefore avoid similar weakness in ourselves. Whereas a Platonic model would say that all lamentation in art would incline us to lament ourselves, Sidney here implies that some form of ethical judgment—in this case, of the justice of the lamentations—precedes and informs our emotional response.

This is a different model of aesthetic experience than the one explored in the previous section. Instead of transmitting a worldview, including the emotions represented, the emotions provoked by literature in these examples register ethical judgments about what we see. We do not live in the world of the text; we exist as observers, rendering decisions about a world we do not participate in. This is particularly clear in the case of comedy. Sidney defines it as "an imitation of the common errors of our life, which [the comic writer] representeth in the most ridiculous and scornful sort that may be, so as it is impossible that any beholder can be content to be such a one" (229–30). Here there is no claim that the audience will imitate what they see represented in the text. Instead, by presenting "common errors" in a way that is "ridiculous" and "scornful," the poem makes us want to avoid such errors.

Arthur F. Kinney notes the contradiction that arises out of these conflicting accounts of mimesis: "on the one hand Sidney supports an aesthetic distance . . . and on the other asks his reader to emulate what he reads."[23] In the examples of elegy and comedy, Sidney does not claim, as he does elsewhere, that the audience will be moved to imitate what they see in the text. Instead, he points to situations that require our judgment as part of the response. We are not imbibing a "medicine of cherries"; we are responding to the scene before us with emotions that register ethical decisions about what we are seeing. To be sure, Sidney suggests that these judgments are encouraged by the poet: it is the work of comedian to represents human errors "in the most ridiculous and scornful sort that may be" so that our response is derisive laughter rather than sympathy. To the extent that Sidney frames emotional responses as ethical judgments in the example of elegy and comedy, however, the audience nevertheless participates in making that judgment by having the appropriate emotional response. The text doesn't simply represent emotions that we in turn feel; its representations demand a response from us that can range from consent to derision, and that response depends on how we judge what we see before us.

These moments are cracks in Sidney's argument about literature's ethical potential insofar as they suggest that the audience does not simply swallow whatever representation is handed to them as truth. The case of elegy, where the audience might have contrasting responses, particularly emphasizes that life does not simply imitate art, the way Sidney suggests in other passages. Where the argument outright breaks, however, is in the example of Alexander Pheraeus, noted above. In this vignette, Sidney appears to provide a demonstration of his claim that even "those hard-hearted evil men" like Alexander can be taught to experience virtuous emotions through the instruction of poetry. The problem, however, is that this teaching doesn't work. Sidney continues, "And if it wrought no further good in him, it was that he, in despite of himself, withdrew himself from hearkening to that which might mollify his hardened heart" (230). Alexander may feel pity for the first time watching a play, but by Sidney's own admission this feeling of pity doesn't follow Alexander out of the playhouse.

Sidney tries to account for Alexander's reaction in religious terms, explaining the lack of change as a result of his aesthetic experience in language that, to sixteenth-century English Protestants, would signal Alexander's reprobation; a victim of double-predestination, Alexander's "hardened heart" can't be saved by poetry.[24] But if this is the case, it raises the question of why Sidney thought this was a good example of the ethical force of aesthetic representations. Indeed, far from showing poetry to be a "medicine of cherries," Sidney here better illustrates the point that even a child knows that what she sees on stage isn't real. Alexander may weep at the play, but that is a response to a fiction and has no bearing on his behavior in his own world.

The telling moment in Sidney's example is his claim that Alexander could not resist "the sweet violence of tragedy." In calling the violence "sweet," he is gesturing at the argument that the delight we experience in watching tragedy is what entices us to swallow the medicine it provides. The incongruity of calling *violence* "sweet," however, echoes Aristotle's insight that "though the objects themselves may be painful to see, we delight to view the most realistic representations of them in art, the forms for example of the lowest animals and of dead bodies"[25]—a claim that aesthetic experience is different from other kinds of lived experience. Instead of delight serving as the vehicle by which art communicates a worldview to us, for Aristotle (and for Sidney's Alexander) it is a response that registers our aesthetic distance from artistic representation.

Because he does not believe that literature simply prompts our imitation, as his teacher does, delight as a marker of aesthetic distance is not a problem for Aristotle. But the kind of problem it might present for an argument like Sidney's is articulated by Augustine. As previously dis-

cussed, the question Augustine asks about his experience of tragedy—
qualis misericordia, what kind of pity does tragedy inspire?—leads him
to the recognition that his experience of pity when he watches a play is
qualitatively different from the kind of pity he thinks a good Christian
should feel, which is to say the kind of pity that leads us to act to alleviate the suffering we see. Significantly, the source of this difference is
aesthetic delight:

> But at that time at the theaters I shared the joy of lovers when they wick-
> edly found delight in each other, even though their actions in the spec-
> tacle on the stage were imaginary; when, moreover, they lost each other,
> I shared their sadness by a feeling of compassion. Nevertheless, in both
> there was pleasure. Today I have more pity for a person who rejoices
> in wickedness than for a person who has the feeling of having suffered
> hard knocks by being deprived of a pernicious pleasure or having lost
> a source of miserable felicity. This is surely a more authentic compas-
> sion; for sorrow contains no element of pleasure.[26]

Whereas Sidney at multiple points treats aesthetic pleasure and the
emotions aroused by literature as allied forces in poetry's ethical potential, here Augustine opposes them. "Authentic" *misericordia* cannot be felt when it is combined with aesthetic delight, because that
delight makes us pursue the experience of grief and pity rather than
seek to end the suffering that gives rise to these emotions. The *qualis
misericordia* of aesthetic experience, then, isn't the kind that is virtuous. The experience of aesthetic delight, for Augustine, draws a clear
line between aesthetics and ethics because that delight mediates our
experience of the emotions stirred by the artwork.

Augustine would tell Sidney that Alexander remains pitiless in his
own life even after leaving the theater in tears because rendering violence "sweet" via aesthetic representation fundamentally changes the
character of the emotion he feels viewing the play. It is Alexander's delight that renders the tragedy's ability to "move" Alexander ineffective
as a form of moral instruction. However much the play might provoke
a pitiless man to tears, those tears are alloyed with literary pleasure,
making this a different kind of pity than the kind Sidney implies should
"move" Alexander's actions in the world. Sidney's strange admission
of the play's inability to save Alexander gestures at the idea, argued by

Augustine, that the emotions literature provokes in us do not translate to our lives in the world because those emotions are *mediated* by delight. That delight is a product of the aesthetic qualities of the work that mark its fictionality, so that delight is at least in part a response to poetry's autonomy. On this account, the reason we are willing to take our "medicine of cherries" and watch a tragic play is because whatever sadness we feel is felt at a distance, mediated by music and plot structures that we recognize as signs of a constructed reality that is not our own. Thus Alexander can, like Augustine, weep at the "sweet violence of a tragedy" without it having the least effect on how he behaves toward actual people.

In making the claim that literature instructs, delights, and moves us, Sidney argues that delight in aesthetic experience holds our attention in order for poetry to show us virtuous representations that provoke virtuous emotions, which in turn move us to do what is right in the world. It is an argument that relies on a continuity between aesthetic and real-world experience in which aesthetic pleasure leads us to imitate what we see represented. But this argument, which adopts the frameworks of poetry's critics, is undercut by Sidney's daring assertions for the autonomy of poetry. These assertions have their root in the source materials of Renaissance aesthetics, but Sidney takes them further than his predecessors by suggesting literature might offer only a world of its own rather than any propositions about the "brazen" world we live in. In this model, the Alexander example suggests, delight qualifies the emotions literature provokes, or at least places us at a sufficient distance from the experience that the life-imitates-art model Sidney adopts from Platonist critics of literature does not hold. It is this distance that allows us to judge whether we should commiserate with elegiac lamentation or see it as a sign of weakness. It is this distance that might also allow us to judge that our aesthetic feelings might have no relevance to our life at all.

The possibility that this raises is that the emotions we feel when we experience art are also something different from the kinds we feel from other kinds of experience. And if that's true, then perhaps Augustine is right: a virtuous emotion like compassion ceases to be virtuous—which is to say that it stops leading to good action in the world—when it is mingled with aesthetic delight. Delight, in this model, only refers us back to the poem, never out into the world. It can "move" us to want to experience

SIDNEY BETWEEN TWO WORLDS

similar imitations—it can keep Augustine and maybe even Alexander going back to the theater—but that is the extent of its powers. However moved Alexander may be watching the play, the emotions don't leave the theater with him, and so they play no role in his ethical life

III. DELIGHT AND PITY IN *ASTROPHIL AND STELLA*

Sidney confronts this problem in considerably more detail in *Astrophil and Stella*. Here, Sidney test-drives the aesthetic theory of the *Defence* and crashes. In particular, his explorations of aesthetic autonomy via the experience of delight in the prose text find a much fuller development in the sonnet sequence. Astrophil opens by articulating a theory of how his sonnets might move Stella that draws heavily on his arguments from the *Defence*. By halfway through, however, Astrophil must confront the failure of his art to produce any change in Stella. Poetry, he eventually decides, can make the audience love the poem but not the poet because the audience's delight in poetry does not allow poetic emotions to travel outward.

Instead of writing *about* how poetry moves its audience, in *Astrophil and Stella* Sidney is writing poetry *in order to* move his audience—specifically, Astrophil writes to move Stella. While these poems aren't about teaching virtue in an obvious way, the sonnet sequence takes as its starting point one of the fundamental claims of the *Defence:* poetry has the power to move people, both inwardly and outwardly.

> Loving in truth, in fain in verse my love to show,
> That she, dear she, might take some pleasure of my pain,
> Pleasure might cause her read, reading might make her know,
> Knowledge might pity win, and pity grace obtain,
> I sought fit words to paint the blackest face of woe[.] 1.1–5

At first glance, Sidney appears to follow the familiar courtly narrative. The beloved takes a perverse delight in the pain of her lover's unrequited affections, while erotic love is raised to the status of theological grace, as Astrophil imagines Stella eventually showing a mercy akin to God's to relieve his suffering by accepting him as her lover. But Astrophil reimagines this courtly narrative somewhat by conjoining it with the power of art to transform the reader. Instead of Stella cruelly taking pleasure in Astrophil's suffering, he says that he wishes "in verse [his] love to show" in order that she will "take some pleasure of [his] pain." His pain, he indicates, is not on its own pleasurable to Stella; he needs to put it in verse for her to enjoy it. It is the lure of the aesthetic, not Stella's courtly cruelty, that will draw Stella in.

The progression Astrophil traces in outlining his hopes for his sonnets follows closely the one we have already seen in the *Defence* when Sidney describes "those hard-hearted evil men" who "despise the austere admonition of the philosopher" but who nevertheless "will be content to be delighted" by poetry (227). In failing to love Astrophil, Stella is cast as the "hard-hearted" audience who can be tricked into engaging with the poet's content—his love and his pain—because she "will be content to be delighted" by the verse. Once she's willing to engage with the verse, Astrophil argues, "reading might make her know, / Knowledge might pity win, and pity grace obtain." Like the "hard-hearted evil men" who "cannot but love" what they find in the verse, Astrophil imagines that Stella's love will grow from the natural force of the content of what she reads.

Unlike the passage from the *Defence*, however, in *Astrophil and Stella* Astrophil is not trying to communicate "the form of goodness." What Stella will instead find in his verse, according to Astrophil, is an emotion that should move a consequent emotion in her: pity. In this sense, the opening of the sonnet sequence also echoes Sidney's clearest articulation of the relationship between delight and moving in the *Defence,* where he says that the best poets "make to imitate, and imitate both to delight and teach, and delight to move men to take that goodness in hand, which without delight they would fly as from a stranger" (218). Delight does not just produce learning, but it *moves* the audience through strong emotion to take action. The aesthetic mimesis of Astrophil's suffering will communicate to Stella, so that in feeling his pain she will experience compassion; and, feeling that compassion, she will want to alleviate Astrophil's suffering and so grant him "grace," which is just to say her love.

This is not entirely what Augustine meant when he defined *misericordia* as "a heartfelt sympathy for another's distress, impelling us to succor him if we can." Yet the pity that Sidney describes in this first sonnet shares with this definition an orientation toward the ethical, insofar as this pity is not supposed to be enjoyed by Stella but instead should move her to take action in the world. More so than the *Defence*, then, Sidney's *poetic* description of an instrumental aesthetics makes very clear how reading poetry creates a specific moral effect in the world. Aesthetic delight induces the reader to engage with the text, which inspires the unsettling emotion of pity, which agitates the reader to remedy the suffering that is the cause of her pity.

But if the first five lines of *Astrophil and Stella* articulate a clearer picture of poetry's ethical potential than the whole of the *Defence*, the sonnet sequence nevertheless runs into many of the same problems with this account as the prose work does. As in the case of Alexander Pheraeus, *Astrophil and Stella* is largely the story of poetry's *inability* to move its audience. Towards the middle of the sonnet sequence, Astrophil returns to the language of the first sonnet to note that his attempts aren't working:

> My words I know do well set forth my mind,
> My mind bemoans his sense of inward smart;
> Such smart may pity claim of any heart;
> Her heart (sweet heart) is of no tiger's kind:
> And yet she hears, and yet I no pity find,
> But more I cry, less grace she doth impart.
> Alas, what cause is there so overthwart,
> That nobleness itself makes thus unkind?
> I much do guess, yet find no truth save this:
> That when the breath of my complaints doth touch
> Those dainty doors unto the court of bliss,
> The heavenly nature of that place is such
> That once come there, the sobs of mine annoys
> Are metamorphosed straight to tunes of joys. (44)

Sidney opens with a failed syllogism: "My words I know do well set forth my mind," and "Such smart may pity claim of any heart," but "yet she hears and yet no pity I find." Astrophil is confident that the problem does not lie in his mimesis—his words "well set forth" how he feels. He is likewise confident that the mechanism he describes in sonnet 1 should work: "any heart" should respond with pity to his poetry. And yet Stella remains unmoved. Despite these contradictory positions—

any heart should pity the pain he skillfully describes, but Stella's heart does not feel that pity—Astrophil cannot seem to bring himself to reconsider his faith in the power of poetry to move a person to action. The sestet simply ignores the problem of the octave entirely, turning instead to the only "truth" he can uncover in his puzzling over this dilemma, which is that "when the breath of [his] complaints doth touch / Those dainty doors unto the court of bliss," then all his suffering will turn into joy. Instead of solving the puzzle, Astrophil just imagines what it will be like "when"—not "if"—his poetry eventually has the intended effect. Astrophil, it seems, has sufficient faith in the ability of poetry to move others, and in his own skill in poetry, that he's just going to keep trying until it works.

That faith in the power of poetry, alongside an acknowledgment of its failure, continues into the subsequent sonnet:

> Stella oft sees the very face of woe
> Painted in my beclouded stormy face;
> But cannot skill to pity my disgrace,
> Not, though thereof the cause herself she know;
> Yet hearing late a fable which did show
> Of lovers never known, a piteous case,
> Pity thereof gat in her breast such place
> That from that sea derived, tears' spring did flow.
> Alas, if fancy drawn by imaged things,
> Though false, yet with free scope more grace doth breed
> Than servant's wrack, where new doubts honour brings;
> Then think, my dear, that you in me do read
> Of lovers' ruin, some sad tragedy.
> I am not I, pity the tale of me. (45)

Stella, we learn here, is not incapable of feeling pity: a "fable which did show / Of lovers never known" elicits that emotion from her. Here Astrophil finds evidence to support his belief in the power of poetry to elicit particular emotions. Thus, if only he can convince her to see him as a fable or "tale," rather than as a real person, he may be able to achieve the desired response to his own suffering. As the Katherine Duncan-Jones notes in the Oxford edition of Sidney's major works, however, *Astrophil and Stella* "as a whole may constitute 'the tale of me'" (363). His suffering already exists in literary form, in the form that he knows can elicit Stella's pity—so why isn't it working?

Sonnet 45 in many ways implicitly identifies the source of the problem, even as it tries to gloss over it. Instead of complaining that his *poetry* is not eliciting the desired effect on Stella, sonnet 45 begins with the failure of Astrophil's *face*—that is, the failure of his physical presence— to cause Stella to pity him. Unlike sonnet 44, then, this sonnet contrasts the effect of his personal sadness with poetry's superior ability to elicit pity. The pain of an actual, suffering human doesn't move Stella, but "a fable which did show / ... a piteous case" does, and so Astrophil argues that the "fancy drawn by imaged things, / Though false" "more grace doth breed" than his own, presumably "true" suffering. Astrophil therefore wants to make himself "false," as well, by saying "I am not I" so that he can become a "tale" capable of drawing her pity. But this pity is merely aesthetic. In noting the difference between Stella's responses to real suffering and mimetic suffering, this sonnet once again points to the difference between aesthetic and ethical response.

The aesthetic pity that Astrophil wants to invoke in sonnet 45 is the same kind that Augustine repudiates in *Confessions,* a pity whereby the audience "is not excited to offer help, but invited only to grieve." It is pity felt at a distance. Stella is able to feel compassion for "lovers never known" *because* these lovers were "never known," because the fact of their status as fiction means that nothing is at stake for her and so her identification with their suffering is never one that compels action. Astrophil's "wrack," on the other hand, is such that "new doubts honor brings" for her; to show Astrophil "grace" by returning his love brings with it the "doubts" that come with entering into a romantic relationship. "Lovers never known" cannot break Stella's heart, or cause her public scorn, but Astrophil can. To pity Astrophil in an ethical sense would oblige her to take on risk. As previously discussed, Aristotle claims that creating too much fear in the audience annihilates the spectator's ability to feel pity; so it seems with Stella, who can only pity those whose suffering does not require her action. Poetry can create aesthetic pity in Stella; but it's not at all clear that it can produce ethical pity in her.[27]

When Astrophil gives up on his muse in sonnet 55—"But now I mean no more your help to try" (55.9)—he has lost his faith in poetic language to "win some grace" from Stella (55.4), seeming to abandon the project of trying to motivate real-world action via aesthetic mimesis.

50   THE ART OF PITY

Sonnet 57, however, goes a step further, taking a position on aesthetic delight that is close to Augustine's repudiation of it.

> Woe, having made with many fights his own
> Each sense of mine, each gift, each power of mind,
> Grown now his slaves, he forced them out to find
> The thorough'st words, fit for woe's self to groan,
> Hoping that when they might find Stella alone,
> Before she could prepare to be unkind,
> Her soul, armed but with such a dainty rind,
> Should soon be pierced with sharpness of the moan.
> She heard my plaints, and did not only heare,
> But them (so sweete is she) most sweetly sing,
> With that fair breast making woe's darkness clear.
> A pretty case! I hoped her to bring
> To feel my griefs, and she with face and voice
> So sweets my pains, that my pains me rejoice.

Here aesthetic delight is weaponized against Astrophil's cause, as Stella is able to use the "sweetness" of art to disarm Astrophil's attempts to move her. The octave describes much of what precedes this sonnet in the sequence, though what had been framed as a plea for grace in many of the earlier sonnets is now refigured as a stealthy assault on the "dainty rind" of Stella's soul. Instead of that soul being "pierced" with pity for Astrophil, however, Stella in the sestet turns around and sings Astrophil's own words back to him, making him the audience for his own depictions of his suffering. Astrophil notes that he had "hoped her to bring / to feel my griefs," but once she allows him to experience his pain in the "sweet" form of song, now Astrophil, like Augustine watching tragedies, enjoys the suffering he finds there rather than trying to end it: "my pains me rejoice." If sonnet 1 laid out a plan by which aesthetic pleasure would elicit ethical sympathy, sonnet 57 rejects that plan by suggesting that aesthetic pleasure "sweetens" the pain of compassion into something to be enjoyed rather than acted upon.

These later sonnets thus recognize a fundamental difference between the general ability of literature to "move" an audience to aesthetic pity and Astrophil's ability to move Stella to ethical pity with his sonnets. Successful imitation can indeed generate pity in the audience, but that pity relies on an aesthetic distance between the characters and the audience that confines the emotions aroused to the aesthetic space without moving the audience to take ethical action as a result. Moreover the delight that comes with successful imitation renders the emotions it arouses, even the painful ones like pity, pleasurable. The audience may be moved to feel pity, but sonnets 45 and 57 suggest that those emotions will never move beyond aesthetic experience. To put it another way, pity's mediation by aesthetic delight renders it inert. *Astrophil and Stella* is one of the most beautiful and complex sonnet sequences of the English-language tradition. Precisely to the extent that it succeeds as art, however, it fails to make good on Sidney's claims about poetry's ethical potential.

Astrophil and Stella tests the ethical claims Sidney makes for poetry in the *Defence* and finds that they fail because we experience fictional worlds differently from our own. In this sense, the sonnet sequence goes even further than the *Defence* in theorizing art's autonomy by demonstrating that even when art *does* seek to represent the world as it is—Astrophil/Sidney is telling the story of his own love-longing—it is experienced by the audience as a world apart. Whereas the *Defence* oscillates between different understandings of how we engage literature, sometimes claiming a continuity between the aesthetic realm and our own and sometimes positing that literature creates a world of its own, *Astrophil and Stella* begins from the proposition that Astrophil can generate pity in Stella by "paint[ing] the blackest face of woe" in verse but finds that whatever pity poetry can generate cannot pass out into the world. In effect, *Astrophil and Stella* take sides on the two positions Sidney tries to walk between in the *Defence* and comes to the conclusion that Sidney in the *Defence* cannot: if poetry's ethical value rests in the continuity between aesthetic emotions and "life emotions," then poetry is a poor teacher.

This does not mean, however, that the only ideas of value in the *Defence* are those moving toward the intuition of literature's autonomy. The *Defence* stands between two worlds: one in which a Platonic framework for understanding how poetry affects us was motivating both criticism and defenses of poetry, and one in which early theorizing about aesthetic distance was starting to push toward the autonomy thesis. If Sidney's work demonstrates the incompatibility of these two worlds, it also reminds us that poetry's ability to rouse powerful emotions is at the center of how and why we engage with literature. At the very least, it should prompt us to ask how those powerful emotions relate to the kind that motivate us to act in the world. If aesthetic autonomy can't be reconciled with a Platonic understanding of emotional transfer from text to audience, we are still left with the question of whether there is an understanding of aesthetic emotions that *would* move outward into our lives. In the next two chapters, we shall see how Spenser and Shakespeare offer very different answers to this question.

CHAPTER 2

Virtuous Pity and Spenser's Aesthetic Doubt

The Rise of Literary Autonomy

To the extent that, as Raphael Falco argues, Elizabethan writers "managed to erect, in Sidney, a homegrown vernacular precursor from whom the national literature could descend,"[1] the tensions and questions explored in Sidney's *Defence* and *Astrophil and Stella* carried substantial influence at the end of the sixteenth century and beginning of the seventeenth. Spenser's admiration of Sidney is well enough attested by the dedication of the *Shepheardes Calender*, and Spenser himself played no small role in assigning Sidney the role of "vernacular precursor." That Sidney's arguments in the *Defence* can be heard echoing in much of Spenser's "Letter of the Authors," appended to the 1590 publication of the three-book *Faerie Queene*, should come as no surprise. At that point, at least, Spenser appears to share with his patron both a Platonic vision of how poetry might communicate ethical ideas and an attraction to an Aristotelian model of aesthetic education.

Spenser also shares with Sidney a belief that emotions are a vital part of ethical life and a recognition that poetry is uniquely positioned to evoke emotions in the reader. But because *The Faerie Queene* explicitly takes virtue as its subject matter, Spenser's poem engages in a much more detailed discussion of the role of emotion in virtue than Sidney does in the *Defence* or *Astrophil and Stella*. By doing so, Spenser is able to explore more fully how *representations* of emotions relate to the *lived* emotions experienced by the audience. This exploration lies at the heart of book 4, the Legend of Friendship, which explores the role of pity in the virtue of friendship.

While many critics have found Spenser rejecting pity through much of his six-book epic, these discussions have tended to focus on books 1, 5, and 6. Book 4, a book that talks about pity and compassion perhaps more than any of the others, is often left out of the conversation. That may be because book 4 develops a significantly different concept of pity than the other books of *The Faerie Queene;* book 4 moves beyond the courtly and Senecan models of pity appearing elsewhere in the poem and, in contrast to those models, takes a distinctly Thomist approach that sees pity as an equalizing force necessary to the strongest kinds of love bonds between people. Particularly in the story of Britomart and Amoret, Spenser follows Aquinas's approach, uniting Aristotelian friendship with Augustine's *misericordia* and, in so doing, conceiving of a pity that is virtuous.

Through this Thomist model of pity, Spenser interrogates and ultimately rejects the notion that poetry can teach us to feel virtuously. As is clear as early as the *Letter,* while Spenser's thinking about the ethical potentials of poetry owes much to Sidney, Spenser does not share the faith that the *Defence* professes in the ability of poetry to move the audience to ethical action. Even as he defends his choice to use "an historical fiction" as a way "to fashion a gentleman or noble person in vertuous and gentle discipline,"[2] Spenser demonstrates considerably more distaste for poetry as a means of instruction than Sidney, appearing to embrace Platonic concerns about poetry's ability to impose its own worldview on the audience. His allusions to Aristotle in the *Letter* additionally indicate an awareness that poetry might be more autonomous than his defense of allegory suggests. By 1596 and book 4 of *The Faerie Queene,* Spenser is using his exploration of friendship and its constituent emotion, pity, to illuminate the aesthetic distance between the world of the text and our own reality.

Book 4 offers multiple examples not just of Thomist pity but of how that pity might be communicated from one person to another via representations of sorrow, seeming to succeed where Sidney's Astrophil failed. At the same time, however, Spenser's narrator interrupts multiple times to wink at aesthetic distance, throwing the ability of the poem to make us feel what its characters feel into doubt. Because Thomist pity entails identification with another, book 4 is able to draw

VIRTUOUS PITY AND SPENSER'S AESTHETIC DOUBT

a contrast between how the characters feel pity and the audience's own pity, which does not and cannot rely on the same identification. The poem thus emphasizes the gap between our aesthetic experience and the characters' ethical one, a gap that cannot be crossed by an act of imaginative identification because of the mediating structure of aesthetic delight. *The Faerie Queene* thus draws our attention to its own autonomy, and in doing so rejects literature's ethical potential.

I. SPENSER'S AESTHETICS: ENSAMPLE VERSUS PLEASING ANALYSIS

Unlike Sidney, Spenser does not give us a treatise in defense of literature. Instead, where Spenser discusses the value of poetry, he simply makes a case for *his own* poetry. E. K.'s epistle to Gabriel Harvey in *The Shepheardes Calender* defends a young poet's choice to step out onto the branches of a literary family tree he traces back to Theocritus, while the "Letter of the Authors" sets out to explain the poem's purpose— "to fashion a gentleman or noble person in vertuous and gentle discipline"—so that he can avoid "gealous opinions and misconstructions" of his work's meaning (451). While Spenser does not set out to defend poetry as such, however, his Letter demonstrates a similar tension between conflicting models of mimesis as we've already seen in the work of literature's defenders.

The Letter presents two different theories of how poetry might provide ethical instruction. The first, instruction by "ensample," draws heavily on Platonic ideas about how poetry transmits ideas deceitfully; the second, instruction by "pleasing synthesis," looks to Aristotle and the experience of aesthetic distance. In his Platonic mode, Spenser expresses considerable distrust of poetry's power, sounding at times more like Sidney's *misomousoi*—the poet-haters—than like Sidney. As in Sidney, the Aristotelian model offers an answer to the problems created by the ensample model. Critics debate to what extent we should understand the Letter as a lens for reading *The Faerie Queene*,[3] and my intent here is not to suggest that the Letter comprehensively summarizes Spenser's aesthetic theory or motivations in writing *The Faerie Queene*. But in exploring these two models of instruction-by-mimesis in the Letter, we can find Spenser setting the stage for the undoing of his ethical project in book 4. His distrust of the idea that poetry might be a vehicle for a worldview leads him toward a vision of aesthetic autonomy whose only lesson to the reader is that we do not live in the world of the poem.

Spenser's central claim about how his "darke conceit" will achieve the ethical ends he lays out for it relies on what I have defined in previous chapters as a Platonist conception of how art can transmit virtue. Just as Plato believed that poetry could be dangerous (and Sidney believed it could be powerful) because it offers examples that audiences will imitate to the extent that the examples are delightful, Spenser focuses on the persuasive force of "ensample" when it comes to instruction:

> To some I know this Methode will seeme displeasaunt, which had rather have good discipline delivered plainly in way of precepts, or sermoned at large, as they use, then thus clowdily enwrapped in Allegoricall devises. But such, me seeme, should be satisfide with the use of these dayes seeing all things accounted by their showes, and nothing esteemed of, that is not delightfull and pleasing to commune sence. For this cause is Xenophon preferred before Plato, for that the one, in the exquisite depth of his judgement, formed a Commune welth such as it should be, but the other in the person of Cyrus and the Persians fashioned a government such as might best be: so much more profitable and gratious is doctrine by ensample, then by rule. (452)

This passage echoes Sidney's claim in the *Defence* that the work of the poet "worketh, not only to make a Cyrus, which had been but a particular excellency, as Nature might have done, but to bestow a Cyrus upon the world, to make many Cyruses, if they will learn aright why and how that maker made him" (216–17). Following Plato's model in *Republic,* life imitates art according to Spenser, and so providing people with good examples to imitate will improve society as a whole, disseminating the virtue of those examples throughout the readership.

In accepting the Platonic notion that people imitate what they see and read in art, Sidney and Spenser both open themselves up to Plato's suspicion of poets, and so both have to focus on what the *good* poet can do. Thus Sidney claims, just before talking about a world of Cyruses, that "the skill of the artificer standeth in that *idea* or fore-conceit of the work, and not the work itself," asserting that good poetry is made good in advance by the ideas the poet seeks to represent, while implying that poets with bad ideas will not be able to produce good poetry (216). For Spenser, who, as DeNeef argues, engages deeply with the Sidnean idea of the fore-conceit, the response to the Platonism of his concept of literature is simply to assert that *he*, at least, has good—that is to say, moral—"fore-conceits."[4] And so he writes his "Letter of the Authors" in order to "avoyd gealous opinions and misconstructions"—that is, to show that his meanings and ideas are virtuous.

The emphasis on the fore-conceit for Spenser creates an even stronger distinction between aesthetic form and the moral content than Sidney espouses with his Horatian take on the physician metaphor in the *Defence*. After stating the purpose of *The Faerie Queene*, Spenser says that he thought his purpose would "be most plausible and pleasing, being coloured with an historicall fiction, the which the most part of men delight to read, rather for variety of matter then for profite of the ensample" (451). Spenser explains his choice to write "an historicall fiction" as a matter of strategy. People enjoy reading historical fictions, so to get people to engage with the instruction in virtue he wishes to provide, he's going to give the people what they want. But Spenser recognizes quite clearly here that people don't read these kinds of poems "for profite of the ensample" but rather "for variety of the matter"—people want aesthetic pleasure, a good story. Without explicitly invoking the Lucretian metaphor of the honey on the rim of the cup of medicine, Spenser nevertheless frames himself here much like the good physician explaining his methods: if you want people to imbibe your moral lessons, you have to administer them with a pleasing delivery system. But this means that the delivery system is separate from the moral content and has no ethical value of its own.

Indeed, as several readers of the Letter have noted, Spenser sounds almost frustrated with the tendencies of his contemporaries.[5] It is merely "the use of these dayes," not a universal truth, that "all things accounted by their showes, and nothing esteemed of, that is not delightfull and pleasing to commune sence." *Kids these days only care about what's delightful* seems to be the tone here. "Shows" in this period and in Spenser's own writing could be an object of suspicion, such that the word often meant "a feigned performance of an action; a pretence, an act."[6] Thus, for instance, we are warned in advance about Duessa and Ate in book 4, who "in outward shew faire semblance . . . did beare"—a "shew," we are told, that is a "maske" for their "Vile treason and fowle falshood" (4.1.17). That people care only for "showes" suggests that they care only for the mask, not the substance underneath it. If this is the case, then Spenser's audience is, as Gosson and others worried, susceptible to imitating the wrong kinds of ideas so long as they are presented in a delightful manner. Spenser claims he is only providing virtuous images, but he explains his purpose in language that suggests that the virtue rests in his intentions, rather than in the art itself.

The art itself, as Spenser describes it, might well be considered with suspicion. Saying that his purpose is "coloured with an historicall fiction" again gestures at art's dangers. On the one hand, "coloured" here can just mean ornamented, and this seems plainly to be Spenser's overt meaning. On the other, however, the verb "color" in the period can also mean "portray in a false light," a double meaning that glances at both the detractions of critics like Gosson and the concerns Plato had about the falseness of poetic mimesis.[7] Saying that this "colour" is "most plausible and pleasing" just muddies the waters further. "Plausible" can be a synonym for "pleasing"; or it can mean "convincing"; or it can indicate, like "shows" and "colour," deceit—what is plausible is what merely *seems* to be true.[8] Even as he promises to deliver instruction in virtue, Spenser keeps gesturing to the idea that the method by which he will deliver that instruction is false, deceiving, and merely a "show." Whereas Sidney tries to defend literature in Platonic terms while rejecting Platonic conclusions, Spenser's argument for the moral value of his work belies a mistrust of his medium that Plato would wholeheartedly endorse.[9]

This mistrust becomes even more pronounced in the poem itself. At the start of book 4, he raises the specter of the *misomousoi* when he refers to his critics' claim that, by poetry "fraile youth is oft to follie led, / Through false allurement of that pleasing baite" (4.Pr.1.6–7). As Joseph Campana notes, Spenser does not defend his poem against this criticism of poetry, choosing instead to defend the value of his poem's content.[10] Spenser furthermore gives life to this criticism elsewhere in the poem, insofar as the characters who most obviously seem to stand in for poet-figures are enchanters working against the various knights of virtue—characters like Archimago, Acrasia, and Busirane. Archimago's first act in the poem is to create "false shewes," in which he teaches a dream "to imitate that Lady trew, / Whose semblance she did carrie under feigned hew" (1.1.46). Acrasia's Bower gilds the lily many times over.[11] And Busirane, as Guenther argues, is a figure for the poet-as-magician, whose words are effective in the world precisely to the extent that they draw on the enchanting—and therefore morally suspect—powers of aesthetic language.[12]

Moreover, when Spenser juxtaposes these characters with "good" versions of the idea, art often gets dropped from the equation. As Peter C. Herman notes, throughout *The Faerie Queene,* "Spenser does not so much contrast good and bad art as imitation with truth, that is, art with non-art." Thus, for instance, he notes that the Garden of Adonis is supposed to be the corrective to the Bower of Bliss. The Bower is characterized by artifice; the Garden by the lack of it: "There was a pleasant arbor, not by art, / But of trees own inclination made" (3.6.44). The Bower's artifice is part of what makes it wrong. The "good" version of it becomes good in part by eliminating artifice. "Like *The Apology for Poetry,*" Herman argues, "*The Faerie Queene* is haunted by the possibility that the charges of the Muse-haters are partially valid, that the distinction between good and evil poetry is hard to maintain, indeed, that 'good' art might not even exist in the world."[13]

This is a problem that Spenser sets up in the Letter as well. The logic of the aesthetic "ensample," while it explains why a poem might be the best way to instruct his readership in virtue, nevertheless relies on the idea that the fiction and the formal features are mere ornament for ethical ideas, making the ornament itself potentially suspect. By casting the choice to write "an historicall fiction" as a necessary evil for reaching an audience that is more interested in pleasing shows than in the "profite of the ensample," Spenser sets aesthetic pleasure up as a concession to "the use of these dayes" rather than, as Sidney did, what sets poetry in preeminence over all other disciplines.

To a certain extent, the Letter thus bears out Tilmouth's claim that Spenser is situated in the rationalist, Stoic tradition that Tilmouth argues will be pushed aside in the seventeenth century for a more passionate ethics (though as we will see, *The Faerie Queene* has a more positive view of emotion than Tilmouth argues).[14] Whereas the delights of poetry were part of its virtue for Sidney, Spenser clearly distrusts aesthetic pleasure, both in the Letter and in *The Faerie Queene*—not because he distrusted emotion more generally but because of the deceptiveness that Platonic models of mimesis attributed to specifically poetic pleasure. It is unsurprising, then, to see Spenser turn to Aristotle later in the letter for a different model of poetic instruction, one that focuses on "pleasing analysis" rather than on the imitation of good "ensamples." In this model, the deceptions of aesthetic delight are replaced by the pleasures of learning that derive from an awareness that one is having an aesthetic experience.

The one moment at which Spenser makes the case for poetry as such, rather than just defending the value of his own poetry, comes when he alludes to Aristotle's argument distinguishing the work of the poet from the work of the historian.[15] Whereas "an historiographer discourseth of affayres orderly as they were donne," Spenser argues, "a poet thrusteth into the middest, even where it most concerneth him, and there recoursing to the thinges forepaste, and divining of thinges to come, maketh a pleasing analysis of all." On the one hand, this is simply a claim about method: the historiographer starts at the beginning while the poet starts in the middle. On the other, however, method shapes content insofar as the ability to "thrusteth into the middest" and to jump around in time allows the poet to make "a pleasing analysis of all." Now, instead of asserting a strong distinction between the precepts and the "historicall fiction" by which they are communicated, Spenser suggests that the way the story is told affects what can be learned from it.

On this reading, Spenser's theory of poetry is more synthetic than it might appear at first glance, insofar as it requires us to engage with the *way* in which the specific story points to universal lessons. Instead of pleasing shows that bypass reason to communicate the poem's "fore-conceit" directly into the mind of the reader, this later moment in the Letter emphasizes the poet's analysis, achieved by his formal choices in how to represent his fore-conceit, as the source of our pleasure. Just as for Aristotle we delight in imitations because we learn from them, here too Spenser suggests that our pleasure is caused by our engagement with the analysis, implying that we comprehend the analysis and therefore also engage in the rational work of analyzing. What begins as a claim about the method of the poet, then, also implies a theory of the method of the reader. Instead of merely imbibing virtue from a virtuous picture, we are being asked to consider the "analysis" being made by the virtue's representation.

In this moment in the Letter we get a hint a conflict that book 4 brings to the foreground. Aristotle's concept of mimesis differs from Plato's, of course, to the extent that Aristotle thinks that we experience art not as an attempt at copying reality but as a union of particular and universal in a representation that we experience differently than we experience events in real life. Put simply, for Aristotle, part of the experience of art is an *awareness* that we are experiencing art. When Spenser's heroes are moved to folly by the "shewes" of his artist-characters, it is often because these knights are unaware that what they are seeing is, in fact, a show rather than a reality. Art is deceptive *when we do not experience it as art.* Unlike Redcrosse's encounters with Archimago's "shewes," an Aristotelian reader of poetry isn't fooled into thinking that what is represented is in fact reality, even when it is represented "with perfect realism." When Spenser discusses poetry as a "pleasing analysis," he suggests that a reader is capable of a different experience, one in which we acknowledge that what we are seeing is a "shewe" and that its truth is therefore analytical and not simply what the surface appearance seems to present. In this juxtaposition of Platonic and Aristotelian models, Spenser suggests that we as readers stand in a different relation to what we experience than the poem's characters do because, unlike his characters, we are aware that we are having an aesthetic experience. This troubles the claim that *The Faerie Queene* will teach us by "ensample" by raising the question of how a character's experience in a fictional world might provide an example that can simply be vicariously experienced by the reader. If our experience is structurally different from theirs, how and to what extent can their experiences translate to ours?

The tension in Spenser's Letter, then, is once again a question about how audiences experience aesthetic objects. Is poetry just an outward "shewe" that hides the truth of what it is really saying, so that the audience imbibes whatever content is offered before their reasoning minds are aware? Or is it a "pleasing analysis" that ties form and content together into an Aristotelian representation, one that "imitates" only insofar as it provides us with plausible understanding of how humans can, do, and/or should act? This tension continues into the poem, particularly into the question of the relationship between the kinds of pity represented in the experiences of various characters and the *qualis misericordia* the audience is invited to experience.

II. SPENSER'S ETHICS AND THE ROLE OF PITY

If Spenser's aesthetic theory is divided and ambivalent, his ethical framework is somewhat clearer. More than any other text discussed in this book, *The Faerie Queene*'s approach to virtue situates itself in the context of Aristotelian virtue ethics, inflected through Christianity. In the Letter, Spenser explicitly states that he intends "to pourtraict in Arthure . . . perfected in the twelve private morall vertues, as Aristotle hath devised, the which is the purpose of these first twelve bookes" (452), and he follows Aristotle in claiming that "magnificence" is the perfection of all the virtues. Within *The Faerie Queene*, Spenser takes the Aristotelian position that emotion plays an important role in the virtues he explores.

Despite his explicit reference to Aristotle's ethics in the Letter, modern critics tend to situate Spenser's ethics within Stoic traditions that reject emotion's role in moral decision-making. For example, Spenser is Tilmouth's example of the rationalist tradition that, he argues, held sway in England through the sixteenth century. Others, as we will see, argue that Spenser rejects strong emotions like pity in favor of Stoic replacements. But *The Faerie Queene* quite explicitly rejects the idea that reason and passion should be in conflict and articulates an alternative that is the cornerstone of virtue ethics. In book 2, for instance, Spenser laments, "What warre so cruell, or what siege so sore, / As that, which strong affections do apply / Against the fort of reason evermore."[16] His solution isn't to banish the "affections" but to bring them under the "goodly government" of reason: "But in a body, which doth freely yeeld / His parts to reasons rule obedient," the whole person experiences "happy peace" (2.11.2.1–4). Instead of a continual war between passion and reason, the proper state of affairs is one in which those two forces are in accord. To be able to *restrain* one's passions for Aristotle is not a virtue: it is mere continence, as opposed to temperance.[17] *Training* the passions to respond in the right way to the right things is, for Spenser as for Aristotle, part of what it means to be virtuous.

Spenser also follows the tradition of Christian virtue ethics by asserting that emotions are felt differently based on the extent to which a person is virtuous. In *City of God*, Augustine claims that "will, caution, and gladness are felt by good and bad alike; and . . . desire, fear, and joy are emotions common to both good and bad. But the good feel these emotions in a good way, the bad feel them in a bad way."[18] Spenser's narrator strikes a very similar note when he remarks, "Wonder it is to see, in diverse minds, / How diversly love doth his pageaunts play." In those with "baser wit," love "stirreth up to sensuall desire," whereas "in brave sprite it kindles goodly fire" (3.5.1). His defense of love goes even further, explicitly rejecting the Stoic tradition for the Peripatetic. After noting how often "brave exploits which great Heroes wonne, / In love were either ended or begunne," Spenser's narrator invokes Plato's *Critias,* which "Of love full manie lessons did apply, / The which these Stoicke censours cannot well deny" (4.Pr.3).

The Faerie Queene thus repeatedly takes the position, which it gets from Aristotle and the subsequent Christian virtue ethics tradition, that well-trained passions are part of the virtuous temperament. For instance, part of Redcrosse's training in virtue is learning to feel the pain of his sins the right way. When Despayre confronts him with the facts of his own deeds up to that point in the poem, "The ugly vew of his deformed crimes" causes Redcrosse to consider killing himself.[19] In the House of Holiness, however, when he is "Greevd with remembrance of his wicked wayes, / And prickt with anguish of his sinnes so sore" (1.10.21), this is part of his process of finding his way back to God. Grief at one's sins experienced by a soul who has lost sight of faith leads to sinful despair; grief at one's sins experienced by one who remembers the promise of God's mercy becomes a step toward regeneration.

If *The Faerie Queene* generally takes a positive view of emotion's role in virtue, however, its treatment of the specific emotion of pity is somewhat more complex. Many passages in *The Faerie Queene* outside of book 4 seem to cast pity in a pejorative light, and there is a significant body of criticism arguing that *The Faerie Queene* rejects pity as an unhelpful or even dangerous emotion. Before we turn to what virtuous pity looks like for Spenser, it is worth examining these versions of nonvirtuous compassion, which explore a variety of courtly and Stoic understandings of pity. Viewed within a framework that sees emotion as a part of virtue that need to be oriented correctly by reason, these moments of "bad" pity can throw into relief what occasions and comportment characterize "good," ethical pity in the poem.

Critical treatments of Spenser's pity have tended to argue either that Spenser's characters must learn to resist pity or that they need to learn to embrace its Stoic counterpart, clemency. As Cynthia Nazarian argues, "Faerielond's knights constantly fall victim to sympathy before they learn how to resist its enticing hues."[20] To be sure, it is not difficult to come up with examples of pity leading Spenser's characters astray. In book I, we see Redcrosse's pity for Duessa—disguised as Fidessa—leading Redcrosse away from the virtuous path. Fidessa asks Redcrosse to act "in pitty of my state," and he takes up her cause, telling her that "hart of flint would rew / The undeserved woes and sorrowes, which ye shew" (1.2.26). Guyon likewise falls prey to Duessa's "shows" in book 2—"Great pitty is to see you thus dismayd," he tells her, believing that she has been raped by Redcrosse (2.1.14)—leading him to attack his fellow knight of virtue. Pity has perhaps its worst moment in book 5 when Artegall, seeing Radigund's face for the first time, "Empierced was with pittiful regard, / That his sharpe sword he threw from him apart."[21] Giving up his sword, and thereby his allegorical and chivalric pursuit of justice, Artegall not only fails to uphold his virtue but also fails to protect his fellow knight; his loss in the fight leads to Sir Turpine's death by hanging.

As Jan Frans van Dijkhuizen notes, part of the problem with pity in *The Faerie Queene* is "its troubling potential to attach itself to those characters which are cast as dangerous or other."[22] Because the poem's "bad" characters consistently command pity from the knights of virtue, many readers see Spenser constructing pity as a force to be overcome. But whether the tendency to feel pity for the wrong people indicates a problem with pity or with the character who feels that pity depends upon the discourse within which that pity operates. Van Dijkhuizen notes that pity functions differently in the context of epic than it does in the context of romance; in romance narratives, it is a motive force that leads knights to great deeds—saving damsels and helping fellow knights— whereas in epic, pity needs to be set aside in order for the hero to complete his task (thus, for instance, Aeneas needs to get over his pity for Dido to found Rome).[23] The context in which a character feels pity matters to the extent that pity drives outcomes that may or may not be at odds with the larger values of the world the characters inhabit.

Moreover, Stoic, Aristotelian, and Christian discourses all define pity and its value differently. In her discussion of pity in *The Faerie Queene*, Nazarian distinguishes between "Greek pity," identified in Aristotle's *Rhetoric* as a concept that "required judgment and evaluation" (specifically of whether suffering is deserved or not) and "vain pity," as defined in Seneca's *De Clementia*, where *misericordia* is opposed to *clementia.*[24] But *misericordia,* too, had a divided history in Spenser's time. On the one hand, Seneca criticized pity for the fact that it causes suffering in the one who pities: "But a mind cannot be both great and also grieving."[25] On the other, Augustine and Aquinas, as well as John Calvin, explicitly rejected this view. Augustine defends the significance of *misericordia* and grief specifically against the Stoic account in *City of God,* and Calvin follows him in his commentary on *De Clementia,* citing Augustine's definition of *misericordia* from *City of God* and claiming, "Obviously we ought to be persuaded of the fact that pity is a virtue, and that he who feels no pity cannot be a good man."[26]

Several recent studies of pity in *The Faerie Queene* have argued that Spenser takes a Senecan, Stoic line on this issue, particularly in book 5.[27] And certainly, in Spenser's own time, Senecan mistrust of pity was influential in political theory. In his 1531 book *The Governour,* Thomas Elyot writes in language very close to Seneca's,

> And if ye aske me what mercye is, it is a temperaunce of the mynde of hym, that hath power to be auenged, and it is called in latine Clementia, and is alway ioyned with reason. For he that for euery lyttel occasion is meued with compassion, and beholdynge a man punysshed condygnely for his offence, lamenteth or waylethe, is called pitiouse, which is a syckenesse of the mynde, wherewith at this daye the more parte of menne be diseased. And yet is the sikenes moch wars by adding to one word, callynge it Uayne pitie.[28]

This rejection of a feeling of compassion for a more rational concept of Stoic mercy or clemency also resonates, as Leah Whittington points out, in Justus Lipsius's 1584 *De Constantia* and, as Colin Burrow notes, in Jean Bodin's 1606 *The Six Bookes of a Commonweale.*[29]

Book 5, the Legend of Justice, clearly engages with Stoic ideas about the relationship between pity and justice. Spenser's rejection of the Stoic position on love in the proem to book 4, however, indicates that, particularly where matters of love are concerned, he was more inclined to side with Augustine's claim that the kind of *apatheia* taught by the Stoics "is a condition to be shunned in this life, if we wish to live the right kind of life."[30] Despite the currency of Stoic rejections of pity, both Whittington and John Staines note that the earlier Christian understanding of *misericordia* remained very much present during the sixteenth and seventeenth centuries,[31] and Ruth Kaplan, in her study of Spenser's *Ruines of Time* and *Amoretti,* notes that "Anti-Stoic Christians saw pity not as an emotion to be overcome by the wise man but as the signal Christian emotion."[32]

Considering how the Christian Aristotelian tradition understood the relationship between passion and virtue as opposed to that of the Stoics provides some different answers to questions raised by *The Faerie Queene*'s representations of pity. First, it reorients our understanding of how pity works. Instead of seeing pity, as Nazarian does, as "unwilling, unreasoned response that threatens agency and identity," we might instead consider to what extent pity functions in conjunction with, rather than in opposition to, reason.[33] Moreover, virtue ethics offers an answer to the problem in the poem that "pity" seems to be felt by and for good and bad characters alike. While many critics for this reason have argued that Spenser's representation of pity is at best conflicted and at worst an outright rejection of pity's role in virtue,[34] reading Spenser in the context of virtue ethics predicts that pity is going to be a force for good in the good characters and a force for bad in the evil ones, simply because passions will be experienced and will signify differently based on the virtue of the person experiencing it. The question, then, isn't whether pity itself is good or bad; the question becomes when and how one should experience pity.

Negative outcomes for the knight who pities thus are not necessarily an indictment of pity but might instead be read as an indictment of the knight's virtue—that knight has not yet learned to feel pity as a virtuous person should. So, for instance, when Redcrosse pities Fidessa/Duessa at 1.2.26–27, the problem is not that it is wrong to pity a damsel in distress and to seek to help her but that it is wrong to pity *Duessa* specifically. As van Dijkhuizen argues, "Redcrosse's failure lies not so much in his pity *per se*. . . . Rather, Redcrosse's pity is deluded because it fails to distinguish between genuine and counterfeit suffering, and because it is rooted in erotic desire."[35] This failure is itself symptomatic of the fact that Redcrosse has already abandoned Una, allegorically leaving the virtuous path to err his way through to canto 10.

The case of Artegall's pity for Radigund is evidence of how far Artegall is from the virtue of justice not because pity is opposed to justice but because pity rightly felt is supposed to serve the ends of justice. Aristotelian pity is a judgment that rests on an apprehension of justice. Augustine similarly explains that *misericordia* "is the servant of reason, when compassion is shown without detriment to justice, when it is a matter of giving to the needy or of pardoning the repentant," a point on which Aquinas follows him.[36] Artegall's pity at 5.5.13 is quite clearly a "detriment to justice," and so this moment demonstrates that he has not adequately trained his passions to respond in the right way to the situation. A virtuous person does not feel pity for Radigund at this moment, but this does not mean that, for Spenser, a virtuous person does not feel pity at all.

III. SPENSER'S VIRTUOUS PITY

Turning to book 4, we find a context in which pity is a crucial component of one of Spenser's key virtues: friendship. Throughout book 4 of *The Faerie Queene*, pity is the force that generates the poem's most stable, unified relationships. But the pity we see here is not the same that we see elsewhere in the poem. In contrast to the courtly, erotic pity Redcrosse feels for Duessa, or the weak, irrational Stoic view of pity that Spenser explores in book 5, book 4 defines a version of compassion that has much in common with Aquinas's discussion of pity as a virtue in *Summa Theologica*, wherein he unites Augustine's definition of *misericordia* with Aristotle's discussion of friendship in *Nicomachean Ethics*. This Thomist conception of *misericordia*—"*heartfelt sympathy for another's distress, impelling us to succor him if we can*" in which "one looks upon another's distress as one's own"—is the means by which Spenser explores what it would mean to have relationships not structured by power.[37] By representing virtuous pity as a way to reorient social relationships around identification with another, the poem sets out to distinguish this kind of compassion from the pity the reader experiences.

When we first see Britomart and Amoret traveling together in canto 4, their relationship demonstrates how the structures of chivalry interfere with the formation of intimate emotional bonds between people. In the first canto, Britomart and Amoret find themselves awkwardly trying to negotiate their courtly relation to each other, sustained by Amoret's belief that Britomart, who saved Amoret from her captor in book 3, is a male knight. Amoret, Spenser tells us, "right fearefull was and faint" because she "feard his mind"—that is, Britomart's—"would grow to some excesse" (4.1.5.4, 4.1.7.9). Britomart, who at this moment is seeking "to hide her fained sex the better," does nothing to disabuse Amoret of her fears, and instead plays the part of the would-be courtly lover: she "both did and sayd / Full many things so doubtfull to be wayd," and to Amoret "purpos made / Of love" (4.1.7.3–8). As a result, their relationship is characterized by each of them being emotionally isolated from the other. Amoret's "doubt of fowle dishonor / Made her not yeeld so much, as due she deemed," while Britomart hides her true intentions toward Amoret in order to hide her identity (4.1.8.7).

Once Britomart reveals herself as a woman, however, the threat that Britomart might try to cash in on the courtly debt Amoret owes to her passes, so that Amoret is "now freed from fear" and can afford "More frank affection" to Britomart (4.1.15.6–7). What marks the transition from fear to affection is mutual pity:

> Where all that night they of their loves did treat,
> And hard adventures twixt themselves along,
> That each the other gan with passion great,
> And griefull pittie privately bemoane. (4.1.16)

Campana argues that "the enigmatic workings of sympathy" are "the basis for social life in *The Faerie Queene*,"[38] and this passage demonstrates how this might be so. In the act of pitiful bemoaning, Britomart and Amoret move beyond themselves and find a basis for community. Whereas before both had suffered silently and individually—Britomart heartsick for Artegall, Amoret missing Scudamor and fearing Britomart—now they "bemoane" "each the other," bonded by a common pain. The inwardly aimed lamentation of Britomart in book 3, in which she "shut up all her plaint in privy griefe" (3.4.6–11), now looks outward, creating a social bond. Pity moves out from the self to another person and so becomes the basis of their friendship.[39]

This is something different from what we've seen elsewhere in the poem. In the passages discussed in the previous section, pity largely exists within power structures that place the supplicant and the one who pities in unequal relation to each other. As Colin Burrow notes, "appeals for pity usually happen when one party is either not suffering from the pain of the other or is capable of alleviating some discomfort that the sufferer is powerless to escape. Pity is consequently a relation founded on a disparity of power between the sufferer and the pitier."[40] When Redcrosse pities Duessa, it is his power as knight, the ability to save the damsel in distress, that drives him. At the same time, however, his pity also becomes a form of self-subjection to the extent that he pledges himself to her. In the later books, where we see a similar dynamic play out between Artegall and Radigund, the idea of pity also gets increasingly bound up with notions of justice. This problem cannot be solved simply by replacing pity with *clementia*. *Clementia*, just like erotic, courtly pity, is bound up in the same dynamics of power. As Seneca explains, *clementia* is "leniency on the part of a superior towards an inferior in imposing punishments."[41]

The pity that unites Britomart and Amoret is something different from either courtly pity or Stoic mercy, undoing the asymmetry of their courtly relationship rather than reinforcing it. Their pity is precisely *not* the kind in which "one party is . . . not suffering from the pain of the other," since they come together over a recognition that both are suffering similarly. And while both of them are "powerless to escape" their suffering on their own, theirs is not a case wherein one party gives and the other receives; it is one in which the relief from suffering derives from the mutuality of their lamentation, from the fact that both give and both receive succor. Thus, unlike Redcrosse's, Guyon's, or Artegall's pity, the compassion Britomart and Amoret feel for each other is a feeling shared between equals. In the recognition that they are the same gender and that they share a common source of suffering, they create community between them, so that Amoret becomes "companion of [Britomart's] care" and "great comfort" to her because Amoret "likewise her lover long miswent" (4.5.30). In this relationship they stand on equal footing.

In basing Britomart and Amoret's friendship on the undoing of power relations between them, Spenser is following Aristotle's discussion of friendship in *Nicomachean Ethics*. For Aristotle, "Friendship is equality and likeness, and especially the likeness of those who are similar in virtue."[42] While he notes that "equality" in friendship does not always mean that friends have equal status, Aristotle's best kinds of relationship are "between good men who are alike in excellence or virtue," in which "each one receives what he gives to the other."[43] Moreover, friendship for Aristotle means a strong identification with the other that leads us to want good things for the other person. After noting that everyone desires what is best for themselves, Aristotle claims that a person "has the same attitude toward his friend as he does towards himself, for his friend really is another self," and so likewise a person wishes for the friend's good.[44] This blurring of the distinction between self and other in friendship suggests that, whatever the social status of two friends, they experience each other and what is good for each other as an extension of their own selfhoods. For Aristotle, this identification with the other differentiates virtuous friendships from the imperfect kind, in which "the friend is loved not because he is a friend, but because he is useful or pleasant."[45] To be a good friend for Aristotle means that the other is not simply a means to something one desires, but rather that the good of one is bound up with the good of the other.

We see Spenser following Aristotle in this notion of identification in friendship more than once in book 4, and the opposed sets of friends in Paridel and Blandamour, on the one hand, and Cambel and Triamond, on the other, speak particularly to the notions of equality and identification that Aristotle develops in *Nicomachean Ethics*. Both pairs of knights take turns fighting for each other, demonstrating on the face of it the desire to do good for the other. But the "left hand rubs the right" relationship between Paridell and Blandamour (4.1.40.9) is revealed to be based on self-interest rather than care for another. These two are a clear example of the friendship based on usefulness, in which "the partners do not feel affection for one another *per se* but in terms of the good accruing to each from the other." Such friendships, Aristotle says, are "easily dissolved."[46] Thus, when it comes time to fight Ferraugh, Paridel complains, "Last turn was mine, well proved to my paine / This now be yours" (4.2.6.4–5), and the two end up falling out as soon as one has something he can't share with the other—the false Florimell (4.2.13).

Triamond and Cambell are set up in opposition to Paridel and Blandamour on this point, demonstrating an identification with the other that the false friends lack. When Triamond falls, Cambell "to salve his name, / And purchase honour in his friends behalve" takes up Triamond's arms and fights in disguise, so that Cambell's victories would accrue to Triamond (4.4.27.2–3). Likewise, when Cambell falls in battle, Triamond ignores his own suffering and puts on Cambell's arms to come to the rescue (4.4.33). These two very literally treat each other as "another self," putting off their own identities to pursue the good of the other. The paired episodes demonstrate that true friendship is based on

Aristotelian principles of mutuality, in which each wills the other's good because of identification with each other, rather than the kind of transactional reciprocity that can only loosely tie Paridel to Blandamour.

If this chivalric pairing demonstrates the importance of seeing one's friend "as another self," however, Cambell and Triamond's story also suggests that friendship within the context of chivalric relationships ultimately fails to achieve the kind of fully loving identification with the other that Britomart and Amoret achieve in their rejection of chivalry through pity. The end result of Cambell and Triamond's self-sacrificing desire to help each others' reputations on the battlefield is their absurd refusal to accept their mutual victory:

> Then all with one consent did yeeld the prize
> To *Triamond* and *Cambell* as the best.
> But *Triamond* to *Cambell* it relest.
> And *Cambell* it to *Triamond* transferd;
> Each labouring t'advance the others gest,
> And make his praise before his own preferd:
> So that the doome was to another day differd. (4.4.36.2–9)

As James Kuzner notes, while the other knights are perfectly happy making a joint award, Cambell and Triamond incongruously now insist upon the individuality of their selfhoods at this moment by refusing to accept the prize together and each insisting on the other's praise "before his own," ignoring the possibility of mutual praise. Self-interest makes a strange reappearance here, Kuzner argues, insofar as "Cambell and Triamond's story shows how others can stand in for us so that we can stand for ourselves . . . creat[ing] a ricochet effect by which, with each blow struck, the reputation of each receives extra marks."[47] The result of their inability to accept the victory *as friends*, their refusal to share the prize by instead insisting on maintaining chivalric notions of individual honor, indicates a failure of their friendship to establish genuine community. Instead, because they cannot agree to accept the victory together, "the doome was to another day differd," and nothing is resolved.

Cambell and Triamond's friendship also differs from that of Britomart and Amoret's in that they never have that moment of mutual recognition of the plight of the other. Throughout canto 3, Cambell and

Triamond are doing their best to kill each other, and only the magical intervention of Cambina—who bonks them on the head and then gives them a sip from her magic cup of forgetfulness—is able to turn them into friends (4.3.38–49). Their friendship does not arise out of anything internal to their relationship but instead appears when the two forget that they have anything to be fighting over in the first place. While the two knights may stand on equal footing socially and in terms of virtue, the eristic structure of chivalry that demands a victor is not undone but merely set aside, only to be taken up again in canto 4 as they each strive to outdo the other in graciousness.

Britomart and Amoret, conversely, find virtuous pity to be constitutive of their friendship. To understand this relationship between friendship and pity, it helps to turn to Thomas Aquinas's work, in which he defines the Christian virtue of pity through Aristotle's definition of friendship. From Augustine through the medieval period, Christianity framed pity as a form of identification with another rather than an exercise of power. This pity-as-identification, however, was not always connected to virtuous activity in the world; the pity for Christian martyrs that Anne Schuurman discusses, for example, or the Marian pity van Dijkhuizen sees in Una, exempt the commiserating party from action because the suffering of those they pity is itself holy.[48] Aquinas, however, provides an account of pity that is based in identification with the other and fulfills Augustine's requirement that pity lead to action on behalf of the other, providing a useful framework for understanding the workings of pity in the Legend of Friendship.

Aquinas develops this account by connecting Augustine's pity to Aristotle's definition of friendship. In his question 30, where Aquinas discusses *misericordia* specifically as a virtue (as opposed to a passion), he describes two different kinds of "union" that occur in the act of pity. One, which he calls "real union," he takes from Aristotle's *Rhetoric*: "Hence the Philosopher says (*Rhet.* ii.8) that men pity such as are akin to them, and the like, because it makes them realize that the same may happen to themselves."[49] But real union, Anthony Keaty argues, is secondary in Aquinas's account to the more important, prior identification that Aquinas gets from Aristotle's *Nicomachean Ethics*.[50] In what Aquinas calls the "union of the affections," "he who loves another *looks upon his friend as another self,* he counts his friend's hurt as his own, so that he grieves for his friend's hurt as though he were hurt himself."[51]

This is a conflation Aristotle himself would not authorize, but it is one that suits Spenser's purposes perfectly.[52] By uniting Aristotle's argument that friends desire the good of the other with Augustine's claim that in pity we suffer for another and therefore seek to act to end that suffering, Aquinas provides an account of how pity can both generate friendship-as-identification and move the one who pities to take action on behalf of another. For book 4 of *The Faerie Queene*, which grapples with the problem of how to produce egalitarian modes of social relations in hierarchical contexts, Thomist pity offers a way to produce Aristotelian friendships.

Thomist elaboration of Aristotle's theory of friendship also differentiates the relationship Britomart and Amoret have from Britomart's earlier relationship with Scudamor. At the end of the 1590 version of the poem, in book 3, Britomart first encounters Scudamor as he lies prostrate on the ground, lamenting the loss of his beloved Amoret to Busirane and groaning "as if his hart were peeces made." We're told his suffering moves Britomart's heart to "pitty," and so she asks the weepy knight to tell his story (3.11.8.7, 9). Scudamor tells Britomart of Amoret's plight and then resumes sobbing in a "ghastly fit" that strikes Britomart "Both with great ruth and terrour . . . / Fearing least from her cage the wearie soule would flit" (3.11.6, 8–9). Britomart, in other words, is moved to compassion by a sadness that seems able to kill Scudamor with its intensity. This pity moves Britomart to behave like an Aristotelian friend to Scudamor, seeking his good: "Which the bold Virgin seeing, gan apply / Fit medicine to his griefe" (3.11.13.8–9).

Unlike the "bad" pity of Redcrosse, Artegal, and others, Britomart shows a virtuous pity here insofar as it moves her to seek remedy for one who suffers unjustly. And like Britomart's eventual friendship with Amoret, Britomart and Scudamor's relationship in book 3 is untinged by the courtly hierarchies and erotic impulses that plague male knights elsewhere in the poem: Scudamor believes he is speaking to another man, and Britomart shows no particular desire for the knight who is bouncing his head off the ground in grief. Like Aristotelian friends, Britomart and Scudamor appear to have much in common—including their chivalric relation to Amoret. Upon hearing the full story of Amoret's situation, Britomart responds, "nothing so much pitty doth implore, / As gentle Ladyes helplesse misery," positioning Britomart as a questing knight driven by pity for distressed damsels, much like Scudamor

(3.11.18.5–6). As Aristotle predicts, this similarity leads Britomart to act as "another self" to Scudamor as she tells him that she will "Deliver [Amoret] fro thence, or with her for you dy" (3.11.18.9). Like Cambell and Triamond, Britomart will take the field of battle—indeed she will risk her life—in Scudamor's place.

All of this is an indication that Spenser was already thinking about the relationship between friendship and pity in 1590. At the same time, however, it's notable that this moment does not, in fact, actually produce a friendship between Britomart and Scudamor. In the 1590 ending to book 3, once Britomart returns Amoret to Scudamor, Britomart all but ceases to exist for the happy couple: "No word they spake, nor earthly thing they felt, / But like two senceles stocks in long embracement dwelt" (3.12.45a.8–9). Rather than fellow-feeling and mutuality, the conclusion of Britomart's quest here leaves her more isolated than when she began, "halfe envying their blesse" because she cannot yet herself achieve a similar relationship (3.12.46a.6). In the 1596 version, the situation is even worse: the impatient Scudamor decides that Britomart has run off with Amoret herself (3.12.45b), and Britomart and Scudamor become rivals for a time in book 4.

The component that is missing in this relationship is Thomist mutuality. Britomart identifies with Scudamor, but Scudamor never returns that sense of identity. Indeed, he barely acknowledges Britomart's attempts to help him. After complimenting her "heroike magnanimity" and acknowledging that she is willing to stand in his place, he rejects the "fit medicine" Britomart is offering, wailing "but let me die, that ought" (3.11.19.2–6). At every moment as Britomart tries to help him, Scudamor's response is despair—even once Britomart has successfully entered the castle. Scudamor thus resists Britomart's attempts for a pitiful identification, refusing to enter into any kind of mutual bond with her. The 1590 book 3 *does* end with mutual identification, but it is between Scudamor and Amoret, who "with sweet countervayle, / Each other of loves bitter fruit despoile" (3.12.47a.1–2). Though in book 3 Britomart's pity is an *instrument* of mutual love, it is not a force that enables to her to *participate* in that love. Only when pity unites with Thomist-Aristotelian mutuality does it produce the kinds of relationships the Legend of Friendship explores.

Britomart and Amoret are Spenser's first "ensample" of this process, in which Thomist pity unites two people through common suffering to seek the other's benefit, but they are not the last. It is their relationship that serves as the pattern whereby Spenser can bring together two other pairs in close mutual bonds: Timias and Belphoebe and the long-suffering Florimell with her Marinell. While these two pairs more clearly fall into the category of "lovers" than "friends," the example of Amoret and Britomart—who engage in their mutual commiseration in bed together—indicates that the distinction between erotic and "friend" relationships is not necessarily a bright line.[53] Moreover, if Amoret and Britomart demonstrate through their relationship a way to defuse the violence of chivalry, the use of the same Thomist pity to reconcile two couples who have been tormented by courtly love demonstrates how the logic of friendship-love can help couples find a happier form of eroticism than the one offered by romance narratives.

The healing of the rift between Timias and Belphoebe follows a pattern very similar to the development of the friendship between Britomart and Amoret, in which, though pity, both pairs transition from an emotionally isolated relationship to a love that prompts them to render aid. The difference in the case of Timias and Belphoebe, however, is the presence of a mediator: a turtledove. Having lost his mind for grief after Belphoebe scorned him for dallying with Amoret, Timias retreats to the woods where he "alwaies wept and wailed night and day" (4.8.2.8). As it was for Britomart and Amoret, mourning alone brings no comfort; nothing changes for Timias until he finds himself in the company of a turtledove that "likewise late had lost her dearest love" (4.8.3). The recognition of shared pain once again leads to shared lamentation:

> Who seeing his sad plight, her tender heart
> With deare compassion deeply did enmove,
> That she gan mone his undeserved smart,
> And with her dolefull accent beare with him a part. (4.8.3.6–9)

The turtledove's response to hearing the "doole he made" (4.8.3.2) is to make dole alongside him, so that the bird's song becomes of form of mutual lamentation: "Her mournefull notes full piteously did frame, / And thereof made a lamentable lay" (4.8.4.2–3).

Though her song causes Timias to "poure so plenteous teares" (4.8.4.6), it nevertheless brings him the same comfort the mutual mourning between Amoret and Britomart brought them. The bird seeks "with her mournefull muse / Him to recomfort in his greatest care," and it works: her song "much did ease his mourning and misfare." As a result, the pair engages in mutual aid. Timias shares his food with her, while "of all his woe and wrong / Companion she became" (4.8.5.3–9). The language here is remarkably similar to the language used to describe the friendship between Amoret and Britomart. The little bird "likewise late had lost her love," just as Amoret "likewise her lover long miswent"; just as Amoret was "great comfort in [Britomart's] sad misfare," the turtledove "recomfort[s]" Timias "in his greatest care"; and both Amoret and the song bird become "companions" to the one they mourn with. Once again, pity is tightly bound up with friendship as a form of sympathetic identification with the other.

The turtledove is then able to transfer this relationship to Belphoebe, thereby repairing the rift caused by Timias's previous failure to contain his sexual desire in the presence of the virginal Belphoebe (4.7.24–41). Seeking to help her friend, the turtledove flies off to Belphoebe and sings her a "mournful plaint ... thinking to let her weet / The great tormenting griefe" that Timias is experiencing (4.8.8.6–8). Belphoebe follows the bird back to Timias, whereupon the turtledove "a piteous ditty new deviz'd" to communicate the story of Timias's suffering (4.8.12.2). Witnessing Timias's wretched plight without recognizing him, Belphoebe in turn "pittied much his case, / And wisht it were in her to doe him any grace" (4.8.12), so that now Belphoebe, like the turtledove, seeks Timias's benefit.

In this movement from the turtledove's "piteous ditty" about Timias to Belphoebe's piteous response to Timias, we see friendship-love enabling erotic love via Thomist pity. What distinguishes Timias and Belphoebe's erotic reconciliation from typical courtly pity is that the hierarchies of courtly love are not initially present in this scene. Because she does not recognize Timias, Belphoebe is not—at least from her own perspective—in the position of courtly beloved who holds power over the supplicant would-be lover. Her pity, in other words, isn't inspired by Timias's pleas for a mercy only she can grant—that doesn't arise for another five stanzas, when she finally comes to know who Timias is. Instead, Belphoebe's pity is evoked *before* Timias begins to supplicate and to reveal himself to her. She wishes "it were in her to doe him any grace" before she realizes that she does, in fact, have that power.

VIRTUOUS PITY AND SPENSER'S AESTHETIC DOUBT

Her pity, informed by the turtledove's own sympathetic identification with Timias, begins as a virtuous impulse to imaginatively create her own identification with a suffering human—and this identification, a Thomist "union of affections," enables the two to move past the courtly motif of the unrequited lover. By canto 17, the two are back in a courtly mode: Timias finally reveals himself, telling her "Ne any but your selfe, o dearest dred, / Hath done this wrong" to him, which "sory words her mightie hart did mate / With mild regard," so that "her burning wrath she gan abate, / And him receiv'd againe to former favours state" (4.8.17. 1–2, 6–9). But the fact that her pity was generated earlier through a compassionate identification inspired by the friendship shown by the turtledove suggests that their erotic relationship now encompasses a friendship relationship as well. There is no indication that Belphoebe abandons her virginity in accepting Timias back to "former favours state," but their reconciliation here suggests that the tension created by his sexual desire and her virginity has been quelled, that their relationship has been made happier by a "union of affections."

The reconciliation of Marinell and Florimell again demonstrates how Thomist pity can overcome the dynamic of lover and scornful beloved. As in the case of Timias and Belphoebe, the process begins when Marinell "heard the lamentable voice of one, / That piteously complained her carefull grief" as he walks alone through Proteus's halls. Listening to this anonymous voice, Marinell's "stony heart with tender ruth / Was toucht, and mighty courage mollified" (4.12.13.1–2). Just as Belphoebe does not recognize Timias before she learns to pity him—and is therefore not seeing him as the scorned lover—so too Marinell and Florimell have been removed from their former relation of lover and scornful beloved by the situation. Florimell is not supplicating Marinell here; she doesn't know he's there. And though Marinell did "inly wish, that in his powre it weare / Her to redresse," indicating the virtuous desire to provide succor to the one who suffers, "he meanes found none" to help her.

Significantly, however, when he finds he has no redress to save Florimell from her prison, he falls back to the same action that Britomart and Amoret took in canto 1: he mourns *with* her. Echoing the sympathetic stone of Proteus's home that "seem[ed] . . . to grone with billows from the maine," Marinell "even for griefe of mind . . . oft did grone," finding that "He could no more but her great misery bemone" (4.12.13). Everything in this scene is united in grief, in the shared sadness that elsewhere in the book has been the hallmark of friendship. It is through this shared sadness, in which all are united not only in pain but in helplessness, that Marinell is able to love Florimell.

The lovesickness Marinell endures afterward returns us to the conventions of courtly love but with important differences. Back at his mother's house, Marinell

> gan record the lamentable stowre,
> In which his wretched love lay day and night,
> For his deare sake, that ill deserv'd that plight:
> The thought whereof empierst his hart so deepe,
> That of no worldly thing he tooke delight;
> Ne dayly food did take, ne nightly sleepe,
> But pyn'd, and mourn'd, and languisht, and alone did weepe. (4.12.19.3–9)

"Empierst" hearts are a common trope of courtly love. Thus, for example, in the house of Busirane we see a Neptune who "did pensive seeme and sad" because "privy love his brest empierced had" (3.11.41.6, 8). What has wounded Marinell's heart, however, isn't love but "the lamentable stowre, / In which his wretched love lay day and night." In other words, even once he's far from the place where Florimell laments, Marinell continues to suffer because of Florimell's suffering, to grieve because she grieves. She remains for him "another self."

Moreover, his suffering isn't like Astrophil's aestheticized display of pain that tries to compel Stella's love (nor like Florimell's earlier attempts to entreat Marinell's love). This suffering resembles much more the suffering of our knight of chastity, Britomart, when she falls in love with Artegall. Both believe they are helpless to relieve their suffering, and both receive aid from their caretakers—Britomart from her nurse and Marinell from his mother—who seek to remedy the suffering of someone they, in their turn, also love. Marinell's resemblance to Britomart, who is supposed to be our "ensample" of a virtuous, chaste love, hints at the notion that the love between Marinell and Florimell is something closer to the ideal of erotic love Spenser has been searching for throughout the middle books of the poem than what we have seen before. Marinell's pity is not that of the courtly lover, who seeks only relief for his own lovelorn suffering; it is the pity of one who genuinely wants what is best for the one he loves.

Thomist pity, based in seeing a person as another self and seeking to remedy their pain because of that sense of identification, is thus the basis of virtuous love—both "friendship" and erotic relationships—in book 4. Because it creates identification with another, a requirement for Aristotelian friendship, this kind of pity offers a mode of relation to another that sidesteps, at least for a moment, the hierarchies of chivalric relationships. Spenser opens book 4 by announcing that love "of honor and all vertue is / The roote" (4.Pr.2.6–7), and later goes on to identify friendship-love as best kind of love (4.9.1–2). From this it is possible to read friendship as the most important virtue Spenser discusses. For while Spenser claims that chastity is "The fayrest vertue, far above the rest" (3.Pr.1.2) and he says of courtesy that there "growes not a fayrer flower, / Then is the bloosme of comely courtesie" (6.Pr.4.1–2), only love is identified as the *root* of virtue, the origin of and what sustains other virtues. For Spenser, Thomist *misericordia* gives rise to all other forms of virtue, reorienting social relationships through acts of identification and mutual commiseration that lead to virtuous action in the world. If the poem can teach this much, can teach the reader to feel this form of pity that enables the "roote" of "vertue" to grow in us, then the ethical project Spenser lays out in the Letter seems likely to succeed.

IV. MIMESIS AND THE GENERATION OF PITY

The remaining question, then, is how (or whether) that virtuous feeling is one that we can learn to feel by reading *The Faerie Queene*. While it might perhaps be enough for the poem simply to show us "ensamples" of how Thomist pity generates bonds of virtuous love between people, the stories particularly of Belphoebe and Marinell suggest that *representations* of pity themselves might be enough to create a virtuous emotion in an onlooker, offering the possibility that Spenser's poem might not just *show* us what virtuous pity is but that it might also *generate* that feeling in us. In both stories, we see a Platonic form of mimesis affecting Belphoebe and Marinell so that they, as Plato claims all readers do, feel the same feelings they see represented. To the extent that what they feel is virtuous pity, Spenser shows his characters undergoing the kind of education by representation he gestures at in the Letter.

The narrator of the poem similarly gestures to the possibility that the poem's reader may, in fact, respond the way Marinell and Belphoebe do to representations of pity. At the same time, however, the narrator also winks at a crucial difference between us as readers and his characters as spectators: we are aware that what we view are characters, while his characters are not. To put it another way, Spenser's narrator goes out of his way to remind us that, unlike his characters who experience representations of pity immediately, we are having an aesthetic experience, and our emotional reactions are mediated by that awareness. This nod to Aristotelian aesthetic distance, the "pleasing analysis" Spenser refers to in the Letter, disrupts any possibility that *we* might feel Thomist pity because it reminds us that we cannot identify fully with characters whose suffering we are, on some level, enjoying. Instead of teaching us to feel Thomist pity, Spenser's narrator ultimately dramatizes for us the difference between a fictional world, in which pity artfully represented transmits that pity directly into the hearts of the characters, and our own experience of pity mediated by delight. In doing so, he rejects the Platonist argument for poetry's ethical power by insisting on his poem's autonomy from the world his readers inhabit.

Unlike Amoret and Britomart, who are able to identify with each other's pain because they both share a similar story, neither Belphoebe nor Marinell come to pity their lovers because they already share that pain. Instead, pity is generated in them through an act of pitiful representation by a mediating entity that *does* achieve identification with Timias and Florimell. In the case of Timias, that entity is the turtledove, who engages in an allegory of aesthetic mimesis. This mimesis has two parts: the adornment of the jewel Timias gives the turtledove and the two songs she sings for Belphoebe. In the first song, it is the jewel that attracts Belphoebe's notice, not the song itself (4.8.10), but because she takes notice of the jewel, she follows the bird back to Timias, where the bird sings again of Timias's sadness, and this generates pity in Belphoebe.

This scene resembles Sidney's claims in the opening sonnet of *Astrophil and Stella*. The method of persuasion Sidney outlines in his first sonnet begins with aesthetic pleasure that leads eventually to pity: "Pleasure might cause her read, reading might make her know,/

VIRTUOUS PITY AND SPENSER'S AESTHETIC DOUBT

Knowledge might pity win, and pity grace obtain." This describes Belphoebe's response to the turtledove more than it does Stella's response to Astrophil. In the same way that both Sidney and Spenser describe aesthetic form as a kind of ornament that leads to delight, the turtledove herself is quite literally delivering her song while adorned: she is wearing the jewel that Timias gave her, making her an allegory of the kind of poetry whose persuasive force is supposed to lie in its ornaments. Belphoebe is drawn into engaging with the situation by first engaging with that ornamentation.

At the same time, however, what distinguishes the turtledove's song from Astrophil's is that, whereas Astrophil attempts to represent his own suffering in order to elicit pity, the turtledove at once represents Timias's suffering *and also her own pity for that suffering*. Belphoebe is not moved to compassion by the song alone; it is only when she hears the second song—the "piteous ditty new"—while in Timias's presence, seeing him "in wretched weedes disguiz'd, / With heary glib deform'd, and meager face" (4.8.12.5–6), that she is moved to pity him. "Piteous" can mean both "apt to arouse pity" and "full of pity."[54] Given that singing lamentations has been the turtledove's mode of showing compassion to Timias, her song to Belphoebe is "piteous" in both senses: she sings a sad song so that Belphoebe will be moved to pity, but the bird also performs her own pity for Timias by singing. In this sense, the turtledove engages in an act of mimesis in the Platonic mode that both Sidney and Spenser discuss, offering an allegorical account of how poetry might teach us to feel virtuous emotions. The turtledove's song is able to generate Thomist pity in Belphoebe not by causing Belphoebe first to identify with Timias but by causing Belphoebe to identify with the turtledove's pity for Timias. Belphoebe thus feels a "union of affections" in a Thomist way with Timias not because she has suffered like he has but because she has seen another relate to him in that way, and that representation of sorrow has inspired a sense of pity in her that causes her to see Timias as another self.

The reconciliation of Marinell and Florimell follows a similar course. Instead of the agency of a bird, however, this time it is the rock of Florimell's prison that represents her suffering to Marinell. Florimell's lament "ruth ... moved in the rocky stone," causing it both "to feele her grievous paine" and to respond with mutual lamentation, "oft to grone with billowes beating from the maine" (4.12.5). Just as Belphoebe's pity for Timias appears motivated by witnessing the pitiful interaction between Timias and the turtledove, so too here Marinell's eventual pity follows from the sense that their environment responds compassionately to Florimell's piteous complaints. Previously, Florimell claims, her laments could not move Marinell: "But his hard rocky hart for no entreating / Will yeeld, but when my piteous plaints he heares, / Is hardned more with my aboundant teares" (4.12.7.3–5). That here we are told that Marinell's "stony heart with tender ruth / Was toucht, and mighty courage mollified" indicates that his pity now is a response not simply to Florimell's lament but to sympathy of the "rocky stone" that expresses pity for Florimell's sadness.[55]

The use of representations to generate pity in these characters is important because it answers the crucial question of how we can learn to feel Thomist pity if we don't already recognize a "union of affections" with another person—that is, if we can't already see ourselves in them sufficiently to see them as "another self." If, like Britomart and Amoret, we can only experience the virtuous compassion that is based in identification with another if that other already happens to be very much like us, then our ability to pity another would be limited to a very small subset of people we encounter in the world. By showing how representations of pity can inspire pity in his characters, Spenser's poem suggests that art (and *The Faerie Queene* in particular) can play a role in helping us feel for those who are not necessarily like ourselves. If pity can communicate as Plato describes, so that we feel what a poem's characters feel, then poetry can bridge the divide between our experiences and others' to broaden our ability to feel virtuous pity.

The narrator himself seems to encourage us at various moments throughout the poem to believe exactly this. Van Dijkhuizen notes that "*The Faerie Queene* not only represents pity in its characters but also imagines the act of story-telling itself as a conduit of compassion."[56] The poem does this through its frequent moments of narrative pity, thereby serving as the mediator that represents a pitiful comportment toward the poem's characters. The first time the narrator breaks into the poem outside of the proems, it is to express pity for Una. He notes that "Nought there under heav'ns wilde hollownesse, / That moves more deare compassion of mind, / Then beautie brought t'unworthie wretchednesse," before announcing that he "feele[s his] heart perst with so great agony, / When such I see, that all for pitty I could dy" (1.3.1). Like Belphoebe watching the turtledove singing to Timias, we as readers here witness the narrator's own "piteous ditty" for Una.

What we find in this "ensample" is a combination of courtly pity and the kind of pity that is consonant with the demands of reason. On the one hand, the narrator notes that his pity is evoked "through allegeance and fast fealtie, / Which I do owe unto all woman kind," suggesting a chivalric form of pity of the stronger for the weaker. On the other, however, the judgments of Aristotelian pity also come into play: what "moves" the "deare compassion of mind" is "beautie brought t'unworthy wretchedness." When beauty suffers, we might pity, but not so much as when that suffering is also "unworthy," which is to say not merited. In this sense, the narrator indemnifies himself against the kind of bad pity that characters like Redcrosse, Guyon, and Artegall all display, when they pity someone who is only beautiful and not also suffering from "unworthie wretchnesse." The narrator's pity, he makes clear, is still allied with reason insofar as it is directed by a judgment of justice, even if it is also inflected by chivalric attachment to beauty. Van Dijkhuizen notes that this is part of a larger strategy in the poem, in which it "repeatedly appeals to the reader's sense of pity" both through multiple such moments of narrative compassion and through claims the poem makes that the narratives it tells could indeed move an audience to pity.[57] By making an "ensample" of his own pity, the narrator suggests to us that we might feel the same. He invites us to identify with *his* virtuous compassion.

Perhaps unsurprisingly, book 4 offers more such moments than any other book in the poem. It opens all but announcing that pity will be a major theme of the Legend of Friendship:

> Of lovers sad calamities of old,
> Full many piteous stories doe remaine,
> But none more piteous ever was ytold,
> Then that of *Amorets* hart-binding chaine,
> And this of *Florimels* unworthie paine:
> The deare compassion of whose bitter fit
> My softened heart so sorely doth constraine,
> That I with teares full oft doe pittie it,
> And oftentimes doe wish it never had bene writ. (4.1.1)

These lines seem to respond to the narrator's earlier comment in book 3, when he left Florimell's story behind, that "the hardest hart of stone, / Would hardly finde to aggravate her grief; / For misery craves rather mercy, then repriefe" (3.8.1). That his heart at the start of book 4 is "softened" indicates a recognition that his own heart has been hard toward Florimell and Amoret in not advancing their narratives sooner. That his "deare compassion" softens his heart reflects a similar comportment to Marinell's, whom pity softens toward Florimell, as well as nodding at the theological notion that "softening" of the stony heart is requisite for Christian virtue.

This pity, he tells us, causes him to be kinder to his characters, to show them "mercy," again modeling the kind of virtuous identification that pity can create. Later the narrator remarks of Amoret "That pittie is to heare the perils, which she tride" (4.7.2.9), and then of Florimell's continued captivity that "even to think thereof, it inly pitties me" (4.11.1.9). Positioning himself as an onlooker, the narrator notes that a reader of the tales is susceptible to pity as well, suggesting that the poem might not simply be teaching us pity by "ensample" but also by communicating that emotional response outward from the text via our identification with the narrator's pity. By representing pity for these characters, the narrator plays the role of the turtledove or the stones of Proteus's palace. As readers, we are offered the opportunity to sympathize with this fellow onlooker's pity and thereby to feel the pity he feels. The poem thus transfers virtuous pity to its readers, just as the turtledove transfers her friendship-pity for Timias to Belphoebe. We learn not just by reading, but by feeling.

All of this is undermined, however, by the irony of the narrator's pity in these lines, an irony that establishes more distance between the narrator and the poem's characters—and therefore between us and the poem's characters—than is suited to the Thomist pity that book 4 depicts. In 4.1.1, his claim that the compassion at their "bitter fit" "constraines" his heart is undercut by the poetic structure. On one line we read the phrase "My softened heart so sorely doth constraine," inviting us to read the "heart" as the subject of "constraine," rather than the grammatically correct but syntactically distant "compassion." In other words, the line fleetingly offers the suggestion of what is, in fact, true: that Florimell and Amoret are being "constrained" in this poem by the desire of the narrator. He furthermore completes this reflection on the pity he feels at the tales of Amoret and Florimell by saying that he "oftentimes . . . wish it never had bene writ," calling attention to the fact that these "piteous stories" require an act of writing to reach us as readers—an act undertaken by the narrator.

He more explicitly acknowledges his role in his characters' suffering in his canto 11 reflection on his pity for Florimell, where he remarks, "But ah for pittie that I have thus long / Left a fayre Ladie languishing in payne" (4.11.1.1–2) before commenting that it would take a "miracle" to save her before canto 12: "unless some heavenly powre her free / By miracle, not yet appearing playne, / She lenger yet is like captiv'd to bee" (4.11.6–8). As Campana muses, "there may be something more than a little disingenuous about a work whose narrator plunges women into distress over and over again only to bemoan their constant peril."[58] Far from pursuing a union of affections in which he would be "impelled to succor" his characters, the narrator calls attention to and even jokes about the fact that his characters are suffering—and that they are suffering at his hands.

Through the irony of these moments of narrative pity, Spenser calls attention to the fact that his relationship to his characters is of a different kind than the relationships the characters have with each other. Within the fiction of the poem, characters like Britomart and Amoret and Marinell and Florimell relate to each other as individuals, as people. Their Christian-inflected pity is evoked by the sense of connection and identification that people can recognize among each other. For the narrator and the reader, however, these same "people" are all characters, a fact to which the narrator, as we have seen, calls our attention.

This distinction disrupts the possibility that we might feel Thomist pity for the characters the way we might for real people. In the figure of the turtledove, Spenser offers the possibility that aesthetic mediation can generate virtuous pity in the audience: the "pitteous ditty" helps Belphoebe reconcile with Timias when she learns to identify with the turtledove's own pity. And in 4.1.1, the narrator likewise notes the way in which the aesthetic representation of suffering generates pity—as van Dijkhuizen notes, the narrator indicates that the "piteous stories" are specifically what generate his response to Florimell and Amoret.[59] But Spenser's narrator doesn't offer us the same pity for his characters that the turtledove displays for Timias, because, unlike the turtledove, the narrator is creating their suffering even as he is pitying it. While both the turtledove and the narrator pity and express that pity through aesthetic representations of suffering, only one of them is responding to the vicissitudes of a world that exceeds her ability to control it. The other is making a world of his own.

As readers, we are of course more in the position of the turtledove than the narrator, insofar as our emotions for Spenser's characters are in the same hand as that which is holding the pen. Spenser's narrator laughs at the fact that he is torturing his characters, and to the extent that we feel pity for his characters, he is torturing us as readers as well: *yes, I could get Florimell out of the cave and then we'd all feel better,* he seems to suggest, *but what fun would that be?* It is a situation that recalls the narrator's question at the end of book 3, when we see Amoret pierced through the heart in Busirane's castle: "Ah who can love the worker of her smart?" (3.12.31.7). But then, as Dorothy Stephens remarks in her note on this passage, "The answer, of course, is, 'Everyone'."[60]

While Busirane's torments may not move Amoret to love, Spenser's figure for the poet-magician makes us love Busirane even as he pierces our hearts with pity for Amoret, just as the narrator does in book 4. He is, after all, one of the "showes" described in the "Letter," designed to be "delightfull and pleasing to commune sence," part of the "historicall fiction" with which Spenser "colours" his "good discipline." Unlike Belphoebe listening to the turtledove, who only pities and seeks to help Timias, as readers we are supposed to enjoy the pity we feel because we are looking at an aesthetic representation, mimesis in the Aristotelian sense more than the Platonic. Returning to Aristotle's key insight about aesthetic awareness, we are reminded that "though the objects themselves may be painful to see, we delight to view the most realistic representations of them in art, the forms for example of the lowest animals and of dead bodies." Painful representations are rendered pleasurable in art.

If we follow the narrator as our point of identification for the pity that we should feel for the poem's characters, then it cannot be the kind of friendship-pity that Aquinas discusses, and instead comes much closer to the kind of aesthetic pity that Aristotle describes in *Rhetoric* and *Poetics:* a feeling that recognizes that we are vulnerable to the same fate as the one we pity but that does not fully achieve the "union of the affections" that characterizes the virtue of friendship in an Aristotelian, Thomist, and Spenserian sense. This aesthetic pity we feel alongside the narrator for Spenser's characters also resembles the kind of pity

Augustine rejects in *Confessions* (which is also to say the kind we saw subverting Astrophil's intentions in the previous chapter). In his repudiation of tragic theater, Augustine complains that "the more anyone is moved by these scenes [of tragic events], the less free he is from similar passions." The danger here is that, by enjoying tragedy, the viewer becomes more inured to suffering—that is, we become more like those characters in the play whose mistakes and passions lead to suffering rather than toward a virtuous life.[61] Moreover, the fact that we enjoy this grief—that we keep seeking out these pitiful displays—only affirms suffering, rather than teaching us to end it. This is the antithesis of the virtuous pity Augustine identifies in *City of God*, which forms the basis for Aquinas's own discussion of *misericordia*.

When Spenser's narrator in book 4 introduces his own pity for the poem's characters, he thus offers us not just an alternate definition of pity, but one which is directly opposed to the ethical vision of pity that he places at the heart of his lessons about love. Instead of showing a compassion for his characters that would, for instance, lead him to find a way to free Florimell at the beginning of canto 11 rather than near the end of the canto 12, his pity is the kind that Augustine experienced when weeping over Dido and watching tragic plays, a kind whose pleasurable component encourages the prolonging of grief rather than its redress. Insofar as Spenser's expressions of pity implicate the reader, this suggests that our own pity for his characters is not the virtuous but the aesthetic kind.

The self-consciousness of the narrator's claims of pity, in which he gestures at the fourth wall to remind us of its presence, emphasizes to us the constructedness of the stories we are hearing. He reminds us that we are reading a poem, that these stories—and therefore the characters—are written, not real, thereby also reminding us of the difference—and therefore the distance—between us as readers and the poem's characters. Nor are the representations the poem provides simply a "golden world" to which we might aspire: they are a world of their own that, the narrator reminds us, we cannot reach because that world operates according to different rules than our own. In other words, he reminds us that we are having an aesthetic experience when reading his book, that the poem is a "pleasing analysis," not a real-life situation. To the extent that we engage that analysis, what we see in the narrator's ironic performance of pity is that there is a difference between how people relate to each other and how people relate to fictional characters. We cannot, after all, save Florimell and Amoret ourselves. And yet, like Augustine reading the *Aeneid,* we keep reading.

All of this denies the possibility that allegory might provide the kind of education in virtue that Spenser claims, in the infinitely quoted letter to Raleigh, to be the purpose of *The Faerie Queene.* Spenser defends the choice to deliver his "precepts" "clowdily enwrapped in Allegoricall devises" by noting that "nothing [is] esteemed of, that is not delightfull and pleasing to commune sence." His audience, he argues, is more likely to learn the lessons he teaches if the manner of the lesson is pleasing. In book 4, however, he creates a crisis by suggesting that poetry cannot actually teach us to follow the ensample of his characters because we do not experience them the way they experience each other. However much we might care about them, we experience Spenser's characters mediated through the experience of delight that comes with fictional narratives. That delight in turn mediates our emotional responses, altering the character of them.

The point of telling "piteous stories" is that it teaches us the benefits of pity as a virtue by making us feel it; but to the extent that we enjoy the piteous stories, as Spenser intended us to, the kind of pity we feel is not the right kind—not the virtuous kind, but instead the pernicious, sinful pity Augustine denounced. The pleasure of the allegorical form means that we take delight in reading about the suffering of Florimell and Amoret; and if we delight in it, then we precisely cannot see them "as another self," we cannot unite our affections with theirs, and we cannot thereby engage in virtuous acts of loving charity. This opposition between two kinds of pity—which is also an opposition between two kinds of experience—is put front and center for the reader in book 4, insofar as the narrator repeatedly calls our attention to the problem, asking us to reconsider in 1596 the aesthetic project Spenser described in 1590. The exclusion of the letter in the 1596 version of the poem is perhaps indicative of the more general cynicism that seems to pervade Spenser's project by the time he publishes the six-book version of the poem. By book 4, *The Faerie Queene* has abandoned the poem's purported ethical project because it has abandoned the theory of poetry that enabled it. Instead, it has fully embraced a self-conscious recognition of its autonomy—and it is demanding that we recognize it too.

CHAPTER 3

Alternate Realities

Shakespearean Aesthetics, Pity, and King Lear

No exploration of sixteenth-century English aesthetics would be complete without an examination of drama. While Sidney and Spenser write nondramatic forms of poetry, the theories they rely on to develop their own sense of the ethical value of poetry are themselves, as we have seen in earlier chapters, largely theories of tragedy. Moreover, the *misomousoi* that Sidney and Spenser both defend themselves against were primarily taking aim at the dangers they believed theater posed to the morals of playgoers. The dramatic work of Shakespeare responds to many of the same dynamics that concerned Sidney and Spenser, particularly regarding the potential ethical effects of the emotional responses evoked in the audience by dramatic representations. In Shakespeare, however, we find a different resolution to the question of how our emotional engagement with art affects our behavior in the world.

Shakespeare differs from Sidney and Spenser in several significant ways. Unlike them, he does not provide us with a prose account of his thoughts on art, and in general when Shakespeare's characters discuss literature, they are not so explicitly focused on its ethical value. But many of Shakespeare's plays, like Sidney's *Defence* and Spenser's *Faerie Queene*, highlight the relationship between the fiction and the audience, overgoing Spenser's winking at the fourth wall by turning directly to the audience to ask us what we're going to do with what we've

89

just experienced. In doing so, Shakespeare's work demonstrates an investment both in the autonomy of the plays and in building bridges between our world and theirs.

Shakespeare's work also explores the relationship between emotion and ethics in ways that demonstrate a kinship with the work of Sidney and Spenser, particularly in the plays' exploration of pity. Critics like David Hillman and Richard Strier have argued that the greatness of Shakespeare's work lies in its embrace of powerful emotion, both in the characters and in the audience.[1] As Heather James has noted, a great many of Shakespeare's plays—largely the tragedies but also *The Tempest*—specifically thematize pity as an ethical, political force.[2] By exploring the ethics of pity in a genre that is historically defined by its ability to produce pity, Shakespeare's plays thus offer a metatheatrical bridge for thinking about the relationship between the pity displayed by its characters and the pity experienced by and inspired in the audience.

Shakespeare takes an approach to this relationship that solves Sidney's dilemma and rejects Spenser's conclusions. Where Sidney struggled to reconcile his desire for literature to provide ethical instruction with his sense of literary autonomy, and Spenser abandoned his ethical project to embrace that autonomy, Shakespeare's work offers a model that emphasizes the autonomously structured world of the artwork while exploring the kinds of real-world effects our encounters with those alternate realities can have on us. His work achieves this in part because, even more than Sidney and Spenser, Shakespeare's plays imply a cognitivist approach to emotion derived from both the Stoic and Aristotelian traditions that preceded him, which allows his works to ask us—and often to ask us explicitly—what our feelings about the plays *mean*. Shakespeare thus offers an aesthetic theory wherein we are affected in our own lives by our emotional experience of the work, not *despite* but *because* of the distance between our world and the text's.

By first examining several explicitly metatheatrical moments in Shakespeare's work, we can apprehend *a*—which is not to say *the*—theory of drama that we might call "Shakespearean." This theory, evidenced in the conclusions to *A Midsummer Night's Dream* and *The Tempest*, as well as in in Hamlet's reflections on the power of theater, at once emphasizes the aesthetic distance between the play and the audience and offers an invitation to close that gap, imposing an alternate reality on us, the playgoers, and then asking us to reconcile that reality with our own. This is a theory that recognizes literary autonomy while articulating how audience engagement with the world of the text might produce real-world effects.

To understand the ethical import of this understanding of drama, an examination of *King Lear* proves enlightening. This play is often recognized as Shakespeare's most powerfully tragic and, as we will see, offers the most sustained theory of pity in Shakespeare's work. *Lear* develops a radical understanding of ethical pity that both speaks to and reorients the same Aristotelian ethical tradition with which Sidney and Spenser engage. Juxtaposing pity with a form of justice that relies on measurements of what is owed versus what has been paid—a form of reason stripped of feeling that I call "calculative rationality"—the play makes a powerful argument for pity as a way of creating community in a way that rationality alone cannot. By refiguring the emotion of pity as a way of *thinking-through-feeling* in the world, *Lear* engages us for the duration of the play in an alternate reality that asks us to rethink our understanding of the relationship between emotion and reason, forcing us to confront our own responses to the kinds of emotions that the play figures as ethical. In doing so, the play offers the potential— though not the promise—of transformation in our own world.

I. "THE PLAY'S THE THING": SHAKESPEAREAN AESTHETICS

Discussions of aesthetics in Shakespeare—particularly his plays—tend to argue either that Shakespearean aesthetics point to or even lay the groundwork for modern aesthetics, or that the concept of art evinced by the plays and other poetical works is specifically early modern in character and requires us to think through a moment prior to the Enlightenment to understand it. In particular, such discussions focus on the status of the artwork as either autonomous or deeply invested and participating in the processes of history, politics, and ideology.[3] But the line between aesthetic autonomy and what Charles Whitney calls an "ante-aesthetics," in which the audience "link[s] the world of the play to the world beyond and to the lives of playgoers, rather than . . . primarily to an aesthetic dimension," is not as stark as it might seem.[4]

Working with an Adornian concept of aesthetic autonomy, in which the artwork is tied to the historical world by its negation of that world, those who find a modern aesthetics in Shakespeare recognize the ways in which aesthetic autonomy interfaces with that "world beyond" and the "lives of the playgoers." As Hugh Grady notes in a discussion of *A Midsummer Night's Dream,* "although the difference between these two realms [of imaginative space, represented by the fairy plot, and 'the familiar world of human experience'] in the play is clear, the barrier between them, like the wall in the inset play, has chinks in it, and within each separate domain there are traces of its excluded Other."[5] Similarly, Whitney notes that, as much as "ante" means "before," it also means "anticipatory,"[6] so that the key question in these debates tends to be not about whether Shakespeare's aesthetics are modern or early modern but where in the development between those two historical moments to locate him.

The answer to that question lies in how Shakespeare's works think about their own status both as plays and as interventions in the lives of their audience. While Shakespeare himself did not leave behind any personal statement on his views of art, his characters have voiced positions that offer us a way to construct a "Shakespearean" theory of art—particularly of theater—that at once recognizes the status of drama as autonomous, which is to say as something distinct from what Grady calls "the familiar world of human experience," and simultaneously emphasizes the effect a play can have on that familiar world—an effect we might call ethical.

More specifically, in some of his many metatheatrical moments, Shakespeare's characters discuss how plays interact with the world specifically *as plays,* as works of fiction. By virtue of their status as autonomous realities, Shakespeare's plays offer alternative visions to the audience that in various ways try to impose themselves on the realities of the playgoers. The theory of aesthetics that grows out of these moments sees tragedy, as Plato did, as "a vehicle for a worldview," but in doing so it asks us to engage in critical reflection on that worldview once we get to the play's end. Via our emotional responses to what we see, the play encourages our sympathy with the values and responses of the play's characters. But because the play always presents itself *as fiction,* our emotional responses do not cause us, as Plato argued, simply to adopt the worldview of the play. Those responses instead ask us to find a reconciliation between the fictional reality of the text and the lived experience of the playgoer.

Two moments, one from the beginning and one from the end of Shakespeare's dramatic career, shed light on the permeability of the barrier between the aesthetic realm and the world of human experience. Both *A Midsummer Night's Dream* and *The Tempest* end with addresses to the audience that recognize the fictive, constructed nature of the preceding narrative while inviting audience participation in a way that supports Whitney's argument that, for Shakespeare, "characters, players, and playgoers are all encompassed in one articulated theatrical continuum, not entirely divided into knower and known."[7] Put another way, these moments highlight the play as an aesthetic experience, something distinct from other kinds of experience in the world, but they do so in a way that constructs the audience members as both subjects and objects of the play's meaning-making, both able to exert power over the fictional world through their responses to it and affected by those responses in ways that might carry out of the playhouse.

A Midsummer Night's Dream concludes with a double-sided invitation to the audience to engage with the play. The character Robin Goodfellow, better known as Puck, turns to the audience to beg forgiveness and ask for approval. "If we shadows have offended," he explains, the audience should take the whole play as a dream: "Think but this, and all is mended, / That you have but slumber'd here / While these visions did appear." After asking for the audience's "pardon," he then promises twice to make amends but asks the audience for their help in this process: "Give me your hands, if we be friends, / And Robin shall restore amends."[8] *A Midsummer Night's Dream* thus ends by building a bridge between the world of the play and the world of the playgoers. This gesture to the audience cuts two ways. On the one hand, Puck's reference to himself and the other characters as "shadows" and the play itself as a dream frames the experience of the audience as a specifically aesthetic one so that this moment is, as Grady argues, "a misleadingly self-deprecatory assertion of the purposeless purposiveness of aesthetic production." On the other hand, however, by seeking to make amends with the audience Puck suggests that even "shadows" can have interpersonal relationships with actual human beings, so what Grady calls the "autonomously structured aesthetic realm" actually interacts with the lives of the audience.[9]

In particular, the request "Give me your hands," while on the face of it a request for applause, also suggests a reaching across the distance between the dream space of the play and the real world, the ability of the audience to touch these shadows with their hands in a way that makes their aesthetic reality also a material reality. This reality may be "autonomously structured," but that does not mean that it exists apart from the lives the audience. To the contrary, the fact that Puck indicates that the play was the *audience*'s dream—"Think . . . that you have slumbered here"—and requires the audience's hands in order to make amends gives the audience a constitutive role in the fictional space of the play.

The same is true at the end of *The Tempest,* when Prospero likewise addresses the audience to solicit their approval. Claiming that, with the play's end, his "charms are all o'erthrown," he now grants magical powers to the audience, asking them, "Let me not / . . . dwell / In this bare island by your spell." To free him and send him back to Naples, he explains, the audience must applaud: "release me from by bands / With the help of your good hands." Unless we do this, Prospero tells us, his "project fails," and so he throws himself upon our mercy, asking us to pardon him just as we "from crimes would pardoned be."[10]

The resonances with the end of *A Midsummer Night's Dream* are several and again highlight a dialectical relationship between fiction and the lives of the audience. Just as Puck connects the audience's experience to one of the play's metatheatrical aspects, referring the experience of the play to dreamers' experience within the play, Prospero's words here highlight the dual role of his "charms" as part of the fiction of the play and as metatheatrical device. And, like Puck, he imputes that device to the audience. By referring to the audience's power to keep him confined to the island as "your spell," Prospero grants the audience the same world-making abilities that the play has used as a metaphor for theatrical production throughout the play. The space of the play may be an enchanted one, but the power for enchantment lies not just within the fictional space of the theater but within the people who themselves move into and out of that space. By granting the audience the same power of magic he has used throughout the play, Prospero, like Puck, confirms what Whitney notes about playgoing practices in the period: "the playgoer is more than a consumer—he or she can re-create the product."[11] Moreover, Prospero *requires* the audience to "re-create the product" insofar as the audience is called upon *either* to send him to Naples through the work of the audience's "hands" *or* to keep Prospero on the island "by your spell." Audience engagement with the fiction is not optional.

This is a different approach to the question of aesthetic delight than we've seen in either Sidney or Spenser. In both of these moments, Shakespeare's characters are asking the audience a simple question: *did you like this play?* By asking for applause, Puck and Prospero take the pro forma response to a play's end and ask the audience to make a choice, to *decide* whether they experienced aesthetic delight or not. This gesture foregrounds the dimension of aesthetic delight in a way that constructs our pleasure as a form of negotiation rather than (as for Sidney and the Platonic tradition of mimesis) a form of consent. To applaud is to allow Puck to "make amends," to give "pardon" to Prospero and their respective plays; the fact of applause at the end of the play becomes a form of reconciliation between the fictional reality of the play and the lives of the playgoers.

This reconciliation does not mean we accept the world of the play as our own, but it does suggest that we take something of the play with us. As Paul Kottman notes, "Prospero accosts us on our way out of the playhouse, to find out what we are going to do next"; this is a gesture that grants the audience the agency to *decide* what to do next—what to take and what not to take from the play.[12] Whatever dream they might weave or spell they might cast on us while we sit in the theater, Shakespeare's characters point out that it's up to us how to respond and what to do afterward. These moments thus figure aesthetic delight not as an automatic response but as a form of judgment. By bringing attention to that judgment and making us aware of our delight, these plays frame that delight as a decision rather than a vehicle that sneaks ideas past the faculty of reason.

At the same time, however, even in these final moments the plays attempt to impose an alternate reality on us. Puck and Prospero construct the audience as participants in the plays' conclusions, but it is the characters, not the playgoers, who ultimately assign meaning to the audience's participation by telling us what our applause will signify. To give the players our "hands" does not just signal our delight, they explain, but our pardon. In this way, these metatheatrical moments assert a power that extends beyond the boundaries of their fictional space even as they recognize that the audience will have the ultimate power to decide whether or not to allow that to happen. By giving meaning not just to their own aesthetic structures but to how the audience *responds* to those structures, the plays claim for themselves the ability to impose their realities—their meanings, their structures, their assignment of values—onto the experiences of the playgoers. For the time we engage with the fiction, we are part of the reality of play.

This tension between the play's ability to create an alternate reality that situates the audience within it and the reflection that is prompted by our delight plays itself out in more dramatic form in *Hamlet. The Mousetrap,* and Hamlet's reflections on the nature of theater and acting surrounding the play-within-a-play, indicate that drama can indeed have real-world effects. Those effects, however, are not necessarily predictable or controllable. From his first conception of *The Mousetrap* plan, Hamlet puts great faith in the ability of acted representations to affect the behavior of the audience:

> I have heard
> That guilty creatures sitting at a play
> Have by the very cunning of the scene
> Been struck so to the soul that presently
> They have proclaim'd their malefactions.[13]

This is not, perhaps, what Sidney meant when he described the ability of tragedy to move an audience, but it does offer one vision for how art, and specifically theatrical production, can affect a spectator. Seeing one's crimes performed, Hamlet indicates, can motivate conscience to "miraculous" confession (2.2.590).

Like Puck and Prospero, Hamlet attempts to affix meaning to Claudius's response to the play in advance: "I'll observe his looks; . . . If a do blench, / I know my course" (2.2.592–93). As with the epilogues, whether that attempt to affix meaning is successful depends on the audience. On the one hand, Hamlet's play achieves what he wants it to. As Grady notes, "the play soon establishes the correctness of Hamlet's and Horatio's surmise, the correctness of the Ghost on at least the central point that Claudius has murdered King Hamlet, when we are presented with the isolated figure of King Claudius confessing his guilt and trying to repent of his sin."[14] On the other, however, as both Grady and Abraham Stoll argue, it's not at all clear that Hamlet should *know* that he's right about Claudius. Grady notes the long history of recognizing the ambiguity of Claudius's response—is Claudius responding to the pangs of his own conscience, or is he responding to the threat implied by this representation of a nephew killing his uncle?—and Stoll argues that, when Hamlet witnesses Claudius's inability to pray and misinterprets it, Claudius's "conscience recedes from Hamlet's understanding, and from ours."[15] Hamlet wants the play to reveal Claudius's inner state, but Claudius's resistance to repentance means we only see part of that inwardness.

This only partial success of *The Mousetrap* to "catch the conscience of the King" (2.2.601) also reveals the incongruity of Hamlet's theorizing about theater as mimesis. As we have seen in the previous chapters, how we imagine literature affects the audience is closely tied to whatever theory of representation—the question of what the artwork *is*—that we are working with. Hamlet's own comments on dramatic representation, as Robert Weimann has demonstrated, are not consistent with the rest of the play (or with Hamlet's own behavior), and in this disparity we can find a theory of drama that is closer to what Puck and Prospero provide than anything Hamlet explicitly says.[16]

Hamlet offers one model of mimesis when he instructs the players that "the purpose of playing . . . was and is, to hold, as 'twere, the mirror up to nature; to show virtue her own feature, scorn her own image" (3.2.20–23). Art, he seems to claim here, merely replicates life, providing its perfect image. *The Mousetrap* can prompt Claudius to confession simply by showing him a reflection of his own iniquity—it will show "scorn her own image"—confronting him with his crimes. The context of Hamlet's claim that art holds "the mirror up to nature," however, indicates that successful "playing" isn't simply about faithful reproduction of real life. Successful art, he explains to the players, requires "temperance":

> for in the very torrent, tempest, and, as I may say, the whirlwind of passion, you must acquire and beget a temperance that may give it smoothness. O, it offends me to the soul to hear a robustious periwig-pated fellow tear a passion to tatters, to very rags, to split the ears of the groundlings, who for the most part are capable of nothing but inexplicable dumbshows and noise: I would have such a fellow whipped for o'erdoing Termagant; it out-herods Herod. (3.2.5–14)

"Passion" is clearly important to Hamlet—it "offends [him] to the soul" when an actor "tear[s] a passion to tatters"—but it requires restraint to represent passion well, which is to say with "smoothness." A few lines later, Hamlet refers to the "modesty of nature" (3.2.19), seeming to indicate that "nature" tends to pull toward the Aristotelian middle, that which is moderate. If this is true, then an actor must show "temperance" in order to mirror nature because nature itself tends in that direction.

As Weimann notes, however, the notion that nature is "modest" doesn't seem to hold up in the case of Hamlet himself.[17] After watching the player's speech in 2.2, Hamlet calls it "monstrous that this player here, / But in a fiction, in a dream of passion" can nevertheless "force his soul so to his own conceit" so that his body shows visible signs of grief—a pale face, tears, "distraction in's aspect, / A broken voice" (2.2.545–50). The player's ability to show grief isn't monstrous because it is fiction but because Hamlet can't force a similar performance out of himself in response to his own real-life grief. Given "the motive and the cue for passion" Hamlet possesses (2.2.555), this actor who can weep for Hecuba would "Make mad the guilty an appal the free, / Confound the ignorant, and amaze indeed / The very faculties of the eyes and ears" (2.2.558–60). The "modesty of nature" seems to fly out the window when Hamlet imagines his own grief represented, and instead he imagines the player behaving not unlike the "robustious, periwig-pated fellow" who "split[s] the ears of the groundlings"—that is to say, he would engage in a demonstration of emotion that is not tempered to "smoothness" by art.

Significantly, it is *this* image of mimetic passion, which lacks the temperance and modesty he instructs the players to have in 3.2, that leads him to the notion that "the play's the thing / Wherein to catch the conscience of the King." It is by "drown[ing] the stage with tears" and "cleav[ing] the general ear with horrid speech" (2.2.556–57) that the actor can generate a reaction in the "guilty" Claudius—or at least so Hamlet believes at the end of 2.2. The disparity between this vision of passionate performance and the one he exhorts the players to demonstrate raises a question about whether art represents nature as a mirror or whether it represents nature cultivated by artifice—"cunning," as he describes it above (2.2.586)—to a "smoothness" that is not quite natural. Successful performance, Hamlet insists in 3.2, is *both* a mirror of nature and temperate, modest; but, as he indicates at the end of 2.2, the nature of his own grief is neither temperate nor modest.

The claim that "the purpose of playing" is "to hold . . . the mirror up to nature" is thus undercut by Hamlet's reaction to the player's speech in 2.2. Theater is not, for Hamlet, merely an exact reproduction of nature: rather, Hamlet wants it to produce an *idealized* version of nature. Ultimately *The Mousetrap* is less about showing Claudius a mirror so that he must face his own iniquity and more about Hamlet seeing a vision of the world that makes sense to him. After watching the player mourn for Hecuba, Hamlet is distressed that the player is able to show intense grief over "a fiction," whereas he, who has a very real, nonfictional reason to mourn, remains a "dull and muddy-mettled rascal" who "can say nothing"—and, more importantly, *do* nothing—to expose Claudius (2.2.561, 563). Just as Sidney's Astrophil cannot grasp why Stella can feel pity for "lovers never known" but not for him, Hamlet struggles to understand why fiction produces a show of passion that reality cannot.

Significantly, however, Hamlet does not attribute the difference to the sources of the grief—this issue isn't, as it is for Sidney, the difference between aesthetic and ethical relations to things—but rather he attributes it to the one who experiences the grief. The player, Hamlet claims, *would* be able to express an appropriate—which is to say an immoderate—level of grief if he had Hamlet's motive and cue for passion. For Hamlet, the player's ability to express emotion at something fictional exposes the defect in Hamlet for his inability to express emotion at something real. This is the "mirror" the player holds up to Hamlet's nature, not by showing Hamlet what he *is* but instead by showing Hamlet what he *should* be, or at least what Hamlet thinks he should be. He is moved by the player's speech, which leads him to reflect on the relationship between the player's show of grief and Hamlet's own experience of it. Through this reflection, Hamlet perceives a discrepancy between the world of the actor and the one he himself inhabits. The actor creates an alternate reality that exposes the lie in Hamlet's own.

The ability of drama to show things that his own world cannot appeals to a figure whose central concern in the play is the inability to produce adequate "shows." Hamlet's greatest frustration through the first half of the play is that, as he explains to his mother, he has "that within which passes show" (1.2.85). The pain he feels so keenly seems unintelligible to those around him, and he is unable to act on it in a way that feels suitable to him. Even before the call to revenge, what Hamlet wants is for things to appear as they are; he wants a world in which grieving sons can express their grief adequately, one in which mothers who appear faithful do not remarry in haste—and, once the ghost intervenes, a world in which murderers look, act, and are seen to be guilty. When Hamlet instructs the players to "suit the action to the word, the word to the action" (3.2.17–18), then, he is asking them to do the thing that he desperately wants to be able to do but cannot. Hamlet's words are evidence of his lack of action—he can only "like a whore unpack [his] heart with words" rather than get revenge (2.2.581)—and so he looks to the players to show him a world in which words and actions align. In this sense, Hamlet looks to the players to produce Sidney's "golden" world, to contrast with the "brazen" one in which he lives.

Fiction is not an escape for Hamlet—he isn't looking to disappear into a fictional world to avoid the misery of his real one. Instead, Hamlet attempts to use the theater to *change* the reality he lives in, to make the "real world" conform to the logic of the theatrical one. Making Claudius "blench" means revealing Claudius for the villain he is, and so for Hamlet it means making Claudius's behavior conformable to what Hamlet believes—but to this point cannot know—is Claudius's inner reality. And by reacting as he does, Claudius carries the play's fictional structure, one in which murderers behave like murderers and not like kings, out into his own reality, confessing to Shakespeare's audience and then behaving through the remainder of the play like the murdering villain Hamlet hoped he really was.

But if we, the audience, can see Claudius's perfidy on full display after *The Mousetrap,* the fact that it is less fully revealed to Hamlet suggests that the play's audience also has a role in deciding how the alternate reality on the stage will be reconciled with the reality of the audience. Claudius does not, after all, confess his crimes to anyone but the audience, and his inability to repent suggests that, although he is willing to accept his role as a murderer after *The Mousetrap,* he is not willing to accept the judgment or consequences that come with that role. Hamlet uses a play to out Claudius as a murderer, and it works—but not in the way that Hamlet seems to intend. What Claudius takes from the play is a negotiation between the reality the play offers and Claudius's own values and desires.

Aesthetic delight, of course, plays less of a role in *Hamlet* than in the epilogues of the other plays—Claudius does not applaud, nor is he meant to. But the workings of the play-within-the-play in *Hamlet* nevertheless dramatize a dynamic similar to the one constructed at the end of *A Midsummer Night's Dream* and *The Tempest*. A play produces a reality of its own, and part of that reality is the audience; the play attempts before the end to interpret *us*, to situate us within its own logic and structures of meaning. But the audience gets the final say in the extent to which we will accept that interpretation. Whether we experience delight and applaud or storm angrily out of the playhouse, we have been affected by the alternate reality; *how* we are affected is our decision, prompted by the kind of reflection Hamlet engages in after the player's performance of Hecuba's speech.

As an account of mimesis, this Shakespearean theory of drama is different from the accounts Sidney and Spenser develop, and it is less full of contradictions. On the one hand, this account is closer to Aristotle than to Plato, insofar as our responses to an aesthetic experience are material for reflection rather than an indication that we have swallowed this new reality whole. It is also one that rejects Plato's claims that literature is merely a copy of a copy and instead more clearly resembles Sidney's claim in the *Defence* that the poet "nothing affirms, and therefore never lieth" (235). Shakespeare's plays do not aspire to a faithful reproduction of the world as is it but instead produce other worlds. On the other, however, it is also not clearly the case, in these examples, that poetry affects us as a union of universal and particular in the way Aristotle argues and both Sidney and Spenser, to varying degrees, claim. What learning we experience, if we take Hamlet and Claudius as examples, is more about the meaning to be found in negotiating the gap between the alternate vision in the play and the one we experience. How Hamlet responds to Hecuba's speech or Claudius to *The Mousetrap* is less about discerning the universal in the particular and more how one particular story can enable us to reflect on our own.

II. THE ETHICS OF ALTERNATE REALITIES
AND SHAKESPEARE'S PITY

This aesthetic theory that we have traced through several of Shakespeare's plays does not, on its own, speak to the ethical value of literature. In outlining how a play might interact with the lives of playgoers, however, Shakespeare's work offers an avenue by which literature might have a significant real-world effect, even if it cannot determine in advance what that effect might look like. Just as Hamlet determines his course of action to "catch" Claudius's conscience as a result of his reflection on the player's performance, so too do moments like the epilogues to *A Midsummer Night's Dream* and *The Tempest* ask us to reflect on the relationship between the alternate realities of those texts and our own in ways that might inspire change in us. But a play does not need to stop and ask us to applaud to prompt this reflection. Our emotional engagements with the plays can, as they do for Hamlet, create a turbulence in us that requires our attention, producing this effect.

The effect of emotion on Shakespeare's audiences has been the focus of some critical attention lately, and unsurprisingly pity and similar forms of fellow-feeling often appear in these discussions.[18] One model for the ethical possibilities of theatrical emotions is James's argument that pity in Shakespeare has "revolutionary potential." Because "the plot builds up sympathy, frustration, and outrage but effects no catharsis,"[19] we leave the theater carrying those strong emotions with us and wanting to *do* something as a result. Her pattern for this is again Hamlet responding to the player's speech, whose "description of Pyrrhus's sword constitutes a meditation on the relation of action to pity, felt not by Pyrrhus but by the unknown viewer." This pity-as-motive translates outward to Hamlet: "As *Hamlet* presents the effects of tragedy, the response to a dramatized regicide might be an actual one: this possibility is, it turns out, the reason Hamlet requests to hear once more a tragic scene that in his recent circumstance doubles for both his father's murder and his own fantasy of murdering Claudius."[20]

If Hamlet wants to see a murderer acting as a murderer in the play, he also wants the play to show him a reality in which a nephew kills the king, to help him manifest his own revenge in the world. What drives him to this desire to use a play in this way, James points out, is the emotional power of the player's rendition of Aeneas's tale. Read in this way, pity elicited by the injustice of Pyrrhus's act, recounted through the passionate performance of the player, motivates Hamlet first to represent the reality he wants to impose on the world aesthetically and then to act out his response to injustice in the real world. Likewise, James argues, Shakespeare's characters on the stage can motivate audiences by stirring us via pity to *do* something about the kinds of problems and injustices we see befalling those characters.

This reading of the transmission of pity from play to person, however, relies on a de-aestheticization of tragic pity that is hard to reconcile with the insistence on drama's fictiveness that we find in the metatheatrical moments. It is also a theory we have seen tested by Sidney and Spenser that has fallen apart each time. My own account is somewhat closer to Richard Meek's analysis of sympathy in Shakespeare, which argues that "Shakespeare was clearly intrigued by ideas of emotional resemblance and mimesis, but he also reminds us that human beings ... are never exactly the same, and that emotions do not simply transfer from one individual to the other."[21] On the one hand, Shakespeare's work, like Spenser's, suggests that representations of pity can elicit a corresponding pity in the viewer; on the other, however, the viewer's pity is not necessarily of the same kind. This is both because, first, as Meek argues, "the sharing of affect is a complex process that involves thought, choice and judgment," so that the audience, as we have already seen, plays a role in deciding how they will respond to a representation of pity, and because, second, our experience is not that of a person confronted with another person's suffering but of an audience encountering a fiction.[22]

Following on Meek's insight that "the most powerful moments of sympathetic transference in Shakespeare's works are not simply instinctive or spontaneous but rather take place 'in thought,'"[23] I find that Shakespeare's plays offer ethical effects not by simply transferring that feeling of pity to the audience but by asking us to think about the significance both of the pity presented on the stage and of our own emotional response to that representation. As James argues, the play can provoke strong emotion that does not simply leave us when the play ends. But based on the theory of drama that Shakespeare's plays suggest, instead of pity in a play simply transferring outward, our own aesthetic pity elicits a reflection response that prompts us to ask why we feel this pity and whether we think we should.

This question of whether we should share the pity of Shakespeare's characters has been the subject of a considerable body of scholarship, itself evidence that our emotional responses to these texts prompt reflection on the value of pity. Meek, for instance, notes that critical discussions of *Richard II* have been deeply divided over the question of whether audiences should sympathize with the titular king.[24] A similar controversy can be found in critical responses to *King Lear*, as we will see. The question of what pity *means* in these plays—both within the texts and as a response to the texts—reflects the fact that pity as an emotional response *has meaning,* which it just to say that it is based on judgments of value that are bound up with the structures of meaning generated by the play. Though our own pity is not the pity of the characters, it nevertheless asks us to consider the relationship between how we feel, how the characters feel, and how the world of the play relates to our own.

To examine how this process works, let us turn to *King Lear,* a play that is deeply concerned not simply with representing pity but with exploring what kinds of cognitive judgments pity can make and how those judgments might provide alternatives to other forms of merely rational judgment. The alternate reality that *Lear* presents draws on the Thomist tradition of pity but goes a step further by using this form of pity to critique traditional forms of justice in ways that have produced significant scholarly controversy.

III. THE FAILURE OF JUSTICE IN *KING LEAR*

The critical debate over the value of pity in *Lear* grows in large part out of the tension in the play between justice and pity.[25] In a text that has been read largely for what it has to show us about power, hierarchy, and social injustice, pity appears to disrupt attempts to critique these forces by troubling the pitier's ability to make moral and ethical judgments. A. C. Bradley may have been the first to identify this problem when he noted that, by the play's end, we have come to view Lear "almost wholly as a sufferer": "His sufferings too have been so cruel, and our indignation against those who inflicted them has been so intense, that recollection of the wrong he did to Cordelia, to Kent, and to his realm, has been well-nigh effaced."[26] The ability of Lear's sufferings to inspire pity in an audience runs the risk of making that audience forget Lear's original sins. If we forget his sins, we cease to be in a position to judge those sins; and, as multiple critics including Bradley have pointed out, losing our ability to judge Lear's sins potentially means losing any sense of justice at all in the play.[27]

The question the play thus raises for audiences is whether we *should* feel pity for Lear. This question in turn arises from the fact that so many of the play's readers *do* feel pity and yet feel that this pity conflicts with their own closely held values, particularly those about what constitutes a just social order. Thus, for instance, Kathleen McLuskie echoes Bradley when she notes that the play's end "obliterates the past action so that the audience with Cordelia will murmur 'No cause, no cause.'" The problem with this, she argues, is that "the most stony-hearted feminist could not withhold her pity even though it is called forth at the expense of her resistance to the patriarchal relations which it endorses."[28] A response like this registers that push-and-pull between the alternate reality of the text and the audience already explored. On the one hand, it demonstrates the extent to which the play is able, like *The Mousetrap,* to impose its reality on an audience, coercing pity even from the unwilling. On the other, it demonstrates the way that imposition requires the audience to negotiate between her own reality and the one imposed. McLuskie's pity confronts her own feminist commitments, and that conflict leads her to a critique of pity's complicity with patriarchal structures in the play.

McLuskie is unusual in naming the conflict she experiences as a reader, but much of the criticism on *Lear* similarly grows out of a negotiation between the pity response the play elicits and readers' commitments to social justice. Jonathan Dollimore, for example, like McLuskie, reads pity as deeply ingrained in the play's ideologies of power, calling Cordelia's pity for her father "precious yet ineffectual" and a "residual expression of a scheme of values" that fail in the play because they are "an ideological ratification of the very power structure which eventually destroys them."[29] Other critics, like Tom McAlindon and Geoffrey Aggeler, have sought to reconcile justice and pity in the play, arguing for instance that "justice itself cannot be achieved without good pity."[30] Despite sometimes opposing valuations of pity's operation in the play, these readings have in common both that pity, whether the audience's or the characters', *means* something in *Lear*—it is a form of judgment that either absolves Lear or reveals the path to justice—and that its value rests in its relation to the reader's, not the play's, concept of justice.

If many readers' own feeling of pity at seeing Lear weeping over Cordelia's body rests in uneasy relation with traditional concepts of justice, it is because the representation of pity within the play asks us to critique those traditional notions of justice. Instead of either trying to reconcile pity with justice or critiquing pity for its opposition to justice, as critical responses have typically done, another alternative is to let pity's resistance to justice prompt us to interrogate the assumptions and structures on which justice is based. *Lear* provides a compelling critique of justice conceived as a system of rational calculations doling out rewards and punishments, a system that the play suggests relies upon and produces violence. Examining this critique in detail demonstrates how much the play's representation of pity has to offer our understanding of pity's ethical value.

Lear himself is (eventually) the play's greatest critic of justice. His act 4 ravings, in particular, suggest that justice is contingent upon the kind of power relations that critics of the play want the text to expose or subvert. In his reunion with the now-blinded Gloucester, Lear asks Gloucester to consider the case of a beggar running from a farmer's barking dog:

> there thou mightst behold the great image of authority: a dog's obeyed
> in office.
> Thou, rascal beadle, hold thy bloody hand;
> Why dost thou lash that whore? Strip thine own back,
> Thou hotly lusts to use her in that kind
> For which thou whipp'st her. The usurer hangs the cozener.
> Through tattered clothes great vices do appear;
> Robes and furred gowns hide all. Plate sin with gold,
> And the strong lance of justice hurtless breaks;
> Arm it in rags, a pigmy's straw does pierce it.[31]

The dog is an "image of authority" because he has the power to make the beggar "obey" him: he can make the beggar run away because the dog strikes the fear of bodily harm into the beggar. And so it is with those who wield whips and nooses in the name of justice, those endowed with power and position by the political hierarchy. They are, Lear proclaims, enforcers: their "authority" derives from their ability to cause harm, to inflict punishment on those who trespass.

Significantly, Lear does *not* say that this is only the case with "bad" rulers, like his daughters. Just before his comments on justice in 4.6, he notes that what makes him "every inch a king" is the fear he inspires in his subjects: "When I do stare, see how the subject quakes" (4.6.106–7).

Lear furthermore depicts the mechanism of "justice" in line 162 as a "lance," a weapon; justice manifests in the world through physical violence. When justice fails, according to Lear, it is because it is unable to cause harm—it "hurtless breaks" against the gold plate of wealth. Lear's point here is, first, that "justice" is bound up inextricably with the violence of hierarchy, and that, second, because of this, justice is merely arbitrary—"None does offend," he concludes (4.6.164). Of course, we might well ask whether we're supposed to trust Lear's assessment at this moment, given that, as Edgar remarks, Lear has lost his mind: "O matter and impertinency mixed, / Reason in madness" (170–71). Yet the play's final scenes seem to bear out Lear's observations in 4.6. Confronted with evidence of her betrayal in the final act, Goneril reasserts Lear's case for the arbitrary nature of justice when she tells Albany, "The laws are mine, not thine. / Who can arraign me for't?" (5.3.156–57).

This arbitrariness also manifests in the way "order" is restored at the play's end. Those who find something positive arising at the end of the play tend to focus particularly on the triumph of Edgar as an agent capable of returning justice to an unjust world order. In such readings, Edgar is described as a "Champion of justice," and "the worthiest successor to the crown" by virtue of being "the agent of personal and political retribution."[32] What earns him these titles, however, is precisely the violence that Lear predicts in in his 4.6 monologue. If the duel between Edgar and Edmund is an act of justice, it is so only in a world where might determines right. Edgar tells Edmund, "Draw thy sword, / That if my speech offend a noble heart, / Thy arm may do thee justice" (5.3.124–26), again tying the ability to "do" justice—to manifest it in the world—to the ability to inflict harm.

As if recognizing the potential danger here—if justice is determined in duels, then justice belongs merely to the stronger and Lear is right that a dog is the image of authority—Edgar and Albany both try to tie the final events in the play to a sense of divine justice, as if the gods supported Edgar's sword. After dealing his brother a killing blow, Edgar tells Edmund, "The gods are just and of our pleasant vices / Make instruments to plague us," a sentiment to which Edmund assents (5.3.168–69, 171–72). Similarly, Albany responds to the news that Goneril has killed both herself and Regan by calling it a "judgement of the heavens" (5.3.230).

As more than one critic has noted, however, these affirmations of a divine justice ordering the world ring especially hollow in *Lear*. Dollimore notes that Albany calls on the same gods whose justice he affirms at line 230 to save Cordelia barely twenty lines later, only to have his prayer met with the presentation of Cordelia's dead body on the stage, thus subverting any attempt to read divine order into the play's final actions. Likewise, Richard McCoy demonstrates persuasively that "*King Lear* repeatedly shatters all faith in providential justice and divine protection almost as soon as it is voiced."[33] Without this divine backing, the duel between Edgar and Edmund marries justice to superior physical violence in a way that makes justice *contingent* on violence, rather than the other way around. As David Lowenthal asserts in a somewhat chilling assessment of the play, "Moral superiority is not enough: the good must also be physically more powerful than the wicked."[34] The play thus shows us a concept of justice that is inextricably linked with violence. This is not because the play or its characters adopt some ideologically fraught definition of justice that lends itself to violence. Instead, the critique of justice leveled by Lear takes aim at the fact that the calculative rationality by which the play's characters determine their own standards of justice is neither grounded in shared values nor persuasive without the threat of violence behind it.

For those who believe in justice—specifically Edgar, Albany, and the early Lear—their definition is entirely straightforward. As Albany explains at the end, justice is simply a matter of everyone getting what they have "merited": "All friends shall taste / The wages of their virtue and all foes / The cup of their deservings" (5.3.301–3). The mistake the characters make, as a result of the ideologies of power at work in the play, is to believe that the calculations of merit and "deservings" are self-evident and self-regulating; justice becomes ideological when characters fail to recognize Auden's insight that "Temporal Justice demands the use of force to quell the unjust."[35] Lear's 4.6 speech is the moment at which he comes to recognize the lie within this ideology of power. The process by which he comes to this moment reveals the necessity of the final scene's violence if justice is to be served, and therefore the inability of justice, as a merely rational construct, to produce community among the play's characters.

Lear has been criticized for what appears, at least in the opening scene, to be a kind of naïve, uncritical faith in his own power.[36] In his quarrel with his elder daughters, however, he demonstrates that his belief in his right to his "reservation of an hundred knights," to be sustained by his daughters, and to "The name, and all th'addition to a king" (1.1.134–37), is based on a fairly conventional sense of justice. At the onset of his madness in act 3, after trying to give commands to the storm into which he has been cast—"Blow winds and crack your cheeks! Rage, blow!" (3.2.1)—Lear pauses a moment to reflect on the presuppositions of his commands:

> Nor rain, wind, thunder, fire are my daughters;
> I tax not you, you elements, with unkindness.
> I never gave you kingdom, called you children;
> You owe me no subscription. Why then, let fall
> Your horrible pleasure. (3.2.15–9)

This passage explains why Lear thought that he could abdicate the throne and still command his daughters' obedience. Lear finds that he has no authority to command the weather—he cannot "tax" the elements "with unkindness"—because the elements "owe" him nothing. By contrast, his language implies, his daughters *do* "owe" him because of what he "gave" them and "called" them.

This logic of "owing" is at the heart of Lear's thinking about the justice of his authority; justice for Lear is about giving people what they deserve according to a standard of measurement that weighs what one owes against what one is owed. This is the same standard according to which Lear attempts to divide the kingdom in act 1, asking his daughters to deserve their portion through a public declaration of love that will reveal their "merit" and, he thinks, justify giving a "third more opulent" to the "last and least" of his daughters (1.1.53, 86, 83).[37] Similarly, in these lines in act 3, his daughters "owe" him "subscription" because of what Lear "gave" them—his kingdom—implying that, in Lear's mind, the rightness of his authority comes not so much from his "natural" position as king but from the fact that he has *deserved* it by giving something away. Obedience is the price of kingdom.

In act 2, we see a poignant demonstration of the failure of that standard of justice to persuade. When Goneril and Regan are attempting to strip him of the hundred knights he kept for his retinue as part of the conditions of his abdication, he appeals to them by reminding them,

> I gave you all –
> – Made you my guardians, my depositories,
> But kept a reservation to be followed
> With such a number. (2.2.439–42)

His argument is twofold: first, he is reminding his daughters that they had an agreement already in place, and in that agreement he "kept a reservation" that they are now attempting to take away (and we in the audience, who saw what transpired at 1.1.128–40, are witness to this contract). But Lear does not merely cite the contract as sufficient proof of the justice of his case—there can, after all, be unjust contracts. Instead, what justifies that reservation, what makes the contract fair, appears to be the fact that he also gave away something in return—in fact, he tells his daughters, he gave away more than he kept, having given them "all" with the exception of these knights.

Lear clearly thinks this is a persuasive argument, and it's hard to argue that he doesn't at least have a point. Even if he has become the cranky, difficult old man Goneril and Regan describe him as, and even if they might have negotiated a contract more to their liking if they'd had more power in the first scene, he has in fact given them quite lot in return for the maintenance of his retinue, making the terms of the contract fair by a rational standard of measurement, if not perhaps as favorable as Goneril and Regan would like. The madness that ensues from this conversation is a symptom of the failure of the argument to persuade his daughters; the rationality of his claims, based on the equity of the original agreement, is not enough to make his daughters uphold that agreement. This becomes painfully obvious after Lear has been cast out into the storm, when he seeks to "arraign" his daughters in an impromptu court of law, claiming to be bringing them before a "most learned justicer" (3.6.20–21). To Lear, his daughters' lack of justice appears self-evident: in giving testimony against Goneril, he claims merely, "'tis Goneril—I here take my oath before this honourable assembly—kicked the poor King her father" (46–48). But it is important that Lear does not merely accuse his daughters of ingratitude. By staging this mock trial in order to prosecute his daughter for kicking "the poor King her father," Lear implies that biting the hand that feeds you is a matter of justice and law, a punishable offense, which emphasizes the extent to which the services bought by the power of kingship are, as Lear calls it, a matter of "subscription." Though the *Oxford English Dictionary* says that this word in *Lear* means "The action of acknowledging allegiance to someone," the word's most common meanings have to do with signatures at the end of documents—that is, with contracts.[38] Kicking the king is an act of injustice because, in Lear's mind, Goneril and Regan are bound to serve him in exchange for the kingdom he gave them. They haven't held up their end of the bargain, and so Lear, in an attempt to demonstrate the injustice of that behavior, attempts to reassert the agreement by invoking the mechanism that is supposed to guarantee justice: a trial.

But as much as this scene suggests that "justice" for Lear entails upholding the terms of the original agreement, this moment in the play also reveals, both to the audience and to Lear himself, the lesson he will articulate in act 4 in the "dog's obeyed in office" monologue. The scene is particularly poignant, as Edgar registers ("My tears begin to take his part so much / They mar my counterfeiting" [3.6.59–60]), not because of the wrongs Lear has suffered, but because of his impotence to correct them. Lear seeks retribution in a court of law, but in this scene Lear, his companions, and the audience are confronted with the realization that Lear no longer has access to this mechanism of justice. No matter how "rational" Lear believes his case to be ("arraign" is from the Latin *ad-rationare,* meaning "to reason with"), he can find no judge to preside over the proceedings; instead, his "most learned justicer," Tom O'Bedlam, is (so far as Lear knows) a madman. Similarly, that the part of Goneril is played by a joint-stool (51) signals Lear's inability to summon his daughters to participate in the arraignment.

Lear may cling to the notion of justice and to the belief that his cause is just, but his inability to prosecute his daughters' violation of the terms of their contract reveals what is missing, a crucial third element in the measurement of equity: the power to enforce. What the mock trial scene demonstrates with aching clarity is that the rationality of his case isn't sufficient to compel his daughters' obedience. In the absence of a judge who commands a hangman, the unjust need not fear those making an argument for fairness—and precisely because they are unjust, they will disregard all such arguments.

Yet we need not even term his daughters "unjust" to see the problem that Lear confronts in this play. When recourse to violence has been stripped from justice, as it is for Lear in the mock trial scene, its only weapon is appeal to some standard of measurement. This is problematic because, as the play demonstrates, calculative rationality can produce a variety of forms of equitable measurement. Lear's way of calculating the debt owed to him by his daughters is one argument we can make. But, as Strier has argued, the greatest proponents for reason in the play are the "villains."[39] Lear's daughters have their own standard of calculation, too, and it is not irrational; in asking their father, "What need you five and twenty? Ten? Or five? / To follow in a house where twice so many / Have a command to tend you?" (2.2.450–52), Goneril and Regan make a reasonable point, merely "proposing . . . to apply a standard of economic rationality to Lear's expenses."[40] Edmund has his own arguments about the arbitrary nature of meritocratic assessment, which he calls "the plague of custom" (1.2.3) and proposes that a standard of value might instead be based on the "natural" superiority that comes with being conceived a bastard, "Who in the lusty stealth of nature take / More composition and fierce quality" than the children produced "within a dull stale tired bed" (1.2.11–13).

Lear's frustration with his elder daughters does not arise from the fact that he is rational and they are not: it arises from the fact that each party is using its own rationally conceived standard of measurement, and neither party is able to convince the other that their system is the *right* system. What Lear discovers is that rational calculation is a tool that cuts many ways, so that his standard of justice is only one possible reasonable way of measuring merit and desert among many possibilities, none of which clearly have any obvious claim to moral superiority in the play. Absent the force of rational persuasion, any standard of justice thus needs violence to create consensus, either through coercion or the elimination of opposing standards of value.

All of this ends up meaning that the ability of justice to regulate a social order in the play depends entirely on the mechanism of justice having violence on its side, thus marrying justice to power in a way that, far from producing equity, in fact *requires* hierarchy. Lear loses the ability to pursue "justice" as soon as he ceases to have the power of a king—which, as Lear demonstrates to Cordelia and Kent, entails the power to punish. For Edgar to bring Edmund to justice, he must both literally and figuratively return Edmund to his place beneath his legitimate brother, causing both Edmund's fortunes and his physical body to fall (5.3.172).

Thus the problem with justice in the play is not that the people who pursue it have no power, but that the idea of justice is inseparable from the violence of hierarchical relations, making any attempt to find "justice" in the sense of equity and fairness in the world of the play automatically self-defeating. For this reason, when Goneril's husband Albany attempts to set the world to rights at the end of the play by restoring power to Lear on the basis of what he has "merited," the effect is less than comforting. Just like Edgar's fratricide, Albany's promise that divides the world into friends and foes forecasts more violence. Justice may be restored at the end of the play, but it is a justice without peace.

IV. CORDELIA'S PITY AND THE REORIENTATION OF REASON

If our pity in response to *Lear*'s final scene seems to resist our ability to judge Lear according to what he deserves, it can thus point us to the fact that this kind of judgment about merit and punishment is deeply mired in violence, domination, and hierarchy. Ultimately justice fails because it cannot create changes that might be meaningful in the tragic landscape of the play. Stripped of power, this justice fails to regulate the behavior of those characters who operate according to a different standard of measurement; armed with power, it reinstates the hierarchies whose abuses it is supposed to redress.

But if our own pity can point us to this critique of justice, it can also ask us to compare that feeling to the pity experienced by the play's characters—particularly Cordelia—and to ask whether the judgments that inform that pity offer something more than just critique. Like book 4 of *The Faerie Queene*, *Lear* shows us a reality in which pity operates in a Thomist fashion, creating union with another through an act of identification that seeks the other's good. By setting up this kind of pity in opposition to its representation of justice, however, *Lear* goes a step further by showing us a pity that reorients our rationality. Instead of the judgments of justice, which are based on retrospective calculation, Cordelia's pity looks forward and asks how the damage can be repaired. This pity is at the same time opposed to the sixteenth-century understanding of Stoic mercy, which looks similarly forward rather than backward but which supports rather than dismantles hierarchies of power. Rather than pitting emotion against rational measurements of merit or the good of the sovereign, *Lear* makes pity a form of thought-as-feeling that is superior to justice and Stoic mercy because it is more transformative.

The moments of pity that have garnered the most critical attention are those in which a character makes some overt commentary about or takes some clear action against the political structures of Lear's world. In act 3, having "Expose[d himself] to feel what wretches feel," Lear first starts to recognize his failures to live up to his own standard of justice as king, regretting that he has "ta'en / Too little care of this" and realizing that he has not done his part to help the "houseless heads and unfed sides" in his kingdom (3.4.28–36). Gloucester similarly excoriates his own moral failings when he describes his own misfortune as divine "distribution," punishing his lack of pity toward the poor—he was the man "that will not see / Because he does not feel" (4.1.69–74). Even Goneril and Regan, who never have a redemptive moment in the play, evince the power of pity in their fear of it. After setting the blinded Gloucester loose, Regan frets, "It was great ignorance, Gloucester's eyes being out, / To let him live. Where he arrives he moves / All hearts against us" (4.5.11–13)—a fact she herself witnesses when Cornwall's own servant kills Cornwall to stop him from attacking Gloucester (3.7.71–97).[41]

None of these political examples, however, fully demonstrate the transformative power of pity because none of them entirely escape the play's logic of justice. The rebellion of Cornwall's servant achieves nothing—Gloucester loses both his eyes despite the intervention—and it relies upon the same violence that makes justice impotent to improve Lear's world.[42] Similarly, criticism in the last several decades been quick to point out that the moments of pity for the poor that both Lear and Gloucester experience reflect a very traditional, hierarchical social worldview, rather than any kind of radical egalitarianism.[43] These moments fall short of creating social transformation not because pity is "precious yet ineffectual," but because, despite the pity they've started to feel, these characters are still bound by a concept of justice as equity or fairness. The servants that survive the rebellion against Cornwall frame the events they have witnessed as an affront to justice: "I'll never care what wickedness I do / If [Cornwall] come to good" (3.7.98–99). Lear recognizes that, in having "ta'en / Too little care" of the poor, he has failed to be "just" (3.4.36), just as Gloucester perceives his own suffering as itself a judgment of the "heavens" (4.1.69).

In the case of Lear and Gloucester, part of the problem, of course, is that Lear's and Gloucester's pity is only partially pity for the poor. Because they cling to the measurements of justice, their pity becomes a kind of *self*-pity in which both get caught up in judging themselves for their failures—specifically their failures as rulers, as men at the top of the social hierarchy. Insofar as both Lear and Gloucester are moved sufficiently by pity to recognize the horror of their political world, we can perhaps agree with Aggeler that in these moments "the emphasis is on feeling as the avenue to an understanding that makes moral activity possible."[44] But Lear and Gloucester still aren't at the point in which they can actually *reach* that understanding; both are still caught up in the same structures of power that produced the inequality they decry. In this sense, pity does not coexist usefully with justice.

Where pity simply abandons justice, however, the results are notably different. Cordelia becomes the play's representative of radical pity—that is, a pity that turns away from the judgments of justice entirely—and her pitiful interaction with her father does more to undo his thinking about power and hierarchy than do any of his meditations on the justice (or injustice) of his suffering.[45] As Lear recovers from his madness at the end of act 4 to find the daughter whom he had banished ministering to him, Lear recognizes his fault in his treatment of her:

> If you have poison for me, I will drink it.
> I know you do not love me, for your sisters
> Have, as I do remember, done me wrong.
> You have some cause, they have not. (4.7.72–75)

At Lear's most poignant moment of self-recognition, the judgments of justice still dominate his thinking. Since even those without a legitimate grievance have seen fit to abuse Lear, he assumes that the one daughter whom he has in fact wronged will also wish him harm. But he is willing to drink Cordelia's poison because hers is the just grievance—she has "cause," a word evoking the legalism of the mock trial scene.

Cordelia's reaction to Lear's words is so swift that it completes Lear's final line: "No cause, no cause" (4.7.75). Rather than explicitly forgiving his actions against her, a forgiveness that would acknowledge the "cause" she has not to love him, Cordelia instead "erases the premise" according to which he submits himself to punishment—that she has cause at all to seek revenge.[46] As a result of her pity, expressed at 4.7.30–31, Cordelia radically revalues Lear's past actions. By telling her father that she has "no cause" to wish him pain, she both denies that his behavior toward her constitutes an actionable offense and, as a consequence, rejects the retributive justice he proposes. Cordelia will not serve as her father's executioner because she denies that there is evidence on which to condemn him.

Cordelia's pitiful response to her father has an almost instantaneous effect on Lear. Only a few lines later, Lear tells her, "You must bear with me. Pray you now, forget and forgive; I am old and foolish" (4.7.83–84). For Lear to ask for forgiveness signals a significant shift in his way of thinking. While he still acknowledges his own wrongdoing by asking to be forgiven, he no longer assumes that the appropriate response to his bad behavior is punishment. The word "forgive," particularly in its older senses, means "To give up resentment against" but also, in its oldest form, simply "To give."[47] In this case, what he asks to be given is precisely *not* what is owed: Lear is owed punishment, but he asks for a gift.

This word "forgive" is also one that, prior to this moment, Lear has not deigned to use except with scorn. In act 2, when Regan suggests that he return to Goneril and apologize, he replies with his only use of the word "forgiveness" prior to his reunion with Cordelia:

> Ask her forgiveness?
> Do you but mark how this becomes the house?
> [*Kneels.*] Dear daughter, I confess that I am old;
> Age is unnecessary. On my knees I beg
> That you'll vouchsafe me raiment, bed and food. (2.2.341–45)

Lear is incredulous here that he would have to ask for forgiveness because he does not believe that he has done anything wrong. Precisely because "age" is *not* "unnecessary," Lear feels he has a right to have his daughters—for whom he once provided—provide for him now. The fact that Lear is willing to ask forgiveness for his old age in act 4 after Cordelia has told him she has "no cause" against him thus marks a change, both in his way of evaluating merit and desert and in his way of thinking about the appropriate response to that evaluation. Lear recognizes that, even though he does not intend to be "old and foolish," he nevertheless is, and he recognizes that this places a burden on his daughter. This suggests that, unlike his earlier response to Regan, where he thinks only of *his* intentions in placing a burden on his daughters, now with Cordelia he thinks about the effect of his situation on *her*. Lear for the first time thinks of his actions not in terms of what he is owed but in terms of what they mean for others.

As Derrida notes in *On Cosmopolitanism and Forgiveness,* "forgiveness has precisely nothing to do with judgment."[48] As long as Lear clings to a juridical accounting of the world of social relations, forgiveness is all but unthinkable to him. When he asks Cordelia's forgiveness, he thus demonstrates an abandonment of the logic of justice in favor of a new way of relating to his daughter. This becomes more apparent in act 5 after Lear and Cordelia have been taken by the English forces. Lear's words to Cordelia reveal a man no longer concerned about anyone getting what they deserve:

> Come, let's away to prison;
> We two alone will sing like birds i'the cage.
> When thou dost ask me blessing I'll kneel down
> And ask of thee forgiveness. So we'll live,
> ...
>   ...And we'll wear out
> In a walled prison packs and sects of great ones
> That ebb and flow by the moon. (5.3.8–11, 17–19)

Lear has lost all interest in meting out the justice he so vehemently argued for earlier in the play; the punishment justice can inflict—prison— is instead to him a place of refuge, one that does not punish him but that is both powerless and, by virtue of being "walled," physically separate from the world of power relations—the "packs and sects of great ones."

This loss of interest in participating in the world of power is furthermore predicated on a very different relationship with his daughter, one that eschews the accounting of a judgment of fairness, of what is owed and what is paid, what is given and what is received. Lear never says whether he will provide his blessing or whether Cordelia will give him her forgiveness. His ability to ask Cordelia's forgiveness therefore does not rely upon her owing him anything since Lear never asserts that he will have given her anything before he makes his own request. Lear will not ask Cordelia's forgiveness in *exchange* for his blessing. Instead, by omitting any mention of either of them receiving what they request, Lear in these lines appears to recognize that both can make requests of each other without assuming the kind of debt that justice would demand be repaid.

This way of thinking about his relationship with his daughter is not just a change of perspective for Lear: it suggests the creation of an entirely different worldview from what we saw in Lear earlier. Prior to his reunion with Cordelia, Lear sees only two alternatives. Either he will inhabit a world governed by the kind of justice he invokes throughout acts 1–3, or he will exit the world of human relations entirely. Having begun to pity those he thought himself above and to recognize the cracks in his notions of justice and authority, Lear looks upon the nearly naked Tom O'Bedlam and proclaims, "Is man no more than this? Consider him well. Thou ow'st the worm no silk, the beast no hide, the sheep no wool, the cat no perfume. Ha? Here's three on's us are sophisticated; thou art the thing itself. Unaccommodated man is no more but such a poor, bare, forked animal as thou art" (3.4.101–6). Gazing at a madman who would be "better in a grave than to answer with [his] uncovered body this extremity of the skies" (99–100)—that is, a madman who would be better off dead—Lear recognizes in him the absence of any relations of "owing" and then promptly tries to join him in this condition—"Off, off, you lendings: come, unbutton here" (104–5).

Lear in 3.4 repudiates the idea of a world governed by just contractual exchanges that he had embraced in 3.2, now seeking to free himself from all owing by sloughing off "lendings," the trappings that tie him to others in the world. Yet these trappings are also what hold Lear *in* the world since, as Lear remarks, to have an "uncovered body" is a fate worse than death (and one that presumably will lead to death). That Lear again tries to remove his "lendings" after his meditation on the failures of justice in 4.6—"pull off my boots; harder, harder, so" (169)—suggests that, in Lear's mind at this point, the only alternative to a world run by justice is a kind of bare, deathly existence outside of the world of human connections. His ability in act 5 to imagine a world in which he and Cordelia are bound *without* the terms of "owing" thus demonstrates that Lear is now open to a new possibility, one that gives him the ability to connect with his daughter outside the hierarchies of justice.

Cordelia's pity is able to transform her father in this way because it interpellates Lear within a different system of value that rejects a merely rational accounting of debts owed. This system of value closely resembles the Thomist pity explored in the previous chapter, which is based on *identification* with the person who suffers and thereby ignores the boundaries of hierarchy and calculations of what a person's previous actions deserve. As our discussion of Spenser described, Aquinas sees in virtuous pity a "union of the affections, which is the effect of love. For, since he who loves another *looks upon his friend as another self,* he counts his friend's hurt as his own, so that he grieves for his friend's hurt as though he were hurt himself."[49] Just as Amoret and Britomart are only able to establish a friendship once they identify with each other on equal ground, Cordelia and (to a lesser extent) Edgar approach their fathers from a position of powerlessness that mirrors their fathers'.

More importantly, however, this union of affections gives rise to Thomist identification of the will. Anthony Keaty writes, "Thomas observes that happiness is the condition of possessing what one wills and that misery is the condition of being subjected to what is against one's will," where "the human activity of willing in its most fundamental sense is that inclining whereby the human agent is directed toward her own perfection, or happiness, or end."[50] When we see someone suffering, it is because she has failed to possess what she wills, which is to say that she has failed to achieve what is best for her. To identify with that suffering is also to identify with the person's will to achieve what is best for her, and so, in grieving with the other, we thereby desire "to act for the friend's good to the extent possible," uniting us in a single act of willing.[51] What it means, then, to treat another person "as another self" is to act on behalf of that person, to direct one's agency according to the needs of the other by willing for her the good that she wills for herself.

This Thomist account of pity is helpful for thinking about *Lear* because it demonstrates how pity can work against the structures of power that dominate the play. What is notably absent in Aquinas's account of *misericordia* is any sense of what is fair or merited; one does not act to help the friend out of the belief that the friend is *owed* anything, but simply out of love. In this sense, pity of the kind Aquinas describes has the potential to oppose the logic of justice that structures and mediates human relations in *Lear*, where bonds between people revolve around obligations policed and enforced by violence.

As Lear's 4.6 speech explains, the activity of justice is differentiation: justice from thief, whore from beadle—and, at its base, rich from poor, powerful from powerless. Pity conceived in Thomist terms, however, achieves the opposite, insofar as it is an act of identification, of the overcoming of difference through an activity of the affections and will. That *this* is the model of pity we see operating in *Lear* is clear enough from Cordelia's interactions with her father. Referring to his "abused nature" and calling him a "child-changed father," Cordelia laments, "Had you not been their father, these white flakes / Did challenge pity of them" (4.7.15–16, 30–31). As a result of her pain over Lear's suffering, she treats her father "as another self," choosing out of pity to unite her agency to his cause.

Repeatedly upon her return to England, Cordelia expresses her sense of self as an agent by taking actions for her father. As she marches with her army into England, she says to the absent Lear, "It is thy business that I go about" (4.4.24); later, having retrieved her father, she asks that "restoration hang / Thy medicine on my lips" (4.7.26–7); and as she faces down her grim fate at the end, she looks at her father and tells him, "For thee, oppressed King, I am cast down" (5.3.5). Whenever she speaks to Lear after her return, "I" goes hand in hand with "thee." By acting always for him, Cordelia bridges the gap between them by making her will—her ability and desire to act in the world—a response to his need. With every action Cordelia takes in the play, she wills her father's good.

While Cordelia's Thomist pity rejects the assumptions of the play's representations of justice, it is worth exploring the notion that it also rejects contemporary Stoic understanding of mercy. English sixteenth-century Stoicism, again, understood *clementia*, usually translated as "mercy,"[52] as superior to what Elyot in *The Governour* called "vayne pity" because mercy is based in rational calculation about the political good. Thus, Elyot argues, Augustus wisely shows mercy to the conspirator Cinna because, by so doing, he "not only vainquished and subdued one mortal enemy, ... but by the same feate excluded out of the whole citee of Rome all displeasure and rancour towarde hym."[53] Elyot takes this story from Seneca's *De Clementia*, where Seneca argues that "Mercy [cle-

mentia] joins in with reason" by considering what course of action will produce the best political outcome—which is just to say what course of action will best uphold the emperor's power over his people.[54]

Like Cordelia's pity, Stoic mercy does not simply rely on a calculation about what debt is owed; what a person deserves for their past actions may be set aside if doing so serves the larger goals of the ruler. Crucially, however, the rational calculations of Seneca's emperor and Elyot's governor are just as deeply couched in hierarchy as *Lear*'s representation of justice. Following Seneca, for Elyot mercy is exercised by the powerful, both in the sense that the one exercising mercy "hath power to be avenged," and in the sense that mercy is the prerogative of rulers, not of the lower classes. In contrast to the example of Augustus, Elyot's example of pity in the same passage is commoners criticizing a "commissioner" who imposes "any sharpe punisshmente" upon "vacaboundes" that, according to Elyot, "dayly do transgresse the lawes." Those who criticize the commissioner "seeke meanes to brynge hym in to the hatred of people."[55] According to Elyot, wise rulers act mercifully to accumulate political capital and discourage rebellion, acting in service to the spirit of the law by bending the letter. Those without power feel pity, he suggests, because they do not like that exercise of power.

For both Seneca and Elyot, pity is divorced from reason. Seneca calls it "ill adapted for seeing how things are, for thinking out what might be useful," while Elyot calls it a "sicknesse of the mynde."[56] At least for Elyot, however, the irrationality of pity appears deeply tied to his disdain for "the people" and the "vacaboundes" whom the law seeks to punish. Pity, in his account, is dangerous because it is tied to a sense of its powerlessness and even lawlessness insofar as those who exercise it are near the bottom of the political and social hierarchy. The form of rationality that determines whether it is right to exercise Stoic mercy is thus one that begins from the premise that supporting the power of the ruler to govern is the larger goal of justice. This is a different orientation of reason than the logic of owing that Lear espouses, but it is one no less embroiled in the justice Lear critiques in 4.6.

Pity in *Lear* rejects this account of the relationship between *clementia* and pity by turning it on its head, reevaluating the value of powerlessness and reorienting the question of *whose good* virtue should pursue. Contrary to Elyot's disdain for commoners pitying "vacaboundes," pity in *Lear* is strong to the extent that it does *not* come from a seat of power. It instead rejects hierarchy in favor of more egalitarian, communal relations. The greatest practitioners of pity in the play, Cordelia and Edgar, act to help others from positions of powerlessness (at least politically speaking): Edgar as a mad beggar, Cordelia after she has abandoned France and his army.

The interactions between Cordelia and Lear at 4.7 and 5.3, moreover, refigure Stoic mercy into forgiveness in order to strip it of its power. Typically conceived, at least in Western thought, forgiveness operates according to similar power structures as mercy. Just as Seneca argues that mercy is "leniency on the part of a superior towards an inferior in imposing punishments,"[57] Hannah Arendt writes, in responding to W. H. Auden's discussion of forgiveness, that the kind of forgiveness he describes—one based in Christian charity—is really just a kind of judicial pardon (we might say of the kind Seneca describes), one that refuses to recognize any vulnerability of the forgiver to the forgiven.[58] Even secular forgiveness, Derrida argues, is an "affirmation of sovereignty": "It is often addressed from the top down, it confirms its own freedom or assumes for itself the power of forgiving, be it as victim or as in the name of the victim."[59]

In *Lear,* however, forgiveness is closer to Derrida's vision of "a forgiveness without power: *unconditional but without sovereignty.*"[60] This is because, in the play, forgiveness appears as a symptom rather than a cause of improved social relationships, and forgiveness is never complete. When Lear asks for—and then imagines asking for—Cordelia's forgiveness, he does so because he has already been affected by her pitiful mode of relation to him. The asking is what is important here, not the granting. As Arendt notes, "it is more difficult to ask than to give forgiveness"; Lear's willingness to engage in "the mutuality of the whole thing," to offer subjection to Cordelia by asking for more than he is owed, marks his transformation.[61] But it is equally important that Cordelia does not accept his subjection—either in 4.7 or in Lear's imagining of their relationship in 5.3—by forgiving him. Lear and Cordelia reconcile, but there is no forgiveness as such because, by the time Lear asks for it, it is no longer necessary. Cordelia's pity prevents her from acknowledging any crime against her that must be forgiven.[62]

Seneca and Elyot reject pity because they see it as mere emotion that opposes a more rational judgment of the larger political picture—it is "ill adapted for seeing how things are, for thinking out what might be useful." The activity of pity depicted in *Lear* critiques this Stoic position by showing that pity can indeed help a person see how things are and be useful. Pity begins as an emotional identification with another, but insofar as the will is engaged to act on behalf of the other, the one who pities must make judgments regarding what constitutes that good. The difference is simply *whose* good our judgment is oriented toward. For Elyot and his reading of Seneca, *clementia* supports the power of the one who wields it. In Cordelia's Thomist *misericordia*, judgments are oriented toward the needs of the one who suffers.

The extent to which rational judgments play a part in the activity of pity is particularly clear in the case of Edgar's dealing with his father. After Gloucester's suicide attempt, Edgar tells his father that he is

A most poor man, made tame to fortune's blows,
Who, by the art of known and feeling sorrows,
Am pregnant to good pity. (4.6.217–19)

Edgar is hiding his identity from his father, but he is not misrepresenting himself in these lines. Through the machinations of his brother, he has experienced "fortune's blows" as much as anyone else in the play, and his pity for his father has been evident since he first saw the maimed old man at the beginning of 4.1. This pity is articulated through identification, where Edgar is "pregnant to good pity" because he recognizes in Gloucester the same suffering he has experienced.

As in the case of Cordelia, this pity leads Edgar to abandon any "cause" he might have against his father. Under the terms of justice, Edgar has a right to demand something of the man who is at least in part responsible for the "blows" of "fortune" Edgar has experienced—an apology, at least, as Gloucester himself recognizes at 3.7.90–91, but perhaps even retribution, as Edgar later seeks of Edmund. Rather than placing demands on Gloucester, however, Edgar instead acts to help his father—in Thomist terms, seeking his father's good—by curing him of his suicidal desire.

As Edgar tricks his father into believing he has thrown himself off a cliff in order to convince Gloucester of the notion that his "life's a miracle" (4.6.55), Edgar pauses to comment, "Why I do trifle thus with his despair / Is done to cure it" (4.6.33–34). Edgar's pity does not lead him to act out of emotion in the absence of reflection. The complexity of his plan to cure his father of his despair signals the amount of thought that has gone into judging the best of course of action—that is, into determining how best to *achieve* his father's good. Cordelia's attempts to do her father's "business" similarly attest to her "best meaning" (5.3.4), her intention to do what is best for her father that bespeaks this same reorientation of reason.

Insofar as this account of pity critiques the Stoic opposition between mercy and pity, however, it also slightly modifies the virtue ethics tradition as Aquinas describes it. For while virtue ethics holds, as discussed at the beginning of this book, that reason and emotion could and, in fact, *must* be allied for a person to be truly virtuous, that alliance is based on a clear hierarchy that subordinates emotion to reason, and in particular that subordinates pity to justice. Thus Augustine writes that *misericordia* should be the "servant of reason" and is only being exercised correctly "when compassion is shown without detriment to justice."[63] Aquinas generally follows Augustine, claiming at one point that "if by pity we understand a habit perfecting man so that *he bestows pity reasonably,* nothing hinders pity, in this sense, from being a virtue."[64]

These claims raise the question of what it means to show compassion "without detriment to justice" or to "bestow pity reasonably," but in *Lear* these are questions that Cordelia and Edgar (at least in dealing with his father) are not interested in. To the extent that justice is incapable of producing anything but violence, justice cannot provide Cordelia and Edgar a way to reconcile with the fathers they love. Their pity, which begins in an identification born of that love, provides a different grounding and orientation for their reason, and one that produces a better outcome. Instead of the calculative activity of justice—which would ask, "What does my father *deserve?*"—both Cordelia and Edgar instead implicitly ask a different question: "What does my father *need?*"

This adjustment to the activity of reason is what ultimately makes pity, and not justice, able to transform others for the better in *Lear.* One of justice's great failures in the play is its inability to create common ground. Evaluations of justice require debates over the standard of judgment: how do we calculate what a "fair" deal is? How do we measure what is owed and what is deserved? These questions do not admit to easy answers, which is why Lear and his elder daughters can never seem to agree on what they owe him (and perhaps, following Paul Kottman's reading, why Lear and Cordelia fall out in the first place),[65] and why violence is necessary to get one group to conform to another group's standard.

In contrast, pity was considered valuable in the early modern period, as David Anderson has argued, for its ability to create community, and in particular in *King Lear* pity "tear[s] down the solipsistic preconceptions of the characters, emphasizing their relationships to their fellows, becoming something common and shared."[66] Pity's more particular focus—what is good for *this person*, what does *this person* need—sidesteps debates about universal standards of measurement and instead creates a community automatically through the identification of both affect and will. Both parties in the relationship are necessarily seeking the same thing. Lear at the beginning of 5.3 can think of a relationship with Cordelia outside relations of power because Cordelia has already created that relationship through her refusal to judge him and her decision to treat her father as another self. She doesn't need to convince him that they can have this relationship: through an act of identification she has made it exist.

Pity is in this sense a more radical force than both justice and mercy, at least as far as the play and Shakespeare's culture constructed those terms. Justice in the absence of violence can only pass impotent judgments on what is owed and what is deserved, but on its own it can *do* nothing; forgiveness and mercy may only *release* us from consequences that fracture community and thereby enable its rebuilding, though only, in Derrida's words, "from the top down."[67] But pity, which does not require any power beyond the desire to seek what is best for another and requires no assertions of superiority because it is an act of identification, necessarily entails action on behalf of that other, action that by its nature *creates* community[68]

V. *LEAR*'S AUDIENCE AND PITY'S ETHICAL POTENTIAL

Of course, the solidarity created by the pity of Cordelia and Edgar does not last. Edgar returns to the judgments of justice and the violence it entails in the final act. Similarly, Lear's transformation lasts only as long as Cordelia's life. When he finds her dead, Lear tells us that he "killed the slave that was a-hanging" her in a return to retributive justice (5.3.272). To the eye searching for political change, the solidarity effected by pity thus appears fragile to the point of uselessness. Yet the worth of pity in *King Lear* need not be limited to the confines of the drama. Even if we cannot feel pity in precisely the same way Cordelia does, James's argument that the strong emotions evoked by our aesthetic experience do not simply disappear after the play's end points to that fictional reality's ability to affect us after we have left the playhouse or closed the book.

What is perhaps most striking about the critical history of *Lear* is the extent to which audiences have found themselves disturbed by their own pity. Famously, the distress caused by the play's final scenes led eighteenth-century audiences to prefer the more palatable, happy ending offered by Nahum Tate. Samuel Johnson felt so much pity after his first time reading it that he was unable to bear to read it again until his edition of Shakespeare necessitated that he do so.[69] Modern readings of the play, as I have shown, likewise struggle with the feelings provoked by the play's conclusion. This is not to say that all audiences of *Lear* feel pity at the play's end—I have had students, for example, who felt that Lear gets what he deserves. But the fact that a great many audiences of the play have both felt this pity and felt compelled to interrogate it speaks to the ability of strong emotions, evoked by aesthetic experience, to provoke a continued response even after the aesthetic experience has ended. This response *after* the play is where its ethical potential rests.

If our emotions are, as ancient and modern philosophers tend to argue, judgments of value, then our emotional response offers a way to understand what we see as valuable in a play—and then to ask why. While we do not experience the same Thomist pity that Cordelia does for her father—we cannot, like she does, unite our will to Lear's or to Cordelia's because they are fictional characters on the stage—our own pity can still register assent to the judgment that Cordelia makes when she asserts that she has "no cause" to punish her father. That assent responds in large part to the fact that *Lear* has shown us a reality in which justice is based on a calculation of what is owed and relies on violence to achieve its ends. To be moved by Cordelia's pity is to respond to the values and structures of the play's reality and to assent to the ethics of Cordelia's attempt to reorder those values.

The question that remains at the play's end, however, is how to reconcile the play's reality with our own and how to respond. I would not, for instance, advocate for abandoning the pursuit of justice in our own world because my pity at the final scene rejects *Lear*'s construction of justice. The play's critique of this one version of justice, however, creates the opportunity for important reflections about the potential limitations of justice in our world and its relationship to power—reflections that might prompt us to rethink the concept in terms of, for instance, restorative justice as a way to avoid these pitfalls. Similarly, the play's representation of pity not as mere emotion but as an orientation of our rational faculties around the desire to help another person can provoke rethinking of the relationship between emotion and reason. For the play's contemporary audience, Shakespeare offered playgoers an alternative to Stoic mercy that might have prompted reflection on the value of the kind of solidarity among the powerless that Elyot was so quick to dismiss. In our own time, in which emotion is still largely pitted against reason in popular conversation, *Lear*'s representation of pity might give us a reason to rethink the role of emotion in ethics, to consider the value that feelings like sympathy and love might have when we make them grounds for our ethical judgments, and how they might produce forms of community via solidarity where "rational debate" cannot.

Even though we cannot fully engage in the ethical, antihierarchical form of *misericordia* that Cordelia displays, to the extent that we are moved by Cordelia's "no cause," we feel—even before we think—that this *misericordia* is a preferable mode of human relationship to the hierarchical judgments of sixteenth-century conceptions of justice or mercy. Moreover, to the extent that we agree when Cordelia refuses to judge her father, we have not only agreed to but adopted the reorientation of our reason that characterizes Cordelia's pity. The "revolutionary potential" of pity in *Lear* is thus not that the play necessarily inspires us to leave the playhouse and go overthrow a government but that it can overthrow in our own minds a way of thinking that perpetuates hierarchy. To the extent that the play imposes its reality on us, it teaches us to think, at least for the duration of the play, according to the "creative power of Cordelia's compassion"[70]—and then to think about what that way of thinking through feeling might mean for our own lives.

This, then, is the character of Shakespearean aesthetics: it imposes its alternate reality upon us and tells us what our responses to that reality—our applause, our anger, our tears—mean within the logic of that fictional reality. But its fictionality never fades from view, and as such we are left to question what the fictional world has to say to our own. As the multiplicity of readings of the value of pity in the play attest, the answers to that question are as various as the audiences. However much McLuskie acknowledges her identification with Cordelia's refusal to indict her father in the moment, she is nevertheless able to step back and perform the "dispassionate analysis" she thinks is appropriate to the play. In my own reading, by contrast, "dispassionate analysis" is precisely what the play critiques: the question *Lear* asks us is whether we *should* pity Lear by the play's end, but it can only force us to confront that question, to think critically about all that pity entails in the play, by making us feel that pity in the first place.

It is this fact—one Shakespeare's plays readily acknowledge—that separates Shakespearean aesthetics from Plato's critique of tragedy. By asking the audience to applaud in order to reconcile the play with the audience, Puck and Prospero acknowledge the distance between the fictional world they create and the reality of the audience. Instead of presenting the audience with a *defective* reality, as Plato would argue, and one that holds itself forth as if it were the real thing, Shakespeare's plays present *alternate* realities, ones that explicitly acknowledge their autonomy from our reality but that nevertheless ask us to close the gap between our world and theirs. The gesture of seeking the audience's "pardon" may be a way of seeking applause, but it also reminds the audience of the power we have once the show is over or the book is closed: the fiction can tell us what it means and what it thinks our responses to it should mean, but what to *do* with that—whether to assent or deny or reconsider—is left in our power. We can refuse to make amends with Puck or to pardon Prospero. Like Lear asking Cordelia's forgiveness, at the end of the play it gives up its claims of power over us.

This may seem almost too obvious to mention. But the fact that Shakespeare's plays make this fact explicit, that they both point to their ability to impose their reality on us for a time *and* to the fact that their reality *isn't* ours, and that it is only in *our* power to decide how to reconcile that fictional reality with our own, implies an aesthetic theory that potentially solves the ethical dilemma troubling Sidney's work and rejected in Spenser's. For both Sidney and Spenser, the question was how the content of a work of literature could travel across the boundary between fiction and reality into the lives of the audience. To the extent that they focus on emotion, and pity in particular, as the vehicle that might make this crossing, their ideas about the ethical value of art run aground on the difficulty of identifying aesthetic emotions with ethical ones. Shakespeare inverts the question and instead gives us a model wherein the *audience* traverses that boundary. We enter into the world of the text, are captivated by its reality, and accept its logic for the time we are in it. Our emotional reactions in this space are reactions to that internal logic; they are judgments of value. But to the extent that the play is constructed to elicit *specific* responses, our pity and our anger and our laughter are largely determined by what is valued within the world of the text, and so they are important indicators of the structure of the fictional world we have experienced. Then we leave, back into the "real world," having experienced another possibility, an alternate reality, another worldview. What we do with it—whether we adopt that worldview as our own or repudiate it or critique it or just chalk it up as a good time—is up to us. But this does not release art from its ethical function: it simply makes us partners in it, compelling us by our emotional experience to consider the structures of value that prompted that experience and requiring that we *do something* with it. If "all the world's a stage," we are asked by Shakespeare's plays and the alternatives they provide to think about the reality *we* want to create—to think about what reality feels right.

⊹꠸ CONCLUSION ꠸⊹

Early modern English writers, as we have seen, struggled to reconcile their belief in literature's ethical value with a nascent conviction of aesthetic autonomy. Their understanding of that ethical value was rooted in an account of poetic mimesis that saw literature as "a vehicle for a worldview," as an experience whose affective power induced life to imitate art. Thus what Sidney and Spenser found as they attempted their own ethical projects was that this Platonic framework for understanding art's ability to change us is incompatible with aesthetic autonomy. This incompatibility led to the notorious inconsistencies of Sidney's *Defence* and convinced Spenser to abandon this ethical project altogether.

While it's easy to read the conflict in these texts as the product of an era standing between the ancient and modern worlds—and this is certainly true to some extent—we lose sight of why these debates matter if we fail to recognize that we continue today to have the same conversations our early modern predecessors were having. While in scholarly circles the autonomy thesis carries the day, the Platonic worldview echoes still in the critics of aesthetic objects who, for example, try to ban books for "immorality" or denounce first-person shooter video games that supposedly teach impressionable minds to love violence. Readers of this book likely find the Platonic framework archaic and hopelessly naive, but it is alive and well among culture war politicians and many of the parents raising the children who will eventually attend our universities.

The struggles Sidney and Spenser experienced demonstrate why the Platonic aesthetic framework remains durable. This view recognizes that most of us don't experience art in some coolheaded, unemotionally analytic way. Sidney is right that, if we did, only the philosophers would read it. We are drawn to art because it engages us emotionally—it delights us and makes us feel strong emotions. And Plato was right that because of that engagement, it affects us beyond the boundaries of the text. It is not a naive reading of literature to believe that something that moves us so entirely cannot leave us untouched. As the current saying goes, stories matter. They matter because they move us, and in that motion we are changed.

Shakespeare offers a framework for aesthetic experience that acknowledges literature's emotional power and its effects on us without accepting the conclusion that our emotional engagement necessarily entails our assent to the worldview of the text. We are changed by what we read or view, but exactly how we are affected depends on our own values, contexts, and histories, as well as our own conscious evaluation of our emotions. The mistake the Platonic framework makes is that it believes our emotions have no commerce with our reason, that emotional response to literature works as a spell to overwrite our conscious minds. What Sidney and Spenser sensed but only Shakespeare fully realized is what philosophers of emotion have recently rediscovered: emotions are judgments. As such, they are subject to the same kinds of rational, ethical reflection any judgment is, and so it is precisely to the extent that literature engages us emotionally that it offers opportunities for critical thought.

We might then argue (and I would) that no other form of experience is so well suited to ethical reflection as literary experience. As Shakespeare's work suggests, it offers both a space to interrogate the alternate systems of value presented by the text and a motive to do so—it moves us in ways that can make us question, that unsettle us and require us to find a way to resettle. In that resettling, literary experience likewise prompts us to negotiate between the values of the text and our own, making it a space not only for reflection on the object, but for self-reflection. It does not move us to virtue by prompting imitation, but neither does it encourage disinterestedness. To the extent that emotions are judgments of value, we never have a disinterested relationship

CONCLUSION 133

with literature if it provokes feelings in us. Our emotions are evidence of interestedness in the sense that what we read matters to us in some way. Answering the question of *how* it matters means unpacking both the text's and our own systems of value, an act that allows us to interrogate our own frameworks by imagining other possibilities.

I began this book by stating that early modern aesthetics has much to offer us in the current moment, and so I will end by noting how I think this framework can affect scholarly and pedagogical practice, as well as how it can cause us—or at least has caused me—to change the way we relate to others. The reconciliation Puck and Prospero seek always happens, whether we are aware of it or not. When we encounter a piece of literature that engages us, it doesn't simply end. We return to it, think about it, turn it around. Something about it sticks until we have settled our way of thinking and feeling about it in some way, and even then its impact continues to resonate with us. One of the tasks of criticism should be to make these impacts and reconciliations conscious, to attend to the way our own critical insights grow out of emotional engagements that reveal to us a crux, a problem we can make meaning from because we have responded to some friction between the values in the text and our own.

This is not to say that the work of criticism should be to write about our feelings. But the question "Why do I feel this way about this text?" should be recognized as a productive starting point for rigorous analysis—analysis that can both tell us something about the text and tell us something about ourselves (which all criticism does anyway, just without usually acknowledging it). An entailment of this is allowing ourselves to be receptive to how literature can change us. I have known scholars who were told in graduate school not to write on what they loved. The presumption underwriting that advice is that we cannot cast a critical eye on texts we have a deep love for, that analysis must be dispassionate, coolheaded, and detached. What the art of pity teaches us is that strong emotion can be a powerful motivator to analysis and critique.[1] As scholars of an art whose power rests largely in its ability to evoke emotion in the reader, we shouldn't turn away from our own feelings as readers. By allowing ourselves to feel—or perhaps more accurately by acknowledging *that* we feel—we open up new ways to think.

For those of us who teach literature, this framework can help us both to connect our students to what they read and to demonstrate the value of what we teach without abandoning any sense of intellectual rigor. Whatever critical lenses or theoretical approaches we may adopt, using our students' (and our own) emotional responses as a starting point for interrogating both the structures in the text and our own relation to those structures provides an accessible way into even difficult literature. The question "How did you feel about the reading?" is often a throwaway, a warm-up to get students talking before we get into thinking about the text. What early modern aesthetics suggests, however, is that this question is already a "thinking about" the text and as such is a fruitful path to analysis. What did you feel? Why do you think you felt it? Do you think you felt that way because of your own values or because of systems of value created by the text? Do you think you would feel this way about an identical real-life situation?

Such an approach also clarifies one of the virtues of studying literature that we often point to but rarely are able to explain: studying literature increases our emotional intelligence, our awareness of our own emotions and those of others. Recent studies have demonstrated that this is probably true, but they don't explain why.[2] We can make instruction in emotional intelligence explicit if we allow student feelings about the text to become a site of exploration and analysis. This is unlikely to make university boards of directors or administrations pour money into literature departments, but it does allow us to make a clear case to our students that studying literature can benefit them in tangible ways.

What those tangible benefits can be will vary from person to person. But to give an example of what this can look like, I close by offering a case in which literature did have a specific, ethical effect—for me. In the years since I wrote the *Modern Philology* article on which the reading of *Lear* in which chapter 3 is based, my work on the play has profoundly changed the way I approach my students. Examining the defects of justice in the play and the failure of judgments about what people might *deserve* resonated with the systems of rewards and punishments I built into my courses. Adhering to the contract of the syllabus was rewarded; failure to comply was punished. Thinking about what it means for Cordelia to reorient the judgment of her father around what he *needs* challenged my sense of justice in my classroom. In analyzing the play and my own instinctive assent to Cordelia's "no cause," I found I agreed profoundly with Cordelia's ethics. At the same time, I realized I was not practicing them with my students.

As a result of this reflection, I have changed my grading practices and my assignment design. The question "What do my students need?" varies from class to class and from student to student, but for all my classes now an assessment of that question is part of the core of the course. In some cases it has meant moving to contract grading or other "ungrading" practices because of the recognition that traditional grading is for many students an impediment to learning.[3] In other cases it has meant providing a wider variety of assignment options as a way to enable students to connect learning in my courses to other interests they have. In all cases, it has meant that I am less quick to punish; when things go wrong, I start with a conversation to find out *why* they've gone wrong and then to try to find remedies for the cause. "What would Cordelia do?" has become a question I ask myself, and I believe it has had a positive effect on my students' experience.

My emotional investment in Cordelia's pity and the reflections on the failings of justice it prompted led me to change the way I relate to students and to others in my life. In arguing that we should be attentive to the emotions literature makes us feel, therefore, I am not advocating a return to "appreciation" as a mode of literary instruction or criticism. But what appreciation tried to rescue—the pleasures of the text, the way it moves us in sometimes difficult to define ways—must have a place in intellectually rigorous critical analysis. It also has a place in our experience as readers more generally and as people seeking to improve our world and our ways of moving through it. Literary autonomy, as much modern criticism recognizes, creates a meaningful friction between the world of the reader and the world the text. The early moderns recognized that we often feel that friction before we explicitly understand it. Literary analysis does not need to be unemotional to be rigorous or intellectual—indeed, to try to make it so cuts it off from questions of value that orient both the text and our relation to it. As scholars, as teachers, and as people, attention to how literature makes us feel attunes us to the ethical potentials it has to offer, and it can drive us to pursue those potentials. And as Sidney tells us, "to be moved to do that which we know, or to be moved with desire to know: *hoc opus, hic labor est.*"

⊹[NOTES]⊹

INTRODUCTION

1. Sidney, *The Major Works*, 235. All subsequent references to the works of Sidney will be cited in the text and refer to this edition.

2. See Kant, *Critique of the Power of Judgment*. Disinterestedness arises from the purposeless of the aesthetic, in his argument: "Thus nothing other than the subjective purposiveness in the representation of an object without end (objective or subjective), consequently the mere form of purposiveness in the representation through which an object is given to us, insofar as we are conscious of it, can constitute the satisfaction that we judge, without a concept, to be universally communicable, and hence the determining ground of the judgment of taste" (5:221). Kant rejected the kind of emotional experience I will be highlighting here, arguing that "Any interest spoils the judgment of taste and deprives it of its impartiality, especially if the purposiveness does not precede the feeling of pleasure, as in the interest of reason, but is instead grounded on it." Aesthetic pleasure must be caused by purposiveness, not the other way around. Moreover, if an aesthetic object "needs the addition of charms and emotions for satisfaction," he claims, that judgment of taste is "barbaric" (5:223).

3. Bowie, *From Romanticism to Critical Theory,* introduction.

4. Guenther, *Magical Imaginations,* 9.

5. Whitney, "Ante-Aesthetics," 40–60.

6. Joughin, "Shakespeare, Modernity, and the Aesthetic," 66–67.

7. Joughin and Malpas, "The New Aestheticism: An Introduction," 7.

8. Adorno, *Aesthetic Theory,* 1.

138   NOTES TO PAGES 5–7

9. Adorno, 1.

10. Joughin and Malpas, "The New Aestheticism," 11.

11. Docherty, "Aesthetic Education and the Demise of Experience," 31.

12. Robson, "Defending Poetry, or, Is There an Early Modern Aesthetic?," 126.

13. Eisendrath, *Poetry in a World of Things,* 80.

14. Grady, *Shakespeare and Impure Aesthetics,* 69.

15. Guenther, *Magical Imaginations,* 4.

16. Lodge, *The Complete Works of Thomas Lodge,* 1:227. Accessed September 20, 2020.

17. Because the passions—"in general the feelings that are accompanied by pleasure or pain" (*Nicomachean Ethics,* 1106b1)—are capable of being guided by reason, ethics for Aristotle is less a matter of learning to ignore the passions in order to do what's reasonable and more a matter of learning to bring one's passions in line with one's reason. Thus, for instance, in his discussion of the virtue of temperance in *Nicomachean Ethics,* Aristotle argues that "the appetitive element in a temperate man should harmonize with the rational principle" (1119b.15–16). Virtuous action in this account arises from reason and the passions working together. As Kamtekar, "Ancient Virtue Ethics," explains, for Aristotle, "virtue is 'concerned with choice,' which means that it is a disposition with respect to our desires on the one hand and reasoning on the other," insofar as we can only achieve our desires by reasoning how to achieve them. As a result, for Aristotle "virtue is a disposition not only of the rational or intellectual faculty but also of the emotional and desiderative one" (ch. 2). In Aristotelian virtue ethics, living a good life isn't about adherence to specific rules of behavior so much as it is about cultivating this harmonization of passion with reason so that the whole person—not just her rational faculties—at all times will choose to act in a manner consistent with living a good life. Thus, according to Russell, "Introduction," "virtue ethics tells us that what is right is to be a certain kind of person, a person of virtue: courageous, modest, honest, evenhanded, industrious, wise. A virtuous person will, of course, express his or her virtue through action. But, for virtue ethics, the specification of rules of right action is largely a secondary matter—one that in many ways presupposes the kind of practical wisdom possessed by the person of virtue."

18. Tilmouth, *Passion's Triumph Over Reason,* vii. Tilmouth argues that, prior to the early seventeenth century, English ethical thought was dominated by "an austerely rationalist model of self-governance, one centred on ideas of psychomachia and a hostility to the passions." Strier, *The Unrepentant Renaissance,* by contrast, argues that, "Both the humanist and the Reformation traditions provided powerful defenses of the validity and even the desirability of ordinary human emotions and passions" (42). Even Tilmouth's examples, however, demonstrate the influence of Aristotelian models in the late sixteenth century, thought those models were placed haphazardly beside Stoic models: see, for example, his discussion of Thomas Roger's 1576 *Anatomy of the Minds* (*Passion's Triumph Over Reason,* 30–32).

NOTES TO PAGES 7–10

19. See, for instance, Robson, "Defending Poetry," and Clark Hulse, "Tudor Aesthetics," 29–63.

20. Eisendrath, *Poetry in a World of Things,* 47.

21. Wilson, "The Arte of Rhetorique," 26–57, 30.

22. Aristotle defines appeal to the emotions as one of three main modes of persuasion in *Rhetoric* 1.2.1356a1–4, and he devotes a substantial section in book 2 of the text on various emotions. But the emphasis on emotional appeals is sometimes seen as contradicted by Aristotle's apparent rejection of "prejudice, pity, anger, and similar emotions" at the very beginning of *Rhetoric* (1.1.1354a16–17). For an overview of the controversy and an argument that Aristotle's discussion of emotion is in fact consistent, see Jamie Dow, "A Supposed Contradiction," 382–402.

23. Tilmouth, *Passion's Triumph,* 30. He notes that "by 1600 it was widely accepted . . . that passions were, physiologically, alternations in the heart," a premise of the Thomist-Aristotelian position on emotions (29). The movements of the heart were themselves linked to action in the world, as I will discuss in the next chapter.

24. Meek and Sullivan, "Introduction," *The Renaissance of Emotion,* loc. 340: "The motive power of the passions, and its seeming incongruity with the word's etymological implications, is perhaps one of the reasons why a new term, emotions, emerged in late sixteenth-century England to signify these mental and physical states."

25. Augustine, *Concerning the City of God Against the Pagans,* 9.5.

26. Calvin, *Calvin's Commentary on Seneca's 'De Clementia,'* II.5.4, II.4.4; Wright, *The Passions of the Minde in Generall,* 17.

27. *Misericordia* is also the word Aquinas uses to translate Aristotle's *eleos,* the word Aristotle uses in his *Rhetoric* and *Poetics.* On the distinction between mercy and pity as translations for *misericordia,* the Fathers of the English Dominican Province who translated Aquinas note a difference between two senses of the *misericordia:* "The one Latin word *misericordia* signified either pity or mercy. The distinction between these two is that pity may stand either for the act or for the virtue, whereas mercy stands only for the virtue." Aquinas, *Summa Theologica,* vol. 3, n. 1311.

28. Seneca, "On Mercy," 161, 162.

29. The key text for this framework is Paster's *Humoring the Body.*

30. Meek, *Sympathy in Early Modern Literature and Culture,* 20.

31. Benedict Robinson, "Thinking Feeling," 111.

32. Benedict Robinson, "Thinking Feeling," traces these premodern ideas through Thomas Wright's *Passions of the Minde* (114–19). Julie Soloman, "You've Got to Have Soul," 195–228, similarly argues that early modern writers drew on Thomist-Aristotelian notions of passions as judgments about the world. See also Meek and Sullivan, "Introduction," *The Renaissance of Emotion.*

33. Robert C. Solomon, "Emotions, Thoughts, and Feelings," 134–55; Nussbaum, *Upheavals of Thought.* In his extended discussion of Aristotle's *Poetics,*

140 NOTES TO PAGES 10–14

Halliwell, *Aristotle's Poetics,* notes that "Aristotle's concept of the emotions, pity and fear, itself rests on a cognitive basis: properly educated, at any rate, these emotions are not arbitrary or irrationally impulsive, but are aligned with the recognition and understanding of certain types and patterns of suffering or misfortune" (77).

34. Nussbaum, *Upheavals of Thought,* 19.

35. Aristotle, *Rhetoric,* 1385b.15. Nussbaum, *Upheavals of Thought,* 306.

36. Joughin and Malpas, *The New Aestheticism,* 14. My emphasis.

37. Halliwell, *The Aesthetics of Mimesis,* loc. 1279.

38. Plato, *Republic,* 575–844, 605d.

39. Plato, *Republic,* 606a–b.

40. Aristotle, *Poetics,* 1449b24–28.

41. As Weinberg, *A History of Literary Criticism in the Italian Renaissance,* vol. 1, discusses, among Renaissance commentators Aristotle's discussion of *catharsis* was allied with Horace's claim that poetry should be useful, and, as Christian poetics came to dominate the discussion, "the question of utility [was] with greater and greater frequency answered by means of reference to the theory of purgation" (129, 347). Hutton, in his notes on Aristotle's text, claims that for Aristotle *catharsis,* both in *Poetics* and in *Politics,* is "without moral consequences" (89).

42. See Halliwell, *Aristotle's Poetics,* 168–201. Reading Aristotle's comments on pity in *Poetics* alongside *Rhetoric,* Halliwell argues that "What is perhaps most important in both cases is the cognitive status which Aristotle attributes to emotions," which is what enables them to provoke the learning that is fundamental to Aristotle's understanding of poetry (173).

43. Aristotle, *Poetics,* 1453a.4–5.

44. Nussbaum. "Tragedy and Self-Sufficiency, 281. Early in the essay, she likewise notes the distinction between Plato's and Aristotle's valuation of emotion in their discussions of literature: "Just as Plato's commitment to the self-sufficiency of the good person led him to reject tragic pity, so Aristotle's commitment to the real importance of *philoi* and other external goods for *eudaimonia* leads him to restore these reactive emotions, and the belief structure that underlies them, to a place of honor" (276). See also Schuurman, "Pity and Poetics in Chaucer's *The Legend of Good Women,*" in which she discusses Aristotle's concept of pity as a virtue to be cultivated and the medieval reception of this tradition (1304).

45. Thus Plato in *Republic* argues, "the mimetic art is far removed from truth, and this, it seems, is the reason why it can produce everything, because it touches or lays hold of only a small part of the object" (10.598b). He continues, "It is phantoms, not realities, that [poets] produce" (599b), because "the imitator . . . knows nothing of the reality but only the appearance" (601c).

46. Plato, *Republic,* 601a–b.

47. As he says earlier in book 3, poetic passages like the one in the *Odyssey* in which Achilles laments his death should be "cancelled," "not that they are

NOTES TO PAGES 14–18   141

not poetic and pleasing to most hearers, but because the more poetic they are the less they are suited to the ears of boys and men who are destined to be free and to be more afraid of slavery than of death" (Plato, *Republic*, 387b).

48. As Halliwell notes, for Plato both music and poetry work in a "magical" manner, and so are dangerous because "both arts are capable of embodying and communicating feelings which can permanently change the soul of the listener" (*Aristotle's Poetics*, 190).

49. Halliwell, *Aesthetics*, loc. 974–75.

50. Halliwell, *Aesthetics*, loc. 1332. Comparing this passage to Plato's discussion of artistic mimesis in book 3, Halliwell writes, "In both cases the argument posits what amounts to a circle of reinforcement between responses to art and experience of life as a whole, a circle in which the former both draws on and in turn nourishes the latter" (*Aesthetics*, loc. 987–95).

51. Aristotle, *Poetics*, 1451a38–39, 1451b.27. The Barnes edition translates this line as "the poet must be more the poet of his plots than his verses," but James Hutton and S. H. Butcher translate "*maker* of plots." The problem, of course, is that "maker" and "poet" in Greek are the same word, but in the context of the sentence the translation "maker" seems to better retain the meaning in English.

52. Aristotle, *Poetics*, 1448b.9–12.

53. Halliwell, *Aristotle's Poetics*, 22.

54. Aristotle, *Rhetoric*, 1386a.18–24.

55. Halliwell, *Aesthetics*, loc. 2687. See also Halliwell, *Aristotle's Poetics*, 176–79.

56. Halliwell, *Aristotle's Poetics*, 173.

57. When Plato finally decides the only thing to do is to banish the poets from the Republic, he does so by arguing, "For if you grant admission to the honeyed Muse in lyric or epic, pleasure and pain will be lords of your city instead of law and that which shall from time to time have approved itself to the general reason as the best" (*Republic*, 607a).

58. Aristotle, *Poetics*, 1448b.

59. Halliwell, *Aesthetics*, loc. 370.

60. Both Halliwell and Nussbaum persuasively argue that the traditional understanding of *catharsis* as "purgation" is incorrect and that instead *catharsis* is tied to the way in which the audience learns from aesthetic *mimesis*. See Nussbaum's reading of *catharsis* in "Tragedy and Self-Sufficiency," in which she advocates for reading the term as meaning a "clearing up" (280–83), and Halliwell's exploration of the meanings of *catharsis* in *Aristotle's Poetics*, 184–201.

61. Augustine, *Confessions*, 3.2.

62. Augustine, *Confessions* 3.2.

63. *City of God*, 9.5, quoted in Aquinas, *Summa Theologica*, II–II.30.1.

64. Aquinas, *Summa Theologica*, II–II.30.2.

65. Aquinas, *Summa Theologica* II-II.30.2, my emphasis. See Keaty, "The Christian Virtue of Mercy," 190–95. In the first article of question 30, Aquinas repeats almost word-for-word Aristotle's claim that we do not feel pity

for those "who are so closely united to us, as to be part of ourselves, such as our children or our parents"; the claim cited above from the second article seems to contradict this directly. The second claim, however, appears to be the more important to Aquinas, insofar as, per Keaty's analysis, it allows him to link pity to Christian charity. Despite the contradiction, the modification to Aristotle still stands, insofar as Aristotle does not have anything like the "union of the affections" in this theory of pity.

66. A person, Aristotle states, "is related to his friend as to himself (for his friend is another self)" (*Nicomachean Ethics,* 1166a.31–32). See chapter 2 for a discussion of this passage.

67. Keaty, "Christian Mercy," 191. Keaty cites *Summa Theologica* II-I.55.2, 4.

68. Augustine, *Confessions* 3.4. Hillman, "The Pity of It," makes a similar point about Augustine and Aristotelian aesthetic distance, citing the same passage from 3.2 that I examine above (148).

69. Gosson, "The School of Abuse," loc. 600–11.

70. Gosson, loc. 645.

71. Lodge, *The Complete Works,* 3, 5.

72. Lodge, 26.

73. Gosson, "The School of Abuse," loc. 594.

74. Weinberg, *History of Literary Criticism,* 294.

75. Puttenham, *Art of English Poesy by George Puttenham,* 93, 94.

76. Puttenham, *Art of English Poesy,* 93–94.

77. "American Library Association Reports Record Number of Unique Book Titles Challenged in 2023 | ALA," accessed May 30, 2024.

78. Wilde, *The Picture of Dorian Gray,* 271.

1. SIDNEY BETWEEN TWO WORLDS

1. On Sidney's engagement with ancient aesthetic theory, see, for example, Forrest G. Robinson, *The Shape of Things Known;* Lazarus, "Sidney's Greek 'Poetics,'" 504–36; Reisner, "The Paradox of Mimesis," 331–49; Alexander, "Loving and Reading in Sidney," 39–66; Hardison, "The Two Voices of Sidney's 'Apology for Poetry,'" 83–99. On Sidney's poetics as distinctly Protestant, see, for example, Mack, *Sidney's Poetics;* Matz's chapter on Sidney in *Defending Literature in Early Modern England,* 56–87; Herman's chapter on Sidney in *Squitter-Wits and Muse Haters.* One part of Sidney's inheritance I will not take up here is his indebtedness to Cicero; for this, see Andrew Shifflet, "The Poet as Feigned Example in Sidney's Apology for Poetry," 18–38.

2. Reisner, "Paradox of Mimesis," 332.

3. Alexander, "Loving and Reading," 40.

4. Jenefer Robinson, "The Art of Distancing," 153–62. Robinson argues that there is no difference between the feelings provoked by literature and those provoked by real world experiences, but that literary form creates "coping"

strategies that enable us to temper our emotional responses by recognizing we are encountering a fiction.

5. See Forrest G. Robinson, *The Shape of Things Known,* which focuses heavily on defining Sidney's concept of the "fore-conceit" and its relationship to philosophies of the visual.

6. See Glimp's chapter on Sidney in *Increase and Multiply,* 37–62; and Ferguson, *Trials of Desire,* 146–47.

7. Weinberg, *History of Literary Criticism,* 71.

8. Horace, *Ars Poetica,* 130.

9. Weinberg, *History of Literary Criticism,* 150.

10. See, however, Guenther, *Magical Imaginations,* who argues that, in describing "those evil hard-hearted evil men" who will "steal to see the form of goodness" when poetically represented, Sidney "attempts to naturalize poetic efficacy by locating poetry's coercive force not in the dangerously contingent power of the operator's eloquence, but rather in the essential beauty of the metaphysical referent that poetry represents" (24). If the form of goodness alone were enough to make men "steal to see" it, however, then philosophy would be just as persuasive as poetry. Sidney makes a variety of comments about the sources of delight, some of which suggest it might be embedded in poetic content rather than form. In noting that delight is not the same thing as laughter, for example, he says, "For delight we scarcely do, but in things that have a convenience to ourselves, or to the general nature" (Sidney, 245) and then he gives examples where what delights us are things that are good for us. What Sidney means, however, when he refers to things that "have a convenience to ourselves" is not entirely clear. Somewhat earlier in the text, he says that "That imitation whereof poetry is, has the most conveniency to nature of all other; insomuch that, as Aristotle says, those things which in themselves are horrible, as cruel battles, unnatural monsters, are made in poetical imitation delightful" (227). Whereas "convenience" in the first example seems to allude to things that are good for us, so that "convenience" means "Morally or ethically suitable or becoming" (*Oxford English Dictionary Online,* "convenience," 5), in this sentence the term seems to means something close to "favourable to one's comfort" (*Oxford English Dictionary Online,* "convenience," 6). If things "which in themselves are horrible" can be made delightful by poetry because it "has the most conveniency to nature," then it is the manner in which content is presented—the aesthetic form—that renders it delightful. As usual, Sidney isn't entirely consistent on this subject, but the bulk of his argument, as I have argued here, tends toward investing poetic form with the ability to create delight.

11. Hegel, *Aesthetics: Lectures on Fine Art,* 11: "In all these respects art, considered in its highest vocation, is and remains for us a thing of the past. Thereby it has lost for us genuine truth and life, and has rather been transferred into our *ideas* instead of maintaining its earlier necessity in reality and occupying its higher place."

144 NOTES TO PAGES 35–42

12. See, for example, Paster, *Humoring the Body,* who argues that "early modern moralists strongly doubted the force of reason as an encompassing or even adequate rationale for behavior" (loc. 251).

13. Wilson, *Arte,* 32. Spellings modernized.

14. Wilson, *Arte,* 27–28.

15. See, for example, Held, *The Ethics of Care,* who notes, "Deontological and consequentialist moral theories of which Kantian moral theory and utilitarianism are the leading examples concentrate their attention on the rational decisions of agents assumed to be independent, autonomous individuals" (loc. 722).

16. Plato, *Republic,* 606a–b.

17. Lucretius, , 28–29. In *De Rerum*'s opening book, Lucretius compares himself to "Doctors who try to give children foul-tasting wormwood [and] first coat the rim of the cup with the sweet juice of golden honey." Such boys are "tricked into applying their lips to the cup" and so gain in health because of the deception. In the same way, Lucretius says, "this philosophy of ours appears somewhat off-putting . . . and most people recoil from it," and so he chooses to "coat it with the sweet honey of the Muses" so that we will take down the bitter but health-giving "medicine" of his philosophy.

18. Guenther, *Magical Imaginations,* 34. For another discussion of the role of magic in Sidney's notions of language, poetry, and rhetoric, see Doring, "Beginning to Spell," 67–84. Sidney is far from alone in noting poetry's coercive effects. For discussion of Renaissance discussions of this topic, see Weinberg's chapter on Platonism and defenses of poetry in *History of Literary Criticism,* 250–96.

19. DeNeef, "'The Ruins of Time,'" 265–66.

20. See, for example, Robson, "Defending Poetry," 125; Glimp, *Increase and Multiply,* 41; Grady, *Shakespeare and Impure Aesthetics,* 55.

21. See Jacobson, "Sir Philip Sidney's Dilemma," who observes that, taken literally, this passage reads as a "thorough-going denial of what are often called *literary statements:* assertions made via a work of fiction (329).

22. Jacobson, "Sir Philip Sidney's Dilemma," 330. Sidney claims that the poet is "labouring not to tell you what is or is not, but what should or should not be" (235), which very much seems to suggest that poems can make "literary statements." Ultimately this inconsistency describes what is for Jacobson "the tension at the heart of" Sidney's *Defence,* between the need to defend literature from the charge of lying while also defending its ethical potential in humanistic terms (328).

23. Kinney, "Parody and Its Implications in Sydney's Defense of Poesie," 13.

24. Others have explored the ambivalence Sidney portrays in the *Defence* between a Calvinist understanding of salvation that would render poetry (along with all other worldly appeals) useless and Sidney's own desire to make big claims for the power of poetry to improve people. See, for example, Herman, *Squitter-Wits,* 61–93; Doring, "Beginning to Spell," 67–84.; Reisner, "The Paradox of Mimesis"; Brian Cummings, *The Literary Culture of the Reformation,*

loc. 3379–548. For a different reading of the failure of the Alexander example, see Ferguson, *Trials of Desire,* who argues of this passage, "It is no accident that the audience which responds to a representation aesthetically but not morally is figured as a tyrant. The allegorist who intends to promote virtue is a slave to the very phenomenon which gives the ironist power: the divorce between intention and discourse" (156).

25. Aristotle, *Poetics,* 1448b.9–12.

26. Augustine, *Confessions,* 3.2.3.

27. Rebecca Wiseman, "Introspection and Self-Evaluation in Astrophil and Stella," 51–77, similarly notes the distance between the actual Astrophil and the effects of fictional representation on the reader, but she looks at the problem as a tension between the persuasive power of image versus narrative (72–73).

2. VIRTUOUS PITY AND SPENSER'S AESTHETIC DOUBT

1. Falco, *Conceived Presences,* 20.

2. Spenser, *The Faerie Queene: Books Three and Four,* ed. Dorothy Stephens. All subsequent references to *The Faerie Queene* are from this edition and will be cited in the text by book, canto, stanza, and line number(s).

3. See, for example, Erickson, "Spenser's Letter to Ralegh," which looks at the "Letter" as "a complex politico-literary act of damage control, cultural criticism, and rhetorical play" rather than as a straightforward summary of the poem's purposes and contents (140); and Buckman, "Forcing the Poet Into Prose," 17–34, which argues that the Letter isn't so much a statement of Spenser's literary theory as it is a response specifically to Ralegh's misreading of *The Faerie Queene.*

4. DeNeef, "'The Ruins of Time,'" 262–71.

5. For a survey of readings that see suspicion in Spenser's treatment of "showes" in the Letter, see Erickson, "Spenser's Letter to Ralegh," 148–52.

6. *Oxford English Dictionary Online,* "show, n1," 3a., accessed July 4, 2018.

7. *Oxford English Dictionary Online,* "colour | color, v.," 2a, 5, 6a., accessed July 3, 2018.

8. *Oxford English Dictionary Online,* "plausible, adj. and n.," 1–3, 4a, accessed July 3, 2018. "Plausible" and "colour" come together in one of the OED's examples of "plausible" indicating deceit: "The narrative . . . hes ane plawsable face to cullour the . . . pretendit forme thairof" (4a). Cf. *Faerie Queene* 3.Pr.3, where Spenser says that, because he cannot "figure playne" Elizabeth's "glorious portraict," he will instead "in colourd showes . . . shadow itt."

9. Cf. Erickson, who notes that "Spenser's tone and emphasis diverge considerably from Sidney's relatively unabashed celebration of fiction" (152). Erickson, following Beach, argues that Spenser's conception of the relationship between fiction and moral precept diverges considerably from Sidney's; whereas Sidney "describes an intrinsic, dynamic relation between the 'general' and the

146   NOTES TO PAGES 58–64

'particular,' issuing in a synthetic image," Spenser in the Letter instead suggests "an extrinsic relationship between 'precepts' and 'Allegoricall deuises,' a relation in which the hidden or veiled meaning takes priority over poetic ornaments that act as metaphoric clothing" (151–52).

10. Joseph Campana, "On Not Defending Poetry," 34.

11. For Acrasia as poet, see Berger, *The Allegorical Temper,* 224, 226.

12. Guenther, *Magical Imaginations,* 55–61.

13. Herman, *Squitter-Wits,* 152, 145. See, however, Borris, "Platonism and Spenser's Poetic," for an argument that sees Spenser differentiating between good and bad art in *The Faerie Queene.*

14. Tilmouth, *Passion's Triumph,* 37–73.

15. I examined his passage in the previous chapter, where Aristotle writes, "The distinction between historian and poet . . . consists really in this, that the one describes the thing that has been, and the other a kind of thing that might be. Hence poetry is something more philosophic and of graver import than history, since its statements are of the nature rather of universals, whereas those of history are singulars" (*Poetics,* 1451b1–6).

16. Spenser, *The Faerie Queene: Book Two,* ed. Erik Gray (Hackett: Indianapolis, IN, 2006), 2.11.1.1–3. All subsequent quotations from *Book Two* will be from this text and cited in the text.

17. See *Nicomachean Ethics,* III, sections 10–12 (1117b-1119b). Against this argument, see Tilmouth's chapter on Spenser in *Passion's Triumph,* in which he argues that Guyon never manages to achieve temperance but only continence, and that therefore Spenser did not believe that human virtue was perfectible in the way Aristotle described.

18. Augustine, *City of God,* 14.9.

19. Spenser, *The Faerie Queene: Book One,* ed. Carol Kaske (Hackett: Indianapolis, IN, 2006), 1.9.48, 51. All subsequent quotations from *Book One* will be from this text and cited in the text.

20. Nazarian, "Sympathy Wounds, Rivers of Blood," 334. Nazarian is in good company in arguing that the poem devalues pity or sees it as harmful; see also van Dijkhuizen, *Pain and Compassion in Early Modern English Literature and Culture,* 173–215; Villeponteaux, "'The Sacred Pledge of Peace and Clemencie,'" 35–65; Staines, "Elizabeth, Mercilla, and the Rhetoric of Propaganda," 282–312; Morgan, "The Idea of Temperance," 11–39; Burrow, *Epic Romance: Homer to Milton,* 101–47. Campana offers a significant counterpoint to this position, arguing that *The Faerie Queene* offers a version of poetry's value at odds with the Sidnean emphasis on moral precepts, one that privileges affect and specifically sympathetic response to suffering ("On Not Defending Poetry," 33–48).

21. Spenser, *The Faerie Queene: Book Five,* ed. Abraham Stoll (Hackett: Indianapolis, IN, 2006), 5.5.13. All subsequent quotations from *Book Five* will be from this text and cited in the text.

22. Van Dijkhuizen, *Pain and Compassion,* 202. Tilmouth makes a similar claim, noting that while pity in some moments in the poem "is celebrated for

its obvious moral worth," it "equally" has "the propensity to lead Spenser's heroes into disastrous error"; ultimately, he argues, pity "blindly leads the mind, its ethical value emerging only in retrospect (and therein lies part of its danger)" (*Passion's Triumph*, 43–44).

23. Van Dijkhuizen, *Pain and Compassion*, 188–89. See also Burrow, *Epic Romance*, for a detailed discussion of the various roles pity plays in the history of epic through the seventeenth century.

24. Nazarian, "Sympathy Wounds," 333. For the Senecan distinction between *misericordia* and *clementia*, see chapter 3 here. Seneca, of course, does not treat emotions as devoid of "judgment and evaluation," but *misericordia* for him constitutes a particularly erroneous form of judgment.

25. Seneca, "On Mercy," II.5.4.

26. Augustine, *City of God*, 9.5, 14.9. Calvin, *Calvin's Commentary*, II.5.4, II.4.4.

27. See, for example, Villeponteaux, "Sacred Pledge"; Nazarian, "Sympathy Wounds."

28. Elyot, *The Boke Named the Gouernour*.

29. Whittington, "Shakespeare's Virgil: Empathy and The Tempest," ch. 4. Whittington quotes Lipsius, who "contrasts the merciful man who 'will look at another man's misfortune with eyes that are humane but, nonetheless, steadfast' with a man in the grips of pity: 'the vice of a petty, insignificant mind, that loses heart at the spectacle of someone else's evil' (1: 12, 55)" (101). Burrow quotes Bodin: "Nothing is so proper unto a prince, as clemencie; nothing unto a king, as mercie; nothing unto majestie, as lenitie ... Now nothing is more contrarie unto true justice, than pitie; neither anything more repugnant unto the office and dutie of an upright judge, than mercie ... So that a prince sitting in judgement must take upon him two contrarie persons, that is to say, of a mercifull father, and of an upright magestrat; of a most gentle prince, and of an inflexible judge" (134).

30. Augustine, *City of God*, 14.9.

31. Staines, "Elizabeth, Mercilla, and the Rhetoric of Propaganda," 292. Staines goes so far as to argue that "To call Seneca's view an Elizabethan commonplace ... is incorrect" (292). I am indebted to Staines's footnote on this claim for leading me to Calvin's commentary on Seneca. See also Whittington, "Shakespeare's Virgil," who cites Lodowick Bryskett as an example of the Augustinian tradition of pity in the early seventeenth century.

32. Kaplan, "The Problem of Pity in Spenser's *Ruines of Time* and *Amoretti*," 264.

33. Nazarian, "Sympathy Wounds," 333.

34. See, for example, van Dijkhuizen, Villeponteux, Nazarian, and Garrison, *Pietas from Vergil to Dryden*. In a particularly memorable moment, Garrison looks at Duessa's descent to appeal to the Queen of the Night and writes, "But the question here is not Priam's—whether there is pietas in Heaven— but rather whether it exists in Hell. The answer, of course, is that it does. And therein lies the problem, as the trial of Duessa in book 5 well illustrates" (189).

148 NOTES TO PAGES 66–73

35. Van Dijkhuizen, *Pain and Compassion*, 194.

36. Augustine, *City of God*, 9.5. Aquinas writes, "Pity is said to be a virtue, i.e., an act of virtue, in so far as that movement of the soul is obedient to reason; viz., when pity is bestowed without violating right . . . as Augustine says" (*Summa Theologica*, III.59.1).

37. Aquinas, *Summa Theologica*, II-II.30.1. As discussed previously, Aquinas is quoting Augustine in his definition of *misericordia*.

38. Campana, *The Pain of Reformation*, 65.

39. Campana says of this scene, "The relationship between Britomart and Amoret is as suggestively erotic as it is useful in providing a model of sympathetic sociality predicated upon neither aggressive appropriation nor sentimentality nor the erasure of the difference between lover and beloved. Like the nymphs in the fountain of the Bower of Bliss, Amoret and Britomart translate conflict into a collaboration as Britomart learns to inhabit masculinity without succumbing to the urge to establish subjectivity through a dialectic of submission and domination. Sympathetic sociality becomes possible as Britomart admits vulnerability and conflict becomes companionship" (201).

40. Burrow, *Epic Romance*, 122.

41. Seneca, "On Mercy," 164.

42. Aristotle, *Nicomachean Ethics*, 8.8.1159b.

43. Aristotle, *Nicomachean Ethics.*, 8.3.1156b, 8.4.1157a. In chapter 7 of book 8, Aristotle discusses "Friendship between unequals." While he acknowledges that there can be a kind of friendship between parents and children, rulers and subject, and husbands and wives, he notes that these are not "perfect" friendships. Moreover, he notes that any time the disparity of status is too great, there can be no friendship (1158b-1159a).

44. Aristotle, *Nicomachean Ethics*, 9.1.1166a.

45. Aristotle, *Nicomachean Ethics*, 8.3.1156a.

46. Aristotle, *Nicomachean Ethics*, 8.3.1156a.

47. Kuzner, *Open Subjects*, 50.

48. Schuurman, in "Pity and Poetics in Chaucer's *The Legend of Good Women*," writes, "The pity of the sinner for Christ or of the lover for her beloved prompts not action but meditation" (1312). Van Dijkhuizen writes of the specifically feminine virtue of pity displayed by Una for Redcrosse in Alma's house, "All she can do is suffer with him, and this is what makes her compassion 'wise'" (*Pain and Compassion*, 197).

49. Aquinas, *Summa Theologica*, II-II.30.2.

50. Analyzing how Aquinas revises Aristotelian pity, which is only a passion, into virtuous pity, Keaty argues, "In Aquinas's view, then, the sorrowful response characteristic of vulnerability is a passion that is to be subordinated to and governed by the virtuously sorrowful response that arises out of friendship love" ("Christian Virtue," 192).

51. Aquinas, *Summa Theologica*, II.II.30.2. My emphasis.

52. As discussed in the introduction, pity for Aristotle is precisely *not* felt by those we are closest to, for reasons that are not hard to extrapolate. As Keaty

NOTES TO PAGES 75–90　　149

notes, in this Aristotelian concept of pity we recognize our own sense of vulnerability to the same fate, and so "I am united to the suffering person primarily because of my concern for my own loss" (192). This kind connection to another resembles the forms of "imperfect" and "easily dissolved" friendship that Aristotle discusses in *Nicomachean Ethics* and that we see in Blandamour and Paridell: each only appreciates the other insofar as the other affects his own life. In genuine friendship, where we see another person "as another self," however, our concern cannot be primarily for ourselves.

53. See, for instance, Goldberg, *The Seeds of Things;* Kathryn Schwarz, *Tough Love,* ch. 4; and Stephens, "Into Other Arms, 190–217.

54. "piteous, adj.," *Oxford English Dictionary Online,* 2a., 1, accessed June 7, 2021

55. Cf. Swarbrick, "The Life Aquatic," whose ecocritical reading of this scene notes the relationship between Marinell's name and his oceanic location as well as between the "rocky stone" of Proteus's palace and Marinell's "stony heart," remarking that, "In Spenser's hands, this sense of homo-ness—of being composed by the same matter as rock and sea that goes beyond man (homo) toward intimacy with inhuman beings suggests a different kind of friendship, one at odds with the regulatory norms of a marriage plot premised on sexual difference, conquest, and hierarchy" (247). For Swarbrick, this scene shows Marinell developing an "unbounded self" through his connection to the environment and to Florimell. This unboundedness, I would argue, depends on the communication of pity and the Thomist identification with the other that pity entails.

56. Van Dijkhuizen, *Pain and Compassion,* 199.

57. Van Dijkhuizen, *Pain and Compassion,* 204.

58. Campana, *Pain of Reformation,* 61.

59. Van Dijkhuizen, *Pain and Compassion,* 200.

60. Spenser, *The Faerie Queene: Books Three and Four,* 3.12.31.7n2.

61. Augustine, *Confessions,* 3.2.

3. ALTERNATE REALITIES

1. Hillman, in comparing Shakespeare to his contemporary playwrights, notes that "Shakespeare, more than anyone else [in his period], plumbs the emotional depths—and concommitantly reaches the affective heights—afforded by the tragic form," and that his "tragic heroes' lack of restraint in embracing their passions is precisely what these tragedies offer us as admirable, as pictures of greatness of the human spirit" ("The Pity of It," 136, 138). Similarly, Strier has argued that figures like Lear offer powerful arguments against reason and in favor of strong emotion, so that Shakespeare, even more than Sidney and Spenser, seems to embrace an anti-Stoic position that recognizes the value of strong emotion in human life (*Unrepentant Renaissance,* 29–58). Compare to Tilmouth's argument that Shakespeare's *Hamlet* calls into question the rationalist ethics of Stoicism and instead paves the way for the turn to a more Aristotelian ethics in the seventeenth century (*Passion's Triumph,* 75–112).

NOTES TO PAGES 90–104

2. James, "Dido's Ear," 360–82.

3. For the former, see, for example, Grady, *Shakespeare and Impure Aesthetics;* Pye, "'To Throw out Our Eyes for Brave Othello'"; Eisendrath, "The Long Nightwatch," 581–606. For the latter, see Guenther, *Magical Imaginations;* Whitney, "Ante-Aesthetics," 40–60.

4. Whitney, "Ante-Aesthetics," 42.

5. Grady, *Shakespeare and Impure Aesthetics,* 59. See also Joughin, "Shakespeare, Modernity, and the Aesthetic," 61–84.

6. Whitney, "Ante-Aesthetics," 42.

7. Whitney, "Ante-Aesthetics," 47.

8. Shakespeare, *A Midsummer Night's Dream,* in The Riverside Shakespeare, 217–49, 5.1.423–38. All subsequent quotations from the text are from this edition and are cited in the text.

9. Grady, *Shakespeare and Impure Aesthetics,* 89.

10. Shakespeare, *The Tempest,* ed. Harold Jenkins, The Arden Shakespeare (London: Thomson Learning, 2001), Epilogue, 1–20. All subsequent quotations from the text are from this edition and are cited in the text.

11. Whitney, "Ante-Aesthetics," 52.

12. Kottman, "Reaching Conclusions," 131.

13. Shakespeare, *Hamlet,* 2.2.584–88. All subsequent quotations from the play are from this edition and are cited in the text.

14. Grady, *Impure Aesthetics,* 171–72.

15. Grady, *Impure Aesthetics,* 171–72; Stoll, *Conscience in Early Modern English Literature,* loc. 236.

16. Weimann, "Mimesis in Hamlet," 275–90. See esp. 282, 284–85.

17. Weimann, "Mimesis," 284.

18. See, for instance, two recent collections: Meek and Sullivan, *The Renaissance of Emotion;* and Craik, *Shakespeare and Emotion.*

19. James, "Dido's Ear," 382.

20. James, "Dido's Ear," 379, 381.

21. Meek, *Sympathy,* ch. 15. It is worth noting, however, that Meek's recent reading of sympathy in *Lear,* in *Sympathy in Early Modern Literature and Culture,* opposes my claims here, arguing that *Lear* stages an exploration of the limitations of sympathy particular across class lines (189–214).

22. Meek, *Sympathy,* 229.

23. Meek, *Sympathy,* 225.

24. Meek, "Rue e'en for Ruth,'" loc. 3055.

25. The arguments here and in the remainder of this chapter are largely based on my earlier essay, "Pity and the Failure of Justice in Shakespeare's *King Lear," Modern Philology* 113.2 (2016): 482–506.

26. Bradley, *Shakespearean Tragedy,* 231. For similar assessments among more recent critics, see, for example, Marianne Novy, *Love's Argument,* and McLuskie, "The Patriarchal Bard." Novy and McLuskie have opposing readings of the value of pity in the play, but they both point to the same circum-

vention of judgment. Novy writes, "There is so much sympathy with Lear at the end that it seems cold to turn from feeling with him to any further analysis of the play in terms of sex-role behavior" (162); similarly, McLuskie notes that the emotional intensity of the final moments between Lear and Cordelia "obliterates the past action so that the audience with Cordelia will murmur 'No cause, no cause.'" But this emotional intensity, for which even "the most stony-hearted feminist could not withhold her pity even though it is called forth at the expense of her resistance to the patriarchal relations which it endorses," is the "antithesis" of "any dispassionate analysis of the mystification of real socio-sexual relations in *King Lear*" (101, 102).

27. Bradley argues that the sense that the world of the play is "a rational and a moral order, that there holds in it the law, not of proportionate requital, but of strict connection between act and consequence" relies on the "perception of [a] connection" between Lear's actions and the consequences he endures (*Shakespearean Tragedy*, 234). Hockey, "The Trial Pattern in *King Lear*," 389–95, states the case somewhat more boldly, asserting that "Forgiveness and love, rather than a demand for personal justice or insight into the world's injustice, are to re-create Lear," and arguing that, when Cordelia forgives Lear, "Justice capitulates to love" (391, 395). For both critics what is at issue is Lear's "redemption," and the abandonment of worldly justice is implicitly legitimated by Christian assumptions about heavenly justice.

28. McLuskie, "The Patriarchal Bard," 101, 102.

29. McLuskie, "The Patriarchal Bard," 100. Dollimore, *Radical Tragedy*, 193.

30. McAlindon, "Tragedy, *King Lear*, and the Politics of the Heart," 85–90; Aggeler, "'Good Pity' in *King Lear*," 321–31, 328. See also, for example, Peter Holbrook's "The Left and *King Lear*," who argues that the play contains "a utopian countermovement" based in "social sympathy" (356).

31. Shakespeare, *King Lear*, R. A. Foakes, ed., The Arden Shakespeare, Richard Proudfoot, Ann Thompson, and David Scott Kastan, eds. (London: Thomson Learning, 2001): 4.6.146–63. All subsequent quotations from the play are from this edition and are cited in the text.

32. Aggeler, "Good Pity," 327 (the phrase Aggeler quotes is from Joseph Hall); Cohen, "*King Lear* and the Social Dimensions of Shakespearean Tragic Form," 106–18, 115. Others who look hopefully on Edgar at the end of the play include Barish and Waingrow, "'Service' in *King Lear*," 347–55; Markels, "*King Lear*, Revolution, and the New Historicism," 11–26, 23; McAlindon, "Tragedy," 88; Holbrook, "The Left and *King Lear*," 355.

33. Dollimore, *Radical Tragedy*, 203; McCoy, "'Look upon Me, Sir': Relationship in *King Lear*," 53. See, too, Beckwith, *Shakespeare and the Grammar of Forgiveness*, in which she contrasts *Lear* to the romance genre, noting that in the play "romance is systematically inverted to indicate that the gods have left the stage. . . . In the play, the gods never answer the prayers of those who call upon them" (92).

34. Lowenthal, "*King Lear*," 391–417, 411.

152   NOTES TO PAGES 108–115

35. Auden, "The Prince's Dog," 201.

36. See, for example, Dollimore, who claims that "Lear's behavior in the opening scene presupposes first, his absolute power, second, the knowledge that his being king constitutes that power, third, his refusal to tolerate what he perceives as a contradiction of that power" (*Radical Tragedy,* 198).

37. Lowenthal provides a more detailed discussion of the rationale behind (and rationality of) Lear's plan to divide the kingdom in a way that acknowledges Cordelia's merit (*"King Lear,"* 393–96); in particular he notes of the love contest, "It is Cordelia's merit that [Lear] wanted to find a way of acknowledging in the allocation, and the 'love speeches' were the secret means he devised to do so" (395). Lowenthal is following Jaffa, "The Limits of Politics," who argues "Lear's original plan, I think, called for precisely equal shares to go to Albany and Cornwall. . . . But Cordelia was to receive a third 'more opulent' than the other two. Lear divided his kingdom into 'three,' but the parts are not mathematical 'thirds'" (413).

38. "subscription, n." *Oxford English Dictionary Online,* accessed July 2021.

39. Strier, *Unrepentant Renaissance,* 48.

40. Delany, *"King Lear* and the Decline of Feudalism," 434–35.

41. As Strier, *Resistant Structures,* notes of Gloucester's blinding and Regan's response, "In Shakespeare, Gloucester 'moves' hearts simply by being in his condition of victimization. . . . It is the moral process . . . by which 'pity' becomes a political force" (227).

42. For an alternate understanding of this scene, however, see, for example, Schalkwyk, *Shakespeare, Love and Service,* who argues that the servant's rebellion "threatens to rip the very fabric of a society founded upon master-servant relations" (241). See also Holbrook, "The Left and *King Lear,"* who points to this scene among others as part of a "catalogue of popular action" that offers hope in the play (356), and Strier, *Resistant Structures,* 192–94, who calls this "one of the most remarkable and politically significant episodes in the play" (192).

43. See, for example, Cohen, who argues that Lear in his "poor naked wretches" speech "still views the misery of the poor from the perspective of the ruling class" (114). Schalkwyk similarly notes that both scenes "do not represent an anarchic or egalitarian levelling of social hierarchy" but rather "perfect service" (243), while Kronenfeld demonstrates that Lear's and Gloucester's ostensibly egalitarian language was often deployed in the service of monarchy and Church power in Shakespeare's time, a fact which shows "how commonplace and nonrevolutionary is this language of distribution and excess." (763). Compare also to Delany, *"King Lear,"* 435.

44. Aggeler, "Good Pity," 328.

45. It is important to note that Cordelia is not *always* engaged in radical pity in the play. In the first scene, her response at 1.1.95–104 to her father's insistence that she speak evinces the same kind of measurement of fairness that underwrites the play's conception of justice. And when she first arrives back in England, she does so with an army, citing both "love" and "our aged father's right" (4.4.28) as her motivations for arriving in this way, demonstrating the mix of pity and justice that prevent Lear's and Gloucester's moments of piti-

ful identification from being transformative. Once we see Cordelia without the army, her language ceases to focus on her father's "rights" and instead focuses on his suffering and how she can remedy it.

46. Barish and Waingrow, "'Service' in *King Lear*," 354.

47. "forgive, v." *Oxford English Dictionary Online*.

48. Jacques Derrida, *On Cosmopolitanism and Forgiveness*, part 2, section 3.

49. Aquinas, *Summa Theologica*, II-II.30.2, my emphasis. On this point, see Keaty, "Christian Virtue," 190–95.

50. Keaty, "Christian Virtue," 186–7.

51. Keaty, "Christian Virtue," 194.

52. See the Introduction for the terminological slippage in the use of "mercy" in the sixteenth century.

53. Elyot, *The Boke Named the Gouernour*, 106.

54. Seneca, "On Mercy," 161.

55. Elyot, *The Boke Named the Gouernour*, 106–7. For the discussion of Augustus and Cinna, see 104–6.

56. Seneca, "On Mercy," 162; Elyot, *The Boke Named the Gouernour*, 107.

57. Seneca, "On Mercy," 164. Seneca also clearly and consistently predicates mercy and its efficacy on the ability to do violence; for example, in arguing that a ruler improves his reputation among the citizens by exercising mercy, Seneca notes, "But those to whom vengeance is easy to do can do without it and gain sure praise for their gentleness" (136).

58. Hannah Arendt to W. H. Auden. Accessed August 3, 2021.

59. Derrida, *On Cosmopolitanism and Forgiveness*. Arendt's own assessment of forgiveness in her letter to Auden confirms a similar position—if it is harder to ask than to give forgiveness, it is because the asker, by asking, must recognize her position of inferiority—just as she notes in *The Human Condition* that "men are unable to forgive what they cannot punish" (241).

60. Derrida, *On Cosmopolitanism*, part 2, section 7.

61. Arendt letter to Auden.

62. Beckwith, *Shakespeare and the Grammar of Forgiveness*, claims that scenes such as this, while not showing "statements of forgiveness," nevertheless offer "the implication of forgiveness" (174n8). If Auden's reading of forgiveness in Shakespeare is correct, however, that drama necessarily conflates pardon with forgiveness, then Cordelia's "No cause, no cause," which does not demonstrate a pardon but rather a dismissal of the case for lack of evidence, would seem similarly to deny that forgiveness has taken place.

63. Augustine, *City of God*, 9.5.

64. Aquinas, *Summa Theologica*, I-II.59.1; my emphasis. In his earlier discussion of God's mercy in I.21.3, Aquinas recognizes the exorbitant nature of *misericordia*, arguing that "God acts mercifully, not indeed by going against His justice, but by doing something more than justice." This does not exactly mean that God's *misericordia* supersedes justice, but rather for Aquinas it is a reconciliation of *misericordia* with justice: "Mercy does not destroy justice, but in a sense is the fulness thereof." I am grateful to an anonymous reader for Kent State University Press for directing me to this passage in the *Summa*.

65. Kottman, *Tragic Conditions in Shakespeare,* argues that Lear's reaction to Cordelia's refusal to participate in the love contest "expresses a tragic collision, an irreconcilable difference, between their principled positions" (104). The "principled positions" Kottman refers to are how relationships between individuals should be structured. While justice is not Kottman's focus, his analysis shows that Lear and Cordelia are operating from conflicting notions of *what should be,* a judgment closely related to the question of justice and standards of measuring what is right.

66. Anderson, "The Tragedy of Good Friday," 266.

67. Arendt makes forgiveness a condition of possibility for continued human relations, noting that "trepassing is an everyday occurrence" and that therefore "it needs forgiving, dismissing, in order to make it possible for life to go on by constantly releasing men from what they have done unknowingly" (*Human Condition,* 240). Beckwith likewise describes the forgiveness as a crucial condition for the possibility of forming social bonds (*Grammar of Forgiveness,* 34–56).

68. Both Kottman and Strier have pointed out a tension in Shakespeare's work between the demands of universal principles and bonds between individuals. Kottman sees much of Shakespeare's tragedy driven by this conflict. He argues that "normative prerogatives and values that we require to reproduce a sustainable form of life" produce a kind of blindness to others: "In Shakespeare . . . such 'universal' principles threaten to blind us to the recognition of those human beings to whom we might wish to be bound" (*Tragic Condition,* 17). Strier, "Shakespeare and Legal Systems," identifies a tension between impartial, impersonal legal systems and the world of actual social relations, creating a conflict in "the relation between justice and friendship (or other personal relations)," 177. The conflict between the judgments of justice and the judgments of pity seem to me a part of this tension, where part of justice's failure in *Lear* grows out of the attempt to subject personal, local relationships to "higher" principles. I see this problem as less aporetic than Kottman does, however; the play less focuses on the tension between universal and particular and instead, I believe, exhorts us to focus our actions on specific, local relationships. *Lear,* on my reading, might thus have something to say to moral particularism; but this is beyond the scope of this project.

69. Johnson, "King Lear," *The Preface to Shakespeare.*

70. Novy, *Love's Argument,* 159.

CONCLUSION

1. Indeed, Jenefer Robinson argues in "Experiencing Art" that all interpretations just are responses to the questions about our emotional responses.

2. See, for example, Kidd and Castano, "Reading Literary Fiction Improves Theory of Mind," 377–80.

3. On the topic of "ungrading," I am deeply indebted to the work of Jesse Stommel. A good starting point on the subject is his "Ungrading: An Introduction," June 11, 2021.

✠ BIBLIOGRAPHY ⊬

Adorno, Theodor. *Aesthetic Theory.* Edited by Gretel Adorno and Rolf Tiede-
mann. Translated by Robert Hullot-Kentor. Theory and History of Literature
88. Minneapolis: Univ. of Minnesota Press, 1997.

Aggeler, Geoffrey. "'Good Pity' in *King Lear:* The Progress of Edgar." *Neophilolo-
gus* 77, no. 2 (1992): 321–31.

Alexander, Gavin. "Loving and Reading in Sidney." *Studies in Philology* 114, no. 1
(2017): 39–66.

"American Library Association Reports Record Number of Unique Book Ti-
tles Challenged in 2023 | ALA." Accessed May 30, 2024. https://www.ala.org/
news/2024/03/american-library-association-reports-record-number
-unique-book-titles.

Anderson, David. "The Tragedy of Good Friday: Sacrificial Violence in *King
Lear.*" *ELH* 78, no. 2 (2011): 259–86.

Aquinas, Thomas. *Summa Theologica: Complete English Editions in Five Volumes.*
Translated by Fathers of the English Dominican Province. Vol. 3 of 5. Notre
Dame, IN: Ave Maria Press, 1948.

Arendt, Hannah. "Hannah Arendt to W. H. Auden," February 14, 1960. Hannah Arendt Papers, Library of Congress. http://memory.loc.gov/ammen/arendthtml
/arendthome.html.

———. *The Human Condition.* Chicago: Univ. of Chicago Press, 1998.

Aristotle. *Aristotle's Poetics.* Translated by James Hutton. New York: W. W. Norton, 1982.

———. "Nicomachean Ethics." In *The Complete Works of Aristotle: The Revised
Oxford Translation,* Vol. 2, edited by Jonathan Barnes. Princeton: Princeton
Univ. Press, 1984.

———. "Poetics." In *The Complete Works of Aristotle: The Revised Oxford Translation,* Vol. 2, edited by Jonathan Barnes. Princeton: Princeton Univ. Press, 1984.

———. *Poetics.* Translated by S. H. Butcher, 1994. http://classics.mit.edu/Aristotle/poetics.1.1.html.

———. "Rhetoric." In *The Complete Works of Aristotle: The Revised Oxford Translation,* Vol. 2, edited by Jonathan Barnes. Princeton: Princeton Univ. Press, 1984.

Auden, W. H. "The Prince's Dog." In *The Dyers and Other Essays,* 182–208. New York: Random House, 1962.

Augustine. *Concerning the City of God Against the Pagans.* Translated by Henry Bettenson. New York: Penguin, 1972.

———. *Confessions.* Oxford World's Classics. New York: Oxford Univ. Press, 1998.

Barish, Jonas A., and Marshall Waingrow. "'Service' in *King Lear.*" *Shakespeare Quarterly* 9, no. 3 (1958): 347–55.

Beckwith, Sarah. *Shakespeare and the Grammar of Forgiveness.* Ithaca: Cornell Univ. Press, 2011.

Berger Jr., Harry. *The Allegorical Temper: Vision and Reality in Book II of Spenser's Faerie Queene.* New Haven, CT: Yale Univ. Press, 1957.

Borris, Kenneth. "Platonism and Spenser's Poetic: Idealized Imitation, Merlin's Mirror, and the Florimells." *Spenser Studies* 24 (2009): 209–68.

Bowie, Andrew. *From Romanticism to Critical Theory: The Philosophy of German Literary Theory.* New York: Routledge, 1997. Kindle.

Bradley, A. C. *Shakespearean Tragedy: Lectures on Hamlet, Othello, King Lear, Macbeth.* New York: St. Martin's, 1966.

Buckman, Ty. "Forcing the Poet Into Prose: 'Gealous Opinions and Misconstructions' and Spenser's Letter to Ralegh." *Studies in the Literary Imagination* 39, no. 2 (2005): 17–34.

Burrow, Colin. *Epic Romance: Homer to Milton.* Oxford: Clarendon, 1993.

Burton, Neel. "Empathy vs. Sympathy." *Psychology Today,* May 22, 2015. https://www.psychologytoday.com/blog/hide-and-seek/201505/empathy-vs-sympathy.

Calvin, John. *Calvin's Commentary on Seneca's "De Clementia."* Edited by Ford Lewis Battles and André Malan Hugo. Leiden, Netherlands: E. J. Brill, 1969.

Campana, Joseph. "On Not Defending Poetry: Spenser, Suffering, and the Energy of Affect." *PMLA* 120, no. 1 (2005): 33–48.

———. *The Pain of Reformation: Spenser, Vulnerability, and the Ethics of Masculinity.* New York: Fordham Univ. Press, 2012.

Cohen, Walter. "*King Lear* and the Social Dimensions of Shakespearean Tragic Form, 1603–1608." In *Shakespeare: Contemporary Critical Approaches,* edited by Michael D. Payne, 106–18. Bucknell Review. Lewisburg, PA: Bucknell Univ. Press, 1980.

Craik, Katharine A., ed. *Shakespeare and Emotion.* Cambridge: Cambridge Univ. Press, 2020. Kindle.

Cummings, Brian. *The Literary Culture of the Reformation: Grammar and Grace.* Oxford: Oxford Univ. Press, 2002. Kindle.

Delany, Paul. "*King Lear* and the Decline of Feudalism." *PMLA* 92, no. 3 (1977): 429–40.

DeNeef, Leigh A. "'The Ruins of Time': Spenser's *Apology for Poetry.*" *Studies in Philology* 76, no. 3 (1979): 262–71.

BIBLIOGRAPHY

Derrida, Jacques. *On Cosmopolitanism and Forgiveness.* Translated by Mark Dooley and Michael Hughes. New York: Routledge, 2003. Kindle.

Docherty, Thomas. "Aesthetic Education and the Demise of Experience." In *The New Aestheticism,* edited by John J. Joughin and Simon Malpas, 23–35. Manchester: Manchester Univ. Press, 2003.

Dollimore, Jonathan. *Radical Tragedy: Religion, Ideology and Power in the Drama of Shakespeare and His Contemporaries.* Chicago: Univ. of Chicago Press, 1984.

Doring, Tobias. "Beginning to Spell: Sidney's *Astrophil and Stella* and the Crux of Protestant Poetics," *Poetica* 45, no. 1/2 (2013): 67–84.

Dow, Jamie. "A Supposed Contradiction about Emotion-Arousal in Aristotle's 'Rhetoric.'" *Phronesis* 52, no. 4 (2007): 382–402.

Eisendrath, Rachel. "Going Outside: Human Subjectivity and the Aesthetic Object in *The Faerie Queene,* Book III." *Spenser Studies* 30 (2015): 343–68.

———. *Poetry in a World of Things: Aesthetics and Empiricism in Renaissance Ekphrasis.* Chicago: Univ. of Chicago Press, 2018.

———. "The Long Nightwatch: Augustine, Hamlet, and the Aesthetic." *ELH* 87, no. 3 (2020): 581–606.

Elyot, Sir Thomas. *The Boke Named the Gouernour, Deuised by Sir Thomas Elyot Knyght.* London, 1565.

Erickson, Wayne. "Spenser's Letter to Ralegh and the Literary Politics of *The Faerie Queene.*" *Spenser Studies* 10 (1992): 139–74.

Falco, Raphael. *Conceived Presences: Literary Genealogy in Renaissance England.* Amherst, MA: Univ. of Massachuesetts Press, 1994.

Ferguson, Margaret W. *Trials of Desire: Renaissance Defenses of Poetry.* New Haven, CT: Yale Univ. Press, 1983.

Garrison, James D. *Pietas from Vergil to Dryden.* University Park, PA: Pennsylvania State Univ. Press, 1992.

Glimp, David. *Increase and Multiply: Governing Cultural Reproduction in Early Modern England.* Minneapolis: Univ. of Minnesota Press, 2003.

Goldberg, Jonathan. *The Seeds of Things: Theorizing Sexuality and Materiality in Renaissance Representations.* New York: Fordham Univ. Press, 2009. Kindle.

Gosson, Stephen. "The School of Abuse." In *Shakespeare's Theater: A Sourcebook,* edited by Tanya Pollard. Malden, MA: Blackwell, 2004. Kindle.

Grady, Hugh. *Shakespeare and Impure Aesthetics.* Cambridge: Cambridge Univ. Press, 2009.

Guenther, Genevieve. *Magical Imaginations: Instrumental Aesthetics in the English Renaissance.* Toronto: Univ. of Toronto Press, 2012.

Halliwell, Stephen. *The Aesthetics of Mimesis: Ancient Texts and Modern Problems.* Princeton: Princeton Univ. Press, 2002. Kindle.

———. *Aristotle's Poetics.* 2nd ed. London: Duckworth, 2009.

Hardison, O. B. "The Two Voices of Sidney's 'Apology for Poetry.'" *English Literary Renaissance* 2, no. 1 (1972): 83–99.

Hegel, G. F. W. *Aesthetics: Lectures on Fine Art.* Translated by T. M. Knox. Vol. 1 of 2. Oxford: Clarendon, 1998.

Held, Virginia. *The Ethics of Care: Personal, Political, and Global.* Oxford: Oxford Univ. Press, 2006. Kindle.

Herman, Peter C. *Squitter-Wits and Muse Haters: Sidney, Spenser Milton and Renaissance Antipoetic Sentiment.* Detroit: Wayne State Univ. Press, 1996.

Hillman, David. "The Pity of It: Shakespearean Tragedy and Affect." In *The Oxford Handbook of Shakespearean Tragedy,* edited by Michael Neill and David Schalkwyk, 135–50. Oxford: Oxford Univ. Press, 2016.

Hockey, Dorothy C. "The Trial Pattern in *King Lear.*" *Shakespeare Quarterly* 10, no. 3 (1959): 389–95.

Holbrook, Peter. "The Left and *King Lear.*" *Textual Practice* 14, no. 2 (2000): 343–62.

Horace. "Ars Poetica." In *The Norton Anthology of Theory and Criticism,* edited by Vincent B. Leitch, 2nd ed., 122–33. New York: W. W. Norton, 2010.

Hulse, Clark. "Tudor Aesthetics." In *The Cambridge Companion to English Literature, 1500–1600,* edited by Arthur Kinney, 29–63. New York: Cambridge Univ. Press, 2000.

Jacobson, Daniel. "Sir Philip Sidney's Dilemma: On the Ethical Function of Narrative Art." *Journal of Aesthetics and Art Criticism* 54, no. 4 (1996): 327–36.

Jaffa, Harry V. "The Limits of Politics: An Interpretation of *King Lear,* Act 1, Scene 1." *The American Political Science Review* 51, no. 2 (1957): 405–27.

James, Heather. "Dido's Ear: Tragedy and the Politics of Response." *Shakespeare Quarterly* 52, no. 3 (2001): 360–82.

Johnson, Samuel. "King Lear." In *The Preface to Shakespeare.* Project Gutenberg, 28 Dec 2020, https://www.gutenberg.org/cache/epub/5429/pg5429-images. html. Accessed October 25, 2024.

Joughin, John. "Shakespeare, Modernity, and the Aesthetic: Art, Truth and Judgement in *The Winter's Tale.*" In *Shakespeare and Modernity: Early Modern to Millenium,* edited by Hugh Grady, 61–84. London: Routledge, 2000.

Joughin, John J., and Simon Malpas. "The New Aestheticism: An Introduction." In *The New Aestheticism,* 1–19. Manchester: Machester Univ. Press, 2003.

Kamtekar, Rachana. "Ancient Virtue Ethics: An Overview with an Emphasis on Practical Wisdom." In *The Cambridge Companion to Virtue Ethics,* edited by Daniel C. Russell. Cambridge Companions to Philosophy. Cambridge: Cambridge Univ. Press, 2013. Kindle.

Kant, Immanuel. *Critique of the Power of Judgment.* Edited by Paul Guyer. Translated by Paul Guyer and Matthews. The Cambridge Edition of the Works of Immanuel Kant. Cambridge: Cambridge Univ. Press, 2000.

Kaplan, Ruth. "The Problem of Pity in Spenser's Ruines of Time and Amoretti." *Spenser Studies* 29 (2014): 263–94.

Keaty, Anthony. "The Christian Virtue of Mercy: Aquinas' Transformation of Aristotelian Pity." *Heythrop Journal* 46, no. 2 (2005): 181–98.

Kidd, David Comer, and Emanuele Castano. "Reading Literary Fiction Improves Theory of Mind." *Science* 342, no. 6156 (October 18, 2013): 377–80.

Kinney, Arthur F. "Parody and Its Implications in Sydney's Defense of Poesie." *Studies in English Literature, 1500–1900* 12, no. 1 (1972): 1–19.

Konstan, David. *Pity Transformed.* London: Duckworth, 2001.

Kottman, Paul. "Reaching Conclusions: Art and Philosophy in Hegel and Shakespeare." In *The Insistence of Art,* edited by Paul Kottman, 116–39. New York: Fordham Univ. Press, 2017.

———. "The Claim of Art: Aesthetic Philosophy and Early Modern Artistry." In *The Insistence of Art*, edited by Paul Kottman, 1–30. New York: Fordham Univ. Press, 2017.

Kottman, Paul A. *Tragic Conditions in Shakespeare: Disinheriting the Globe*. Baltimore: Johns Hopkins Univ. Press, 2009.

Kronenfeld, Judy. "'So Distribution Should Undo Excess, and Each Man Have Enough': Shakespeare's *King Lear*—Anabaptist Egalitarianism, Anglican Charity, Both, Neither?" *ELH* 59, no. 4 (1992): 755–84.

Kuzner, James. *Open Subjects: English Renaissance Republicans, Modern Selfhoods and the Virtue of Vulnerabilit*. Edinburgh: Edinburgh Univ. Press, 2011.

Lazarus, Micha. "Sidney's Greek 'Poetics.'" *Studies in Philology* 112, no. 3 (2015): 504–36.

Lodge, Thomas. *The Complete Works of Thomas Lodge*. Vol. 1 of 4. Hunterian Club, 1883. https://sourcetext.com/complete-works-of-thomas-lodge/.

Lowenthal, David. "King Lear." *Interpretations* 21, no. 3 (1994): 391–417.

Lucretius. *On the Nature of Things*. Translated by Martin Ferguson Smith. Indianapolis, IN: Hackett, 2001.

Mack, Michael. *Sidney's Poetics: Imitating Creation*. Washington, DC: Catholic Univ. of America Press, 2005.

Markels, Julian. "*King Lear*, Revolution, and the New Historicism." *Modern Language Studies* 21, no. 2 (1991): 11–26.

Matz, Robert. *Defending Literature in Early Modern England: Renaissance Literary Theory in Social Context*. Cambridge: Cambridge Univ. Press, 2000.

McAlindon, Tom. "Tragedy, King Lear, and the Politics of the Heart." *Shakespeare Survey* 44 (1991): 85–90.

McCoy, Richard. "'Look upon Me, Sir': Relationship in *King Lear*." *Representations* 81 (2003): 46–60.

McLuskie, Kathleen. "The Patriarchal Bard: Feminist Criticism and Shakespeare: *King Lear* and *Measure for Measure*." In *Political Shakespeare: New Essays in Cultural Materialism*, edited by Jonathan Dollimore and Alan Sinfield, 88–108. Ithaca: Cornell Univ. Press, 1985.

Meek, Richard. "Rue e'en for Ruth': *Richard II* and the Imitation of Sympathy." In *The Renaissance of Emotion: Understanding Affect in Shakespeare and His Contemporaries*, edited by Richard Meek and Erin Sullivan. Manchester: Manchester Univ. Press, 2015. Kindle.

———. "Sympathy." In *Shakespeare and Emotion*, edited by Katharine A. Craik, Kindle., 224–37. Cambridge: Cambridge Univ. Press, 2020.

Meek, Richard. *Sympathy in Early Modern Literature and Culture*. Cambridge: Cambridge Univ. Press, 2023.

Meek, Richard, and Erin Sullivan. "Introduction." In *The Renaissance of Emotion: Understanding Affect in Shakespeare and His Contemporaries*. Manchester, U.K.: Manchester Univ. Press, 2015. Kindle.

———. *The Renaissance of Emotion: Understanding Affect in Shakespeare and His Contemporaries*. Manchester, U.K.: Manchester Univ. Press, 2015. Kindle.

Morgan, Gerald. "The Idea of Temperance in the Second Book of *The Faerie Queene*." *The Review of English Studies* 37, no. 145 (1986): 11–39.

Nazarian, Cynthia. "Sympathy Wounds, Rivers of Blood: The Politics of Fellow Feeling in Spenser's *Faerie Queene* and *A View of the Present State of Ireland.*" *Modern Philology* 113, no. 3 (2016): 331–52.

Novy, Marianne. *Love's Argument: Gender Relations in Shakespeare.* Chapel Hill: Univ. of North Carolina Press, 1984.

Nussbaum, Martha C. "Tragedy and Self-Sufficiency: Plato and Aristotle on Fear and Pity." In *Essays on Aristotle's Poetics,* edited by Amelie Oksenberg Rorty, 261–90. Princeton: Princeton Univ. Press, 1992.

———. *Upheavals of Thought: The Intelligence of Emotions.* Cambridge: Cambridge Univ. Press, 2001. Kindle.

Paster, Gail Kern. *Humoring the Body: Emotions and the Shakespearean Stage.* Chicago: Univ. of Chicago Press, 2004.

Plato. "Republic." In *The Collected Dialogues of Plato Including the Letters,* edited by Edith Hamilton and Huntington Cairns, translated by Paul Shorey, 575–844. Bollingen Series 71. Princeton: Princeton Univ. Press, 1973.

Puttenham, George. *The Art of English Poesy by George Puttenham: A Critical Edition.* Edited by Frank Whigham and Wayne A. Rebhorn. Ithaca: Cornell Univ. Press, 2007.

Pye, Christopher. "'To Throw out Our Eyes for Brave Othello': Shakespeare and Aesthetic Ideology." *Shakespeare Quarterly* 60, no. 4 (2009): 425–47.

Reisner, Noam. "The Paradox of Mimesis in Sidney's *Defence of Poesy* and Marlowe's *Doctor Faustus.*" *The Cambridge Quarterly* 48, no. 4 (2010): 331–49.

Robinson, Benedict. "Thinking Feeling." In *Affect Theory and Early Modern Texts: Politics, Ecologies, and Form,* edited by Amanda Bailey and Mario DiGangi, 109–27. New York: Palgrave MacMillan, 2017.

Robinson, Jenefer. "The Art of Distancing: How Formal Devices Manage Our Emotional Responses to Literature." *The Journal of Aesthetics and Art Criticism* 62, no. 2 (2004): 153–62.

———. "Experiencing Art." *Proceedings of the Eleventh International Congress in Aesthetics, Nottingham Polytechnic, English,* 1988, 156–60.

Robinson, Forrest G. *The Shape of Things Known: Sidney's Apology and Its Philosophical Tradition.* Cambridge, MA: Harvard Univ. Press, 1972.

Robson, Mark. "Defending Poetry, or, Is There an Early Modern Aesthetic?" In *The New Aestheticism,* edited by John J. Joughin and Simon Malpas, 119–30. Manchester: Manchester Univ. Press, 2003.

Russell, Daniel C. "Introduction." In *The Cambridge Companion to Virtue Ethics,* edited by Daniel C. Russell. Cambridge Companions to Philosophy. Cambridge: Cambridge Univ. Press, 2013. Kindle.

Schalkwyk, David. *Shakespeare, Love and Service.* Cambridge: Cambridge Univ. Press, 2008.

Schuurman, Anne. "Pity and Poetics in Chaucer's *The Legend of Good Women.*" *PMLA* 130, no. 5 (2015): 1302–17.

Schwarz, Kathryn. *Tough Love: Amazon Encounters in the English Renaissance.* Series Q. Durham, NC: Duke Univ. Press, 2000. Kindle.

Seneca. "On Mercy." In *Moral and Political Essays,* edited by John M. Cooper and J. F. Procopé. Cambridge Texts in the History of Political Thought. Cambridge: Cambridge Univ. Press, 2010.

BIBLIOGRAPHY

Shakespeare, William. *A Midsummer Night's Dream.* In *The Riverside Shakespeare,* edited by G. Blakemore Evans, 217–49. Boston: Houghton Mifflin, 1974.

———. *Hamlet.* Edited by Harold Jenkins. The Arden Shakespeare. London: Thomson Learning, 2001.

———. *King Lear.* Edited by R. A. Foakes. The Arden Shakespeare. London: Thomson Learning, 2001.

———. *The Tempest.* Edited by Virginia Mason Vaughan and Alden T. Vaughan. The Arden Shakespeare,. London: Thomson Learning, 2007.

Shifflet, Andrew. "The Poet as Feigned Example in Sidney's *Apology for Poetry.*" *Modern Philology* 14, no. 1 (2016): 18–38.

Sidney, Philip. *The Major Works.* Edited by Katharine Duncan-Jones. Oxford World's Classics. New York: Oxford Univ. Press, 2002.

Soloman, Julie. "You've Got to Have Soul: Understanding the Passions in Early Modern Culture." In *Rhetoric and Medicine in Early Modern Europe,* edited by Nancy S. Struever and Stephen Pender, 195–228. Burlington, VT: Ashgate, 2012.

Solomon, Robert C. "Emotions, Thoughts, and Feelings: Emotions as Engagements with the World." In *Thinking about Feeling : Contemporary Philosophers on Emotions,* edited by Robert C. Solomon, 134–55. Oxford: Oxford Univ. Press, 2004.

Spenser, Edmund. *The Faerie Queene: Book Five.* Edited by Abraham Stoll. Indianapolis, IN: Hackett, 2006.

———. *The Faerie Queene: Book One.* Edited by Carol Kaske. Indianapolis, IN: Hackett, 2006.

———. *The Faerie Queene: Book Two.* Edited by Erik Gray. Indianapolis, IN: Hackett, 2006.

———. *The Faerie Queene: Books Three and Four.* Edited by Dorothy Stephens. Indianapolis, IN: Hackett, 2006.

Staines, John D. "Elizabeth, Mercilla, and the Rhetoric of Propaganda in Spenser's Faerie Queene." *Journal of Medieval and Early Modern Studies* 31, no. 2 (2001): 282–312.

Stephens, Dorothy. "Into Other Arms: Amoret's Evasion." In *Queering the Renaissance,* edited by Jonathan Goldberg, 190–217. Durham, NC: Duke Univ. Press, 1994. Kindle.

Stoll, Abraham. *Conscience in Early Modern English Literature.* Cambridge: Cambridge Univ. Press, 2017. Kindle.

Stommel, Jesse. "Ungrading: An Introduction," June 11, 2021. https://www. jessestommel.com/ungrading-an-introduction/.

Strier, Richard. *Resistant Structures: Particularity, Radicalism, and Renaissance Texts.* Berkeley: Univ. of California Press, 1995.

———. "Shakespeare and Legal Systems: The Better the Worse (but Not Vice Versa)." In *Shakespeare and the Law: A Conversation Among Disciplines and Professions,* edited by Bradin Cormack, Martha C. Nussbaum, and Richard Strier. Chicago: Univ. of Chicago Press, 2013.

———. *The Unrepentant Renaissance: From Petrarch to Shakespeare to Milton.* Chicago: Univ. of Chicago Press, 2011.

Swarbrick, Steven. "The Life Aquatic: Liquid Poetics and the Discourse of Friendship in *The Faerie Queene.*" *Spenser Studies* 30 (2015): 229–53.

Tilmouth, Christopher. *Passion's Triumph Over Reason: A History of the Moral Imagination from Spenser to Rochester.* Kindle. New York: Oxford Univ. Press, 2007.

van Dijkhuizen, Jan Frans. *Pain and Compassion in Early Modern English Literature and Culture.* Studies in Renaissance Literature. Cambridge: D. S. Brewer, 2012.

Villeponteaux, Mary. "'The Sacred Pledge of Peace and Clemencie': Elizabethan Mercy in *The Faerie Queene.*" In *The Queene's Mercy: Gender and Judgment in Representations of Elizabeth I,* 35–65. Queenship and Power Series. London: Palgrave MacMillan, 2014.

Weimann, Robert. "Mimesis in Hamlet." In *Shakespeare and the Question of Theory,* edited by Geoffrey H. Hartmann and Patricia Parker, 275–90. New York: Routledge, 1986.

Weinberg, Bernard. *A History of Literary Criticism in the Italian Renaissance.* Vol. 1 of 2. Chicago: Univ. of Chicago Press, 1961.

Whitney, Charles. "Ante-Aesthetics: Towards a Theory of Early Modern Audience Response." In *Shakespeare and Modernity: Early Modern to Millennium,* edited by Hugh Grady, 40–60. Routledge, 2000.

Whittington, Leah. "Shakespeare's Virgil: Empathy and The Tempest." In *Shakespeare and Renaissance Ethics,* edited by John D. Cox and Patrick Gray, 98–120. Cambridge: Cambridge Univ. Press, 2014. Kindle.

Wilde, Oscar. *The Picture of Dorian Gray,* edited by Norman Page. Broadview, 2005.

Wilson, Thomas. "The Arte of Rhetorique." In *English Literary Criticism: The Renaissance,* edited by O. B. Hardison, 26–57. New York: Appleton Century Crofts, 1963.

Wiseman, Rebecca. "Introspection and Self-Evaluation in Astrophil and Stella." *Sidney Journal* 30, no. 1 (2012): 51–77.

Wright, Thomas. *The Passions of the Minde in Generall.* Early English Books Online, 1604.

INDEX

Adorno, Theodor, 5, 6, 91
aesthetic delight: Aristotle on, 86; and *Astrophil and Stella* (Sidney), 31, 45–52, 80–81; autonomy model of aesthetics leading to, 44–45; and *Defence* (Sidney), 31–37, 42, 46–47; defined, 24, 31; and *The Faerie Queene* (Spenser), 55, 57–61, 80–81; and modern vs. early modern aesthetics, 6–7; and Shakespeare's works, 95–96, 100–101; Sidney on, 23; tragedy and, 12, 43, 86–88
aesthetic distance: in *Astrophil and Stella* (Sidney), 23, 51–52; and autonomy thesis, 11; in *Defence* (Sidney), 38, 41; defined, 11, 15–16; and ethical emotion, 17; in *The Faerie Queene* "Letter of the Authors" (Spenser), 55, 80; in *The Faerie Queene* (Spenser), 54; in Shakespeare's dramas, 90–91; and tragedy, 15–16, 42
aesthetic emotion: Christian Pity vs., 17–19; defined, 11; ethics, distance from, 11, 24; Lodge on, 20; as motive to act, 26; Sidney on, 31. *See also* aesthetic delight
aesthetics: in *Defence* (Sidney), 31–37; in *The Faerie Queene* (Spenser), 55–61; instrumental, 4–6, 24, 31, 47; in *King Lear* (Shakespeare), 24–26, 91–101, 127–28; modern vs. early modern, 1–11; Shakespearean theory of, 25–26, 127–29; and value of literature, 1–3. *See also* aesthetic delight; aesthetic distance; aes-

thetic emotion; autonomy model of aesthetics; early modern aesthetics
Aggeler, Geoffrey, 105, 115
Alexander, Gavin, 29
Alexander Pheraeus, 34, 42–45, 47
alternate realities: ethics of, 101–4; and *Hamlet* (Shakespeare), 90–91, 99–100; and *King Lear* (Shakespeare), 91; and *A Midsummer Night's Dream* (Shakespeare), 95–96; real-world effects of encounters with, 90–91; and Shakespearean theory of aesthetics, 127–29
Amadis de Gaule, 33, 40
American Library Association, 26
Amoretti (Spenser), 66
anachronism, 4
Anatomie of the Minde (Rogers), 8
Anderson, David, 125
Aquinas, Thomas: Aristotle, influence of, 9; on Christian pity, 17–18; *The Faerie Queene* (Spenser), influence in, 54; on friendship, 86; on pity, 65, 67, 72–77, 79–82, 84, 85; and pity in *King Lear* (Shakespeare), 104, 113, 119–20, 123, 124; on the soul, 9; *Summa Theologica*, 67; and virtue ethics, 7
Arendt, Hannah, 122
Aristotelian virtue ethics, 7, 10, 62
Aristotle: cognitive view of emotions, 10; *Defence* (Sidney) indebted to, 29, 32, 38–39; and delight in tragedy, 42; on ethical

164 INDEX

Aristotle (*cont.*)
action, 35; and ethical value of literature, 1, 3, 7–8; on friendship, 70–74; on
function of poetry, 15; mimesis theory
of, 14–17, 61, 86; *Nicomachean Ethics*, 18, 67, 69–70, 72–73; on pity, 19, 49,
64, 66, 83; on pity as motive to act, 25,
26; *Poetics*, 12, 13–16, 86; poetry as instructive through evoking emotions,
11, 13, 16; *Rhetoric*, 10, 15, 18, 64, 72, 86;
Shakespeare, influence on, 91, 98, 101;
Spenser, influence on, 54, 55, 60–63, 70,
80; Thomist ideas influenced by, 9
Ars Poetica (Horace), 32
art. *See* literature and art
Arte of Rhetoric (Wilson), 7
The Art of English Poesie (Puttenham),
21–22
Astrophil and Stella (Sidney): aesthetic
distance in, 23, 51–52; delight and pity
in, 31, 45–52, 80–81; *The Faerie Queene*
(Spenser) compared, 54; *Hamlet*
(Shakespeare) compared, 99; inconsistency in, 30–31; Spenser, influence on,
53, 80–81
Auden, W. H., 108, 122
Augustine: aesthetic vs. ethical emotion,
11, 17; autonomous art and ethics, reconciling, 22; *City of God*, 8, 17, 62–63, 65,
87; *Confessions*, 17, 18–19, 49, 50, 87; and
ethical value of literature, 1, 3; *The Faerie Queene* (Spenser), influence in, 54;
on pity, 17, 18–19, 42–44, 46, 49, 65, 67,
72–73
autonomy model of aesthetics: aesthetic
vs. ethical emotion, 11, 23–24, 131; and
Aristotle's poetics, 39; and *Astrophil and
Stella* (Sidney), 45; and *Defence* (Sidney), 30–31, 32, 37, 38–39, 51–52, 90; defined, 2; and early modern aesthetics,
4, 6, 19–20, 22; and emotions provoked
by literature, 2–3, 135; and ethical value
of individual judgments, 10–11; and *The
Faerie Queene* "Letter of the Authors"
(Spenser), 55–56; and *The Faerie Queene*
(Spenser), 55, 80, 88, 90; mimesis theories, replacing, 23; and modern aesthetics, 1; and Shakespeare's works, 90–94,
128; Spenser on, 24

Bodin, Jean, 65
book bans, 26, 131
Bowie, Andrew, 4

Bradley, A. C., 104
Burrow, Colin, 65, 68–69

Caesar, Julius, 8
Calvin, John, 8, 65
Campana, Joseph, 58, 68–69
catharsis, 13, 16, 102
Christian ethics: Augustine on, 42–44, 72;
in *The Faerie Queene* (Spenser), 62–63;
forgiveness, 122; on pity, 8, 17–19, 42–44,
65–66, 72–74; Sidney on, 23
Cicero, 7, 8
City of God (Augustine), 8, 17, 62–63, 65, 87
clemency, 63–65
clementia, 8–9, 69, 120. *See also* mercy
cognitive theory of emotions, 10
comedy, in *Defence* (Sidney), 41
compassion: and aesthetic delight, 43, 44,
50; in *Astrophil and Stella* (Sidney), 46,
49, 50; Augustine on, 8, 124; and Christian ethics, 8; and elegy, 33, 40; in *The
Faerie Queene* (Spenser), 67, 69, 81–84;
and Stoicism, 63, 65, 67; and tragedy, 14.
See also pity
Confessions (Augustine), 17, 18–19, 49, 50, 87
Critias (Plato), 62
Critique of the Power of Judgment (Kant), 5
culture wars, 26, 131–32

De Clementia (Seneca), 9, 64–65, 120–21,
122–23
De Constantia (Lipsius), 65
Defence of Poesy (Sidney): aesthetics, ethics, and emotion in, 31–37, 54; autonomy, reflection, and delight in, 37–45,
90, 101; and autonomy of art, 6, 30; and
autonomy vs. ethical effects of art, 23,
131–32; on emotions taught through
literature, 7; and ethical value of literature, 2, 8, 30, 51; "golden world" section,
38–39; inconsistency in, 29–31, 40–42,
131; Spenser, influence on, 53, 56–57;
theory of art in, 23
delight. *See* aesthetic delight
DeNeef, Leigh A., 37–38, 57
De Rerum Natura (Lucretius), 36, 57
Derrida, Jacques, 117, 122, 125
Dollimore, Jonathan, 105, 108
drama, Shakespearean theory of, 90–92, 101
Duncan-Jones, Katherine, 48–49

early modern aesthetics, 1–27; and art of
pity, 23–27; defined, 1–2; and emotional

INDEX

experience of art, 11–19; modern aesthetics vs., 1–11; past, engagement with, 19–23; and value of literature, 1–3, 133, 135

Eisendrath, Rachel, 6

elegy: and compassion, 33, 40; in *Defence* (Sidney), 41–42

Elyot, Thomas, 65, 120–21, 122–23, 127

emotional intelligence, 134

emotions: cognitive theory of, 10; in *Defence* (Sidney), 31–37; early modern aesthetics and focus on, 11–19; ethics, role in, 3, 13; frameworks for, 9–10; and literary analysis, 133–35; literature and teaching, 7–8, 24, 26, 30–31, 132–35; and modern vs. early modern aesthetics, 6–9; poetry and dangers of evoking, 11, 12–14, 16, 17, 20, 21; reason vs. passion, 62–63; virtue, role in, 1–2, 10, 63. *See also individual emotions*

Enlightenment, 4

ethical action: and *Astrophil and Stella* (Sidney), 46–49; Augustine and Christian ethics, 43–44, 72; and *Defence* (Sidney), 30–31, 34–36, 54; defined, 7; and Shakespeare's works, 102; and virtue ethics, 7–9

ethical pity: and Shakespeare, 24–26, 90–91, 101–4, 125–29; and Sidney, 23, 49; and Spenser, 62–67

ethics: aesthetic emotion and distance from, 11, 24; aesthetics, modern vs. early modern, 4, 6; in *Defence* (Sidney), 31–37, 40, 51; in *The Faerie Queene* "Letter of the Authors" (Spenser), 55, 57–59; in *The Faerie Queene* (Spenser), 23–24; individual judgments, value of, 10–11; role of emotion in, 3, 13; and value of literature, 1–3, 5, 7–8, 23, 26–27, 30, 51, 55, 131–33, 135. *See also* Christian ethics; ethical action; ethical pity

The Faerie Queene "Letter of the Authors" (Spenser): Aristotle, influence of, 54, 55, 60–63, 70, 80; on ethical instruction of poetry, 55, 59–62, 80; on ethics, 55, 57–59; exclusion from publication, 88; purpose of, 55, 57; Sidney, influence of, 53; on value of aesthetic aspects of literature, 24

The Faerie Queene (Spenser): autonomy of, 90; and autonomy vs. ethical effects of art, 131–32; ethical framework in, 23–24; ethics and role of pity in, 62–67; friend-

ship in, 67–76, 83–84; *King Lear* compared to, 113; love in, 74–79; mimesis and pity, 79–88, 131; on pity, 53–55, 67–79, 85–86; reflection in, 84–85; teaching ethical lessons through example, 57–61

Falco, Raphael, 53

fear vs. pity, 13, 15

Ferguson, Margaret, 30

forgiveness, 115–18, 122, 125

friendship: in *The Faerie Queene* (Spenser), 67–76, 83–84, 86–87; and union of affections, 119

Galen, 9

Gauthier, Théophile, 5

Glimp, David, 30

Gosson, Stephen, 5, 6, 20–22, 29, 58

The Governour (Elyot), 65, 120–21, 122–23

Grady, Hugh, 6, 92, 93, 96–97

grief: and aesthetic delight, 43, 87; in *The Faerie Queene* (Spenser), 63, 68, 73, 78; in *Hamlet* (Shakespeare), 98–100; tragedies, emotional responses to, 12, 14, 17, 87

Guenther, Genevieve, 4–5, 6, 37, 59

Halliwell, Stephen, 10, 12, 14–16, 30

Hamlet. The Mousetrap (Shakespeare), 96–101, 105

Hamlet (Shakespeare), 25, 90, 102

Hegel, Georg Wilhelm Friedrich, 35, 37

Herman, Peter C., 59

Hillman, David, 90

Horace: and aesthetic delight, 6, 7; *Ars Poetica*, 32; and ethical value of literature, 2; Sidney, influence on, 36, 57

instrumental aesthetics, 4–6, 24, 31, 47

Jacobson, Daniel, 40

James, Heather, 90, 102–3, 126

Johnson, Samuel, 126

justice: and aesthetic vs. ethical value of literature, 13; in *The Faerie Queene* (Spenser), 65–66, 69, 83; in *King Lear* (Shakespeare), 25, 91, 104–13, 114–15, 117, 120, 124–27, 134–35; restorative, 127

Kant, Emmanuel, 1, 3, 4–5

Kaplan, Ruth, 66

Keaty, Anthony, 18, 72, 119

King Lear (Shakespeare), 104–29; aesthetics of, 24–26, 91–101, 127–28; and Cordelia's pity, 113–25; and ethical pity, 125–29;

INDEX

King Lear (cont.)
and justice, 91, 104–13, 114–15, 117, 120, 124–25, 134–35; pity in, 104–6; and sympathy, 102–3
Kinney, Arthur F., 41
Kottman, Paul, 95, 124
Kuzner, James, 71

"l'art pour l'art" thesis (Gauthier), 5
Lipsius, Justus, 65
literature and art: aesthetic texts, 33; autonomy of, 5–6; and dangers of evoking emotions, 11, 12–14, 16, 17, 20, 21; ethical value of, 1–3, 5, 7–8, 23, 26–27, 30, 51, 55, 131–33, 135; social function of, 5; teaching emotions through, 7–8, 24, 26, 30–31, 132–35. *See also* aesthetics; autonomy model of aesthetics; early modern aesthetics; mimesis theories; *and individual works*
Lodge, Thomas, 5, 6–7, 20–22, 32
love: in *The Faerie Queene* (Spenser), 68, 74–79, 86; and pity, 74–75; Spenser on, 63, 65. *See also* friendship
Lowenthal, David, 108
Lucretius, 36, 57

McAlindon, Tom, 105
McCoy, Richard, 108
McLuskie, Kathleen, 105, 128
Meek, Richard, 8, 9, 103
mercy, 8–9, 65–66, 84, 113–14, 120–25
A Midsummer Night's Dream (Shakespeare), 6, 25, 90, 92, 93–96, 101–2
mimesis theories: aesthetic autonomy replacing, 23; of Aristotle, 14–17, 61, 86; and *Astrophil and Stella* (Sidney), 46, 49; and *Defence* (Sidney), 32, 36, 38, 39–41, 131; defined, 16–17; and *The Faerie Queene* "Letter of the Authors" (Spenser), 55, 61, 80; and *The Faerie Queene* (Spenser), 79–88, 131; and *Hamlet* (Shakespeare), 97–98, 101, 103; and modern vs. early modern aesthetics, 4; of Plato, 13–14, 15, 22, 26, 58, 60, 79–82, 131–32
misericordia, 8–9. *See also* pity
modern aesthetics, 1–11
mutuality, 71, 74

Nazarian, Cynthia, 63, 64, 66
Nicomachean Ethics (Aristotle), 18, 67, 69–70, 72–73
Nussbaum, Martha C., 10, 13

On Cosmopolitanism and Forgiveness (Derrida), 117

passion, 8, 62–63, 97–99
Passions of the Minde (Wright), 8
patriarchy, 105
Philebus (Plato), 14
physician metaphor, 21–22, 32–33, 36, 57
pity: and aesthetic vs. ethical value of literature, 2–3, 13; art of, 23–27; and *Astrophil and Stella* (Sidney), 31, 46–51; and Christian ethics, 8, 17–19, 42–44, 65–66, 72–74; and *Defence* (Sidney), 31, 34, 40, 42; defined in *Rhetoric* (Aristotle), 10; and early modern aesthetics, 25–26; evoked by tragedy, 12, 14–15, 17, 20, 25–26, 86–87; and *The Faerie Queene* (Spenser), 53–55, 62–67; fear vs., 13, 15; and *King Lear* (Shakespeare), 104–6, 113–25; mercy vs., 8–9, 113–14, 120–24; and mimesis in *The Faerie Queene* (Spenser), 79–88; and Shakespeare's dramas, 90–91; and union of affections, 18, 72, 77, 81, 85; virtuous pity in *The Faerie Queene* (Spenser), 67–79. *See also* ethical pity
Plato: *Critias*, 62; *Defence* (Sidney) indebted to, 29, 37, 39, 51–52; and ethical value of literature, 1, 3, 6; mimesis theory of, 13–14, 15, 22, 26, 58, 60, 79–82, 131–32; *Philebus*, 14; on pity, 40; poetry and dangers of evoking emotion, 11, 12–14, 16, 17, 20, 21; on power of poetry, 37; *Republic*, 12, 36, 56; Shakespearean theory of drama and rejection of, 101; Spenser, influence on, 53, 54, 55, 56; on tragedy, 12–13, 92, 128; worldview, persistence in modern issues, 131–32
Plutarch, 33–34
poet-as-maker metaphor, 21–22
Poetics (Aristotle), 12, 13–16, 86
poetry. *See* literature and art; *and individual works*
Puttenham, George, 21–22

real union, 18, 72
reason vs. passion, 62–63
reflection: and aesthetic distance, 16; of author, 135; in *Defence* (Sidney), 37–45; in *The Faerie Queene* (Spenser), 84–85; and Shakespearean theory of drama, 101; and Shakespeare's works, 25–27, 92, 96, 102–3, 127, 132

INDEX

Republic (Plato), 12, 36, 56
restorative justice, 127
Rhetoric (Aristotle), 10, 15, 18, 64, 72, 86
rhythm and delight, 33
Richard II (Shakespeare), 103
Robinson, Benedict, 9
Robinson, Jenefer, 29
Robson, Mark, 6
Rogers, Thomas, 8
Ruines of Time (Spenser), 66

sadness, 9, 25, 43–44, 78. *See also* pity
The School of Abuse (Gosson), 6, 20–22, 29
Schuurman, Anne, 72
Seneca, 9, 64–65, 69, 120–21, 122–23
Shakespeare, William, 89–129; autonomy
   of works, 90–91; and ethical pity, 24–26,
   90–91, 101–4, 125–29; and ethical value
   of individual judgments, 10–11; and ethical value of literature, 1–3; framework
   for aesthetic experiences, 132; frameworks for emotions, influences of, 9;
   Hamlet, 25, 90, 102; *Hamlet. The Mousetrap*, 96–101, 105; *A Midsummer Night's
   Dream*, 6, 25, 90, 92, 93–96, 101–2; pity
   as motive to act, 26–27; and reflection,
   25–27, 92, 96, 102–3, 127, 132; *Richard II*,
   103; Sidney and Spenser compared to,
   54, 89–90, 99, 101, 103, 128–29; *The Tempest*, 25, 90, 93, 94–96, 101, 102; and virtue ethics, 7. See also *King Lear*
Shakespearean theory of aesthetics, 25–26,
   127–29
Shakespearean theory of drama, 90–92, 101
Shepheardes Calender (Spenser), 53, 55
Sidney, Philip, 29–52; and aesthetic emotion as motive to act, 26; on delight,
   6–7; on ethical action, 7; and ethical
   pity, 23, 49; and ethical value of individual judgments, 10–11; and ethical value
   of literature, 1–2, 5, 135; frameworks for
   emotions, influences of, 9; Halliwell influenced by, 15; mimesis, understandings of, 16; poet-as-maker metaphor,
   21–22; poetry, defense of, 5, 8; Shakespeare's works compared, 89–90, 95, 99,
   101, 128–29; Spenser, influence on, 53,
   56–57; and virtue ethics, 7. See also *Astrophil and Stella; Defence of Poesy*
The Six Bookes of a Commonweale (Bodin), 65
social value. *See* ethics
Socrates, 12, 14
Solomon, Julie, 9

Solomon, Robert C., 10
Spenser, Edmund, 53–88; and aesthetic
   emotion as motive to act, 26; *Amoretti*,
   66; on autonomy of art, 6; "ensample"
   vs. pleasing analysis, 24, 55–61; and ethical value of individual judgments, 10–
   11; and ethical value of literature, 1–2;
   on ethics and role of pity, 62–67; frameworks for emotions, influences of, 9; on
   historians vs. poets, 60; mimesis and
   the generation of pity, 79–88; *Ruines
   of Time*, 66; Shakespeare's works compared, 54, 89–90, 101, 103, 113, 128–29;
   Shepheardes Calender, 53, 55; Sidney, influence of, 53, 56–57; and virtue ethics,
   7; and virtuous pity, 67–79. See also *The
   Faerie Queene; The Faerie Queene* "Letter of the Authors"
St. Hilaire, Danielle A., 134–35
Staines, John, 65–66
Stephens, Dorothy, 86
Stoicism: cognitive view of emotions, 10;
   and pity vs. mercy, 8–9, 113–14, 120–24;
   Spenser, influence on, 62–66; and vir-
   tue ethics, 7
Stoll, Abraham, 96–97
Strier, Richard, 7, 90, 112
Sullivan, Erin, 8
Summa Theologica (Aquinas), 67
sympathy: ethical, 50; in *The Faerie Queene*
   (Spenser), 64, 68; and pity, 2, 15, 17, 46, 67;
   in Shakespeare's works, 92, 102–4, 127

Tate, Nahum, 126
The Tempest (Shakespeare), 25, 90, 93, 94–
   96, 101, 102
Tilmouth, Christopher, 7, 8, 59, 62
tragedy: and aesthetic delight, 12, 43, 86–
   88; and aesthetic distance, 15–16, 42;
   autonomy model of aesthetics leading
   to, 44; in *Defence* (Sidney), 42, 44; pity
   evoked by, 12, 14–15, 17, 20, 25–26, 86–87;
   Plato on, 12–13, 92, 128; and Shakespeare's works, 25–26

union of affections: Aquinas on, 72; in *The
   Faerie Queene* (Spenser), 77, 81, 85; in
   King Lear (Shakespeare), 119; and pity, 18

Van Dijkhuizen, Jan Frans, 64, 66, 72, 82–83,
   85
villains, 100, 112
violence, 107–8, 111–14, 120, 125, 131

virtue: Aristotelian virtue ethics, 7, 10, 62; Augustine and Christian ethics, 43–44; and *Defence* (Sidney), 34, 40, 42, 44; emotion's role in, 1–2, 10, 63; and ethical action, 7–9; and *The Faerie Queene* (Spenser), 54, 62, 66–67; literature and teaching, 7–8, 24; virtuous pity in *The Faerie Queene* (Spenser), 67–79, 85–86; virtuous pity in *King Lear* (Shakespeare), 124

Weimann, Robert, 97, 98
Weinberg, Bernard, 21, 32
Whitney, Charles, 5, 91, 92, 94
Whittington, Leah, 65–66
Wilde, Oscar, 26
Wilson, Thomas, 7, 35–36
Wright, Thomas, 8